VOLUME EDITORS

LON S. NEASE is a PhD student in the Philosophy Department at the University of Cincinnati. He holds an MA in Philosophy from the University of Kentucky, where he studied phenomenology and existentialism. Nease has published on post-Kantian ethical theory.

MICHAEL W. AUSTIN is an Associate Professor of Philosophy at Eastern Kentucky University. His books include *Running and Philosophy* (Wiley-Blackwell, 2007), *Conceptions of Parenthood* (2007), *Football and Philosophy: Going Deep* (2008), and *Wise Stewards* (2009).

SERIES EDITOR

FRITZ ALLHOFF is an Assistant Professor in the Philosophy Department at Western Michigan University, as well as a Senior Research Fellow at the Australian National University's Centre for Applied Philosophy and Public Ethics. In addition to editing the *Philosophy for Everyone* series, Allhoff is the volume editor or co-editor for several titles, including *Wine & Philosophy* (Wiley-Blackwell, 2007), *Whiskey & Philosophy* (with Marcus P. Adams, Wiley, 2009), and *Food & Philosophy* (with Dave Monroe, Wiley-Blackwell, 2007).

PHILOSOPHY FOR EVERYONE

Series editor: Fritz Allhoff

Not so much a subject matter, philosophy is a way of thinking. Thinking not just about the Big Questions, but about little ones too. This series invites everyone to ponder things they care about, big or small, significant, serious ... or just curious.

Edited by Lon S. Nease and
Michael W. Austin

FATHERHOOD

PHILOSOPHY FOR EVERYONE

The Dao of Daddy

Foreword by Adrienne Burgess

A John Wiley & Sons, Ltd., Publication

Blackwell Publishing was acquired by John Wiley & Sons in February 2007. Blackwell's publishing program has been merged with Wiley's global Scientific, Technical, and Medical business to form Wiley-Blackwell.

Registered Office
John Wiley & Sons Ltd, The Atrium, Southern Gate, Chichester, West Sussex, PO19 8SQ, United Kingdom

Editorial Offices
350 Main Street, Malden, MA 02148-5020, USA
9600 Garsington Road, Oxford, OX4 2DQ, UK
The Atrium, Southern Gate, Chichester, West Sussex, PO19 8SQ, UK

For details of our global editorial offices, for customer services, and for information about how to apply for permission to reuse the copyright material in this book please see our website at www.wiley.com/wiley-blackwell.

Library of Congress Cataloging-in-Publication Data

Fatherhood – philosophy for everyone: the Dao of daddy / edited by Lon S. Nease and Michael W. Austin.
    p.   cm. – (Philosophy for everyone)
    Includes bibliographical references.
    ISBN 978-1-4443-3031-1 (pbk.: alk. paper)   1. Fatherhood.   2. Philosophy.
I. Nease, Lon S.   II. Austin, Michael W.   III. Title: Fatherhood – philosophy for everyone.
    HQ756.F38246 2010
    173–dc22

                                                            2010004719

A catalogue record for this book is available from the British Library.

Set in 10/12.5pt Plantin by SPi Publisher Services Pondicherry, India
Printed in Singapore

1   2010

To my daughter Leona, who has made this experience
so wonderful.
Lon

To Sophie, Emma, and Haley, for the patience they show
and the joy they bring.
Mike

CONTENTS

ADRIENNE BURGESS

FOREWORD

In my own writing and research on fatherhood, I've explored the roles played by fathers in the past and present, the impact of fathers for both good and ill on their children and their children's mothers, whether good fathers are born or made, and many of the related public policy issues. One thing that I have discovered is that we can learn a lot by identifying and reflecting on our assumptions about fatherhood. By examining the different ideas about fatherhood in the ancient and modern worlds, studying the diaries of fathers, interviewing present-day fathers, and making use of other kinds of empirical research, we learn something that most of us already knew: fathers matter. When we consider fathers and their roles in these ways, we can gain a deeper appreciation for what it means to be a father as well as some significant insights into how to be a good father. The fantastic book in your hands shares these same goals.

You might be wondering what Aristotle or Confucius has to say to contemporary fathers, or whether the ideas of philosophers can be useful to men navigating the life of a dad in the twenty-first century. Do the thoughts of such people have any relevance for the dads of today? Perhaps surprisingly, the answer is a resounding yes. The writers in *Fatherhood – Philosophy for Everyone* offer us their thoughts about the impact of being a father on children and on men, ethical issues related to different parenting styles, what it means to be an authentic father – and wrap up with advice for dads on some of the dilemmas that they face. They address such questions as:

- How can fathers instill values in their children while also giving them the freedom to choose their own values?
- What is involved in the art of raising a good person?
- How can dads with daughters deal with the particular challenges they face?
- How can fathers instill a passion for social justice in their children?
- How can psychology help fathers excel in the role of "Dad"?
- How should fathers deal with the influence of popular culture in the lives of their children?

These are just the sorts of issues that contemporary fathers care about, and the answers given in this book by men and women from different cultures, professions, and perspectives will give fathers and fathers-to-be (and the mothers of their children) much food for thought.

As you'll see, this isn't dry academic philosophy. This book is practical, insightful, and even fun. Drawing on the insights available from philosophy, psychology, religion, and anthropology, the contributors to this book have provided dads with help and insight from the collective wisdom of the ages that can better enable them to understand, appreciate, and fulfill their roles. Any father who takes the time to think about and then put into practice some of the ideas in the pages that follow will be glad that he did – and so will his children!

ACKNOWLEDGMENTS

First off, we would like to thank each of the contributors for being a part of this book. They are philosophers, psychologists, and anthropologists; but also fathers, mothers, sons, and daughters, each bringing their own unique perspective to what it means to be a dad and how to be the kind of dad that children need. The wisdom, insight, and practical help found on the pages that follow are a result of their hard and excellent work. We have learned much about fatherhood from each one of them.

We are also grateful to Fritz Allhoff, Jeff Dean, Tiffany Mok, and everyone at Wiley-Blackwell for their advice, enthusiasm, and support. We appreciate the part that each of them played in the creation of this book.

Finally, we would like to thank our families. Their patience and support were invaluable from start to finish. They have made fatherhood one of the greatest privileges we could imagine.

Lon S. Nease
Michael W. Austin

INTRODUCTION

Fathering the Idea

*The father who does not teach his son his duties
is equally guilty with the son who neglects them.*
Confucius

*When one has not had a good father, one must
create one.*
Friedrich Nietzsche

What does it mean to be a dad? Strangely enough,
throughout the world and throughout history, this
question has often been neglected. For one of the most important roles
that a man can take in life, relatively little has been put to paper. Sure,
we've all encountered the stereotypes of family protector, breadwinner,
and disciplinarian, but that only begins to scratch the surface. And it's
not even clear that those are essential to being a father – especially now.

Over the last half century there have been so many social and economic changes, that it's not an exaggeration to say the concept of fatherhood is being recreated or even created before our eyes. Families have
typically become smaller and more mobile, with little or no support net-
work close by. Women are working as much as men in many societies.
Studies are increasingly showing the importance of a father's presence to
the wellbeing of a child.

So not surprisingly, dads are becoming much more involved in their
children's lives, doing tasks their dads never did and their granddads

never even dreamt of doing, and wondering, frankly, "What *are* fathers after all?" As parents, are we simply interchangeable with mothers or do we bring something different to the table (other than burnt toast)? Are there unique aspects of our traditional parenting role that are going to be lost if we don't take stock of them? Is there baggage from that past role that is counterproductive today? Is there something else we need to be doing as fathers that we haven't realized yet?

In short, fatherhood is a role in transition. And while social, political, and economic factors will continue to influence how it evolves, the needs of our children also play a very big part. However we conceive of fatherhood, it's got to be grounded in what's best for children. They are, after all, what being a dad is all about.

Do we understand what their needs are? Findings from the social sciences and getting to know our children certainly help with this. But some of those needs – ones we take very seriously, such as the need to lead a meaningful and fulfilling life – seem to take us beyond what is and into the world of our values, what *should* be. What constitutes a meaningful life and how do our childrearing practices affect whether our children can achieve that? How do we figure that out and how do our answers change the way we raise our kids? Where should we look for guidance on all of this?

Certainly, there are many self-help books on fatherhood out there. There were over eighty parenting books with "fatherhood" in the title published in the last five years alone! Scanning through these volumes, however, reveals a variety of different background assumptions about what children will ultimately need in life and what fatherhood should look like. How do we know which of these books is going to help us go down the right path as fathers? Many of them sound convincing and have great stories to tell. And it seems everybody's got impressive credentials. What's a man to do?

To figure this out, we need to step back and reflect on life, children, and especially fatherhood to better understand these deeper concepts and values. And when we're talking about what we *should* do, a matter of values, ethics, and wisdom, then *philosophy* becomes an indispensable resource for our inquiry. Throughout its history, from Socrates through Descartes and right up through today, philosophy has offered a wealth of insights, reflections, and practical advice that can help us become the kinds of fathers our children need.

And that's where *Fatherhood – Philosophy for Everyone* comes in. This volume represents an attempt to think through the role of fatherhood by looking deeper at the experiences, issues, and dilemmas facing dads today. While most of the chapters are written by professional philosophers, we've got psychologists and anthropologists on board as well, all presenting their ideas in an accessible and fun style. What did Plato and Kant have to say that fathers can still make use of today? What are the philosophical issues that affect our everyday parenting decisions? Throughout this book you'll find insights and advice useful to anyone on or about to embark on the wonderful journey of fatherhood.

What does it mean to be a dad? At the end of our inquiry we may find there aren't many clear cut answers, but each of us will arrive at our own deepened convictions. And these will help ground and guide all of our decisions in our role as "daddy."

In the second half of this introduction, we'd like to provide a brief guide as to what you'll find in the pages of this volume. As you've no doubt noticed, the book is divided into four sections, each containing four to five chapters. Each unit has a theme reflecting some aspect of fatherhood, but each chapter is self-contained and not dependent on any other. There's a benefit to reading the chapters of a unit together, as their related ideas tend to lead the mind to further reflection on that section's theme. But you can feel free to skip around, reading the chapters in whatever order you like.

To start off the book we are thrilled to have a foreword written by Adrienne Burgess, the Director of Research and founding member of the Fatherhood Institute in England. Her 1997 landmark book *Fatherhood Reclaimed: The Making of the Modern Father* explored the changing roles of fathers in Britain, Australia, and the United States, and led to the founding of Fathers Direct, an organization devoted to tackling the social, educational, and legal obstacles that keep fathers from being more involved in their children's lives. Fathers Direct organized the first World Summit on Fatherhood in 2003, which brought over fifty experts from five continents together, and more recently the organization became known as the Fatherhood Institute. We can hardly think of anyone more fitting than Burgess to put this volume's aspirations into their proper perspective.

After the foreword, our first unit, "The Impact of Being a Father," gathers together chapters devoted to a man's transition into fatherhood and the impact this new role has on his life. Scott Davison leads this off with a fine essay showing how our sense of time is altered by fatherhood and how to get it back under control so we don't miss out on the precious moments we have with our children. Next, Ammon Allred investigates what fatherhood means to a person's world by looking at the philosophy of Martin Heidegger, the characters of actor Seth Rogan, and the poetry of Paul Celan. Allred finds that fatherhood means more than taking on new tasks. A new father's world is fragile, depending forever thereafter on the child's wellbeing. Third, we have a fascinating essay by Kimberley Fink-Jensen highlighting some of her research into the stories fathers share as part of their transition into fatherhood. Through telling these stories, men solidify their own perception of their new role, and the more involved they get during the pregnancy and birth, the more they identify themselves as fathers after the child is born. This segues nicely into Michael Barnwell's look at what it means to say fatherhood is the meaning of someone's life. Barnwell finds fatherhood is not only compatible with a meaningful life, but given our need to have an impact in the world, it is perhaps one of the noblest ways of instilling meaning into our lives.

The next unit of the volume, "Ethics and Parenting Styles," focuses on fathers' contributions to childrearing, the different ways and the related issues dads face. Is there a value to discipline? How can you raise a child to truly become free? What are our goals in bringing up children? One of the book's co-editors, Lon Nease, starts us off with a philosophically grounded game plan for raising ethical children, drawing from the works of Aristotle, Kant, and Nietzsche among others. In addition to the virtues, a child needs to develop empathy and the underlying skills that make it and the virtues possible. Andrew Terjesen then breaks new ground with an exploration of paternalistic *caring*. While we're quick to acknowledge caring as a mother's way of relating to children, Terjesen feels we've overlooked the caring that is distinctive to the way a father relates to his children. The next essay by Dan Florell and Steffen Wilson takes us straight to the heart of how to raise children, as they analyze the pros and cons of different styles of parenting and offer lots of valuable advice for fathers. Finally, J. K. Swindler examines the nature of autonomy and how fathers are in a special role to lead their children toward this independence of spirit.

This leads us to our third section, "Keeping It Real: Authentic Fatherhood," where we focus on what it really means to be a father. What is an authentic dad, a real dad? Is there a certain form or style to the role? Are there images or traditions that we should look toward to better grasp the nature of fatherhood? Dan Collins-Cavanaugh begins this unit by looking closer at what it means to be an authentic dad. Drawing on the philosophies of Jean-Paul Sartre and Charles Taylor, Collins-Cavanaugh argues that the key to being an authentic father is to make choices that are knowingly your own, but also to make ones that are in line with the needs of your children. The next two essays take us to other continents to explore alternative views of authentic fatherhood that might help us critique our own culturally contingent ideas. Andrew Komasinski shows us that fatherhood is central to the philosophy of Confucius, and that if fathers stay true to their role and teach by example, they can bring out the best in their children and people around them. Then Abiodun Oladele Balogun explains the fascinating and unique aspects of authentic fatherhood in the traditional Yoruba culture in Nigeria. We find their model is a collective one, spreading the paternal responsibilities to all male members of the family as the need arises. Additionally, Balogun emphasizes the role of storytelling and proverbs in the moral education of their children. The last essay in this unit is by Stephen Joseph Mattern in which he examines the nature of mercy and maintains that a real father is one that engages a child in a relation of compassionate caring, responding to their needs and feelings.

In our last unit, "Dilemmas for Dad," we offer a showcase of compelling essays addressing various ethical and practical issues that fathers can face. Leading this off, Joshua Baron considers how much of the popular media fathers should let their kids engage in given how it might impact them. Baron advises dads to focus on experiencing movies, television, video games, and the like with their children, relying on their own good sense as fathers rather than merely trusting the various ratings systems currently in place. David Owen then offers excellent advice to fathers who want to help their children become people who are concerned about social justice. Owen's chapter is very practical, and his encouragement to dads is to become the kind of people who cultivate within themselves and their families the knowledge and character needed to break the cycle of oppressive injustice that is so prevalent in our world. In the next two essays, we return to the theme of autonomy. Anthony Carreras addresses the tension that many fathers are keenly aware of as they seek to impart their values to their children while also respecting the child's present and future autonomy. Jeffrey Morgan also discusses the ideals of fathers as they relate to the lives of their children, and claims that paternalism, rightly understood, is a good thing. Morgan argues that fathers should guide their children and help them achieve goals that are best suited to their individual character and disposition. The book's final chapter, by co-editor Michael Austin, explores some of the unique challenges faced by dads and their daughters. His chapter includes a discussion of moral development and self-knowledge as it relates to the father-daughter relationship, with a focus on the virtues of humility, courage, and wisdom.

As we all know, we live in an information rich age. We have access to a lot of facts, but rarely do we take the time to think about the significance of those facts in a deeper way. There is an all too prevalent poverty of wisdom, especially with respect to fatherhood. Our aim in the pages that follow is to provide you with something more than mere information. Each of the contributors to this book has something important to say to dads who want to think in deeper ways about fatherhood. Our hope is that as you consider the ideas they offer, you will find some wisdom that is helpful to you and the children you love.

PART I

THE IMPACT OF BEING A FATHER

SCOTT A. DAVISON

CHAPTER 1

FATHER TIME AND FATHERHOOD

I am lying in bed with my daughter Grace, who is three years old. She has just fallen asleep on my arm after our usual ritual of stories and songs. It is 1:00 in the afternoon, and I am thinking about how to spend the next hour or so. Grace is the youngest of my children, and she will be the last one. Her older brothers Ben and Drew also took naps with me when they were this age. (I can hear the parenting experts complaining to me about the dangers of sleeping with young children – don't worry, my children sleep alone at night, in their own beds!)

Ben and Drew are in school for most of the day. Before long, Grace will join them. I have been lucky enough to care for all of my children for some part of the day ever since they were born. But soon they will all have busy schedules during the day (thanks to school), and my flexible work schedule won't make much of a difference. We will go our separate ways early in the morning and come back together again late in the afternoon.

As I lie in bed with Grace, I think about what to do for the next hour or so. I could answer email, work on some papers whose deadlines are approaching, or make progress (quietly!) on one of the many home improvement projects underway in every single room in our house (a fact that my wife recently pointed out to me; thanks for that, Becky). But I could also stay here and take a nap with Grace, or just enjoy the experience of watching her sleep.

The reasons that pull me out of bed are all about Father Time: I'm worried about completing projects on time, anxious about being efficient, and hoping to be productive so that I can relax this evening. If I had indefinitely many hours in each day, I would not be faced with such choices, because I could do everything at some point. Father Time imposes limits that force me to make choices, hard choices that reflect, and partly determine, my values. In this essay, I discuss what fatherhood is teaching me about the nature of time.

The Present Moment

People often say that there is no use crying over spilled milk. But sometimes there is a point; maybe crying over spilled milk today will help me to avoid spilling more milk tomorrow. It is important to consider the past carefully in order to learn from it. Sometimes we also need to consider the future carefully. Planning for the future is an important part of life and something that all parents try to teach their children (with mixed results, of course).

But dwelling on the future can become overwhelming. We can be paralyzed by worry or we can get lost in fantasy. With regard to the past, we can become so stuck on pleasant memories ("glory days") or so paralyzed by regrets that we become insensitive to what is happening in the present moment. If we dwell on some past or future event over and over again like a tape loop, we can create a mental habit with momentum, a habit that takes away from our present attention even when this is unwelcome. So we must be careful that our attention in the present moment is not completely taken up by our attention to the past or the future. After all, only the present moment is real; past moments of time no longer exist, and future ones do not exist yet.

Or at least this is what St. Augustine thought. He argued famously that only the present moment is real.[1] Past times, he said, no longer exist, and future times do not exist yet. The only real moment, then, is the present one. We experience past times in memory and future times in anticipation, but only the present moment can be experienced directly. This is because only the present moment is real.

SCOTT A. DAVISON

The contemporary Benedictine monk David Steindl-Rast seems to agree. In our peak experiences, in which we feel most alive and present, we experience a distorted sense of time:

> Our sense of time is altered in those moments of deep and intense experience, so we know what now means. We feel at home in that now, in that eternity, because that is the only place where we really *are*. We cannot *be* in the future and we cannot *be* in the past; we can only *be* in the present. We are only real to the extent to which we are living in the present here and now.[2]

Even if St. Augustine and Steindl-Rast are wrong about the unreality of past and future times, they are right to point out that we experience the present moment very differently than we experience past times (through memory) and future times (through anticipation). The present moment is available to us in a direct and vivid fashion. But sometimes we are so preoccupied with past or future times that we fail to notice what is happening in the present.

Have you ever experienced this? Have you ever discovered, after the fact, that you did not fully experience something wonderful because you were either too preoccupied with the past or too focused on the future? I confess that I have missed many wonderful meals, movies, conversations, and milestones in the lives of my children in just this way. For some reason, I have a mental habit of responding almost instantly to the demands of the past or future regardless of what is going on in the present. Maybe my preoccupation with past and future times gives me a sense of control that is lacking in the present, since I can conjure up memories or anticipations at will. I'm not sure. But I am determined to develop more control over the objects of my attention, so as to not let my life pass me by in this way.

Simpler animals apparently do not have this problem, because they do not have the ability to fixate on past or future times in the same way. Snowball, my children's pet rabbit, never seems to be lost in thought when a piece of celery comes within range. And my children themselves have a share of the rabbit's focus on the present: it is hard to persuade them to wait until later to have a snack, for instance. Perhaps there is something valuable in this ability to ignore the past and the future. Maybe I have something to learn from my children in this regard, like the ability to see things freshly and with wonder.

Sterner on Returning to the Present

In a highly practical and provocative book, Thomas M. Sterner argues that it is possible to return to a childlike focus on the present.[3] As I understand his presentation, there are two main strands to his argument. One of them starts with the observation that we all experience total immersion in the present from time to time. Drawing upon a concept from Zen Buddhism, Sterner describes this state as "beginner's mind." When we do things for fun, for instance, we focus almost exclusively on what is happening in the present moment. If you want to see a case of complete and total immersion in the present, just watch a child play a video game. Sterner also claims that the distinction between work and play is an arbitrary one. What we call "work" and what we call "play" depend on cultural conventions, personal choices, and habits of language. He concludes that as long as we remain immersed in the present moment, we can enjoy doing almost anything, even those things that we typically consider unpleasant work.

The second strand in Sterner's presentation complements and illuminates the first one. It involves the distinction between focusing on the process as opposed to focusing on the end product. Sterner notes that if we focus on the end product, then our minds are on the future, whereas if we focus on the process currently underway, then our minds are in the present. If we shift our goal away from arriving at the end product as quickly as possible and instead make our goal immersion in the present process, we can be content in the present moment without worrying about the future or regretting the past. (My children demonstrate this pattern by focusing on the process of eating the ice cream cone, not the end goal of finishing it.) It's not that we should forget the end goal altogether. In fact, Sterner claims that we should use it as a kind of rudder to steer our activity in the right direction. But our focus should be in the present, on the process in which we are engaged.

Sterner describes several examples of this process oriented focus that are helpful to consider. The first involves Japanese piano makers, who focus completely on the process of making the parts of a piano without regard to considerations of time or efficiency. A worker in such a factory might spend all day working on one part and not find this frustrating, because the goal is to engage in the process of finishing a part, not to produce as many parts as possible. This approach results in the manufacture of very high quality pianos, not to mention highly contented workers who require almost no supervision.

SCOTT A. DAVISON

A second example involves Sterner's own experience as a veteran piano tuner for concert pianists. One day he was expected to tune three concert pianos in a single day. Frustrated by the prospect of a very long and tedious day ahead, he deliberately slowed everything down, focusing on each task one at a time, expecting the day to drag ahead indefinitely. Much to his surprise, as he focused on the present moment and ignored the end product, he found himself really enjoying his work. He continued doing this all day long, simplifying each task and working as slowly as possible, only to find that he had completed tuning all three pianos hours ahead of schedule. He has been able to repeat this result regularly, noticing the difference in cases in which he is expected to do the very same tasks over and over again, such as tuning the same concert pianos.

This kind of focus and simplicity is alien to contemporary Western culture, which celebrates the person who accomplishes more than one task at one time. The allure of multitasking is almost irresistible for me when I am home alone with my children. I have changed many diapers, prepared many meals, and solved many problems over the years while also working on other projects at the same time. My children are still young, yet I regret already not focusing during the times I am doing activities with them. I even wish that I could revisit them at younger ages, to appreciate them for what they were at the time, instead of impatiently hurrying them along to the next developmental stage for the sake of my convenience.

Perhaps because it is so highly valued in our culture, multitasking also has an addictive quality. We experience some kind of thrill in connection with doing many things at once, and this makes us feel empty when we have only one thing to do. Technology encourages us here by providing machines everywhere that we can use to do work or to communicate with others. Unfortunately, this means that we are often literally unable to focus on just one thing, because we cannot be content with it. We cannot do any single thing all by itself without feeling restless, inefficient, and unproductive.

Once again, we can learn something from children, who find it unnatural to try to do more than one thing at once. In the same way that my children have time limits for playing computer games and watching television, often I need to separate myself from information technology in order to focus on the present moment. I need to put away the cell phone, step away from the computer, turn off the television, and stop the music in the background.

Of course, our educational experiences, work expectations, and the messages we receive from the media also play roles in developing a focus on end products instead of processes. In the media, for instance, we are often bombarded with images designed to highlight the difficulties of parenting successfully, together with a solution that is cheap and readily available in the form of some product or service for sale.[4] How many times have you seen children making a mess of something on television, only to see their mother swoop in with the latest cleaning product to save the day? These images play on our product oriented focus, which takes perfect parenthood as an end product that we think we should have already attained.

My response to these images is that becoming a good parent is itself a process, just like the process of a child's growth to maturity. And if we focus on this process instead of the final product, we can let go of the disappointment of having failed to achieve perfection already. As Sterner points out, our own ideas of perfection are constantly evolving over time. Perfection is always moving away from us. Perhaps we should revise our idea of perfection so that it is relative to a particular time or stage of development. In this sense, a flower is just fine at every stage in its development and not just the final stages. As parents, we can admit that there will always be more progress to be made at any point in the future, no matter how far away. We will never arrive at a state that cannot be improved upon. This should diminish the impact of the media images in question.

Sterner also claims that when we experience impatience, frustration, or worry, this is a sign that we are focused on an unrealized product instead of a present process. My worst moments as a parent fit this pattern perfectly. They have all occurred at bedtime, when my obsession with the final product of sleeping children (in their own beds!) has led me to be harsh and unreasonable. If only I could have appreciated what they were experiencing at that moment instead of focusing on the unrealized goal, I could have avoided saying and doing things that I will always regret. Perhaps this would have meant some very late bedtimes on some occasions, but it would have prevented some truly regrettable moments and probably would have resulted in earlier bedtimes on other occasions (in the same way that Sterner's deliberately slowed-down experience as a piano tuner did). I will try to follow the advice of Sterner and St. Augustine by appreciating the difference between the past, the present, and the future. Another source of help lies in different views of the nature of time itself, to which I shall now turn.

Clock Time and Experienced Time

What is time? St. Augustine said famously that he knew exactly what time was until someone asked him to explain it.[5] In the modern Western world, we typically view time in terms of what Steindl-Rast calls "clock time." According to this view, time is a limited commodity that is always running out, like a spilling juice box that cannot be refilled. Time is linear, extending from the past through the present and into the future. The passage of time is uniform and can be measured objectively by clocks.

The Western idea of clock time, a limited commodity that is always running out, leads to the idea of the efficient use of time, the idea of "wasting" time, and to much anxiety and regret about how we spend our time. These ideas make it difficult to recognize the importance of living in the present moment. They also make it more difficult to emphasize quality time rather than a quantity of time. Let me explain these ideas by contrasting clock time with an older view of time that I shall call "experienced time."

In the ancient world, the concept of an hour was very different than it is today. An hour of a day was defined in terms of the activities and opportunities that were appropriate then. In this sense, an hour of a day was not a specific length of time as measured by a clock at all, but rather a vague portion of a day defined in terms of how it is usually experienced. As Steindl-Rast notes, in the same way that the experienced seasons of the year do not always correspond to their officially defined dates ("Is it summer already?"), the hours of the day, in this ancient sense, depended on the actual flow of life, including the rising and setting of the sun, but not on the number of minutes that passed.

Given this ancient sense of the concept of an hour, we can imagine a different sense of time itself. Instead of being a long line that is always getting shorter, like the last piece of licorice disappearing slowly into my son Ben's mouth, time can be viewed as a cycle of similar activities and opportunities, a cycle that is relatively independent of clock time. Let's call this "experienced time." Unlike clock time, which proceeds at the same rate objectively all the time no matter what is happening, experienced time seems to move quickly or slowly depending on what we are doing. Waiting for my children to finish using the bathroom seems to take forever, for example, but laughing at my son Drew's funny faces makes time fly, even on a long road trip. If my wife Becky has been at the office from nine until five (a rare occurrence, thankfully, for both of us), then the day seems like it lasted longer than eight hours of clock time. However, sleeping later that night seems to take no time at all.

So clock time involves the objective, mechanical measure of time independently of what is experienced, whereas experienced time concerns the ebb and flow of life independently of what the clock says. Which kind of time is more important to us? As a father it is my job to attend to the basic needs of my children, including food, shelter, clothing, security, attention, play, and hygiene. Because my children are still young, these basic needs divide the day into segments organized around certain activities. For example, there is breakfast time, play time, snack time, quiet time, nap time, dinner time, and (finally!) bedtime. Although some parents schedule these activities rigidly around specific clock times, we all know that there is a rhythm to them that varies from day to day. Sometimes nap time comes earlier rather than later. Sometimes snack time cannot be postponed any longer. Sometimes it is not clear when bedtime will actually arrive. As Steindl-Rast notes, in a monastery, monks must be ready to drop their tools and move on to the next task when the bell rings to signal a new hour of the day. In the same way, parents must be responsive to what is happening in the present. We must be able to drop what we are doing in order to attend to the needs of our children. (Of course, in my house, instead of a bell ringing, we have different grades of shrieking and screaming, which only the experienced parent can distinguish with accuracy.) So experienced time seems to be more important to me, as a father, than clock time.

Of course, clock time is an important tool. It is necessary for coordinating one's activities with others, for instance. But even if we are not parents, we all seem to care more about experienced time. In order to see this, suppose that you have contracted some rare disease, and you are told that drug therapy is needed for you to survive. Imagine that there are two very different drugs that would cure you, each of which will distort your sense of experienced time in a different way, and each of which will be very painful to administer. Here is the difference between them: drug one will cause you one solid hour of clock time of painful discomfort, but it will distort your sense of experienced time so that this hour of clock time will appear to take only five minutes to pass. By contrast, drug two will cause you only five minutes of clock time of painful discomfort, but it will distort your sense of experienced time so that these five minutes of clock time will appear to take an entire hour to pass. Which drug would you choose to take? Assuming that all other things are equal, of course we would all choose drug one. This shows that experienced time is more important to us than clock time.

To put things differently, it's the quality of our time that counts, not so much the quantity. Who would choose to live for a hundred years of boredom? Wouldn't you rather live a full and complete life that occupied only a short amount of clock time? Fatherhood is teaching me that the most satisfying way to spend my time is to live in the present, not to think too much about the past or future, to focus on the process and not the end product, and not to worry too much about clock time.

So as I watch my children play soccer, or wait with them in the lobby at the dentist's office, or help them do homework, I have to remind myself that this is part of the only time we have together. Sometimes it seems to creep along imperceptibly, but sometimes it flies. Technology is making it more difficult to draw the line between being at home and being at work, and making it fashionable to work just about everywhere and all the time. Years from now, when I look back on these times, I want to remember being present with my children, not frantically trying to do other things while they happen to be in the same room. Let's hope I can make progress before they are completely grown and out of the house![6]

NOTES

1   My discussion of St. Augustine in what follows comes from his *Confessions*, trans. Henry Bettenson (London: Penguin, 2003), book XI, chapters XIV and XXVIII.
2   David Steindl-Rast and Sharon Libell, *The Music of Silence* (New York: Harper Collins, 1995), p. 12, italics in the original.
3   Thomas M. Sterner, *The Practicing Mind* (Wilmington: Mountain Sage Publishing, 2005), pp. 37–42. My description below of Sterner's views is based on this work.
4   It must be admitted though, that our society's standards for being a good mother are considerably higher than those for being a good father. For a humorous but highly insightful discussion of this, see Ayelet Waldman, *Bad Mother* (New York: Doubleday, 2009).
5   St. Augustine, *Confessions*, book XI, chapter XIV.
6   I wish to thank Layne Neeper, Glen Colburn, Tim Simpson, Chris Stewart, and my wife Becky Davison not only for helpful comments and questions concerning earlier drafts of this essay, but also for helping me to learn these things in my day-to-day life.

CHAPTER 2

HOW FATHERHOOD WILL CHANGE YOUR LIFE

When I found out that my proposal for this collection had been accepted, I was quite happy. Nonetheless, I quickly put it out of my mind because I did not have time to think. My daughter wanted her lunch, my son was waking from his nap, and it wouldn't be until later that I'd have to decide between watching TV or starting an outline before going to bed. Being a father changes how we spend our time.

This is a truism. Everybody already knows it (my 5-year-old once told me, "After you have a baby, things get tricky"). Parenthood changes one's life. But how? In this essay, I will address that question by examining how it changes what one's world means. It does this not merely by presenting us with something infinitely more significant, but by showing us the potential meaninglessness of everything. This potential meaninglessness changes the shape of the world by showing us that nothing matters so much as the mere fact of having time. I use the philosophy of Martin Heidegger to develop a project oriented understanding of the world, paying particular attention to the world of fathers. I then contrast the world of fathers to the world of the "man-child," exemplified in the characters of actor Seth Rogan.

By showing the sense of the world in both of these figures and seeing how they offer competing conceptions of masculinity, I suggest that what is distinctive to the father's world is an acute realization of the fragility of all projects. This is seen most clearly in the possible death of the child, as I show by contrasting the worlds of the father and the man-child with the world as presented in a poem by Paul Celan, written after the stillbirth of his son. This poem profoundly expresses the emptiness of the world. This emptiness is a fundamental aspect of the world of all parents, related at bottom to the fact that our children's world is different than our own. After the child is born, the world will be haunted by the possibility of emptiness. But this isn't all bad; it is also what allows children to have a life of their own beyond ours.

The Meaning of the World in Heidegger

Soon, I'll talk about Seth Rogan, but first we need to get some technical matters out of the way. First, defining what we mean by "world." Heidegger elaborates what it means to have a world in the context of what it means to be human. In his most important work, *Being and Time*,[1] the world isn't to be understood as bare physical reality. Rather, it is the meaningful context in which human beings live. Whatever we consider, we discover that things in the world have some particular significance. This piece of plastic I'm touching is a keyboard. The black lines I'm staring at are words. I look out my window at the meadow where I play with my children. These are not just bare things. I encounter them in the context of a whole meaningful life. The world is the place where that encounter happens. What the world means depends upon *how* that happens – the reason I encounter the meadow as a place to play with my children and not, for example, to engage in amateur botany.

Heidegger argues that we encounter things in the world primarily as tools, as means toward ends. But what kind of tools? Means toward what ends? That depends upon what we try to do, what kinds of goals we have, what projects we have. This means that we can best understand what the world means through our projects. Being a father happens to be far more important for me than botany. Consequently, I primarily see the meadow through the lens of fatherhood. Before my dog died, the meaning of the meadow was closely linked with various doggie projects, like walking her and cleaning up after her (its meaning is still linked to her memory). Often, my doggie projects and my daddy projects over-lapped, but not always. We might say that they both fit into some bigger set of projects, domestic projects perhaps. Indeed, many of our projects are parts of bigger projects. I have domestic projects and professional projects. I have hobby projects and entertainment projects, although they occupy a smaller part of my world than they once did. Presumably even these big categories are interlinked, the way this essay links my domestic and professional worlds. We might suspect, therefore, that there may be some sort of overarching, mega-project that integrates the various elements of my life and which makes sense of the world consid-ered as a whole.

What, then, is the biggest project of all? Some famous answers phi-losophers have given include happiness (Aristotle), the well-being of civil society (Kant), and, oddly enough, for Plato, immortality. The project of fatherhood could certainly be the answer many men would give. Heidegger isn't saying that any one of these answers is right; just that each answer describes a different kind of world.

Each of these big projects impact how we deal with things we encoun-ter in the world. What a thing is in a particular world depends on the project we are involved in. Heidegger gives the example of a hammer.[2] What is a hammer? It isn't just metal joined to wood with a certain kind of shape. If I defined it like that, I wouldn't know what a hammer is at all. A hammer is a construction tool that I use to pound things. Of course, that isn't all it is. In a pinch, I could use it as a paperweight or as a backscratcher, or even to make a point in a philosophy essay. Exactly what it is *now* depends upon what I need it for, and that depends upon who I am and how I relate to the world around me. The fact that I'm a philosophy professor means hammers are generally much more useful to me as examples when talking about Heidegger than they are for pounding things. But sometimes they are useful for that too. Ever since we've had kids, I've had to do more home improvement projects.

The point is that things don't have just one meaning and there isn't just one kind of project we use them for. There are many possible uses for things and lots of possible activities, and each of these reveals a different world of sorts. When my kids make me use the hammer in a way that I wouldn't have before, it means my world has changed because of them. But I still haven't explained how.

AMMON ALLRED

Immortality

Above, I described fatherhood as a project on its own and tried to make sense of how it shapes my world. Another way of understanding fatherhood is to fit it into one of the big projects philosophers propose. Take Plato's answer as an example. Immortality is one of the answers Plato proposes to the question of what could be the biggest project of all. That's less weird than it sounds at first. None of us wants to die or to have those we love die. Mortality means that we are each going to die. Before that, we are going to lose things and people who matter to us. Some people try to get around this by becoming famous, so their memory will live on, or by creating beautiful things worth preserving. Plato naturally assumes that the greatest people achieve immortality by studying philosophy (don't ask how). But by far the most common, and least successful, route to immortality is having children. We have children, Plato suggests, so that we can keep a part of ourselves alive through them, in the resemblance of their body to ours, in the place that we occupy in their memory and in the life lessons that we imprint on their souls. Certainly, this speaks to a common experience of parenthood. Isn't one of the reasons we invest so much of ourselves in children because we see ourselves in them, because we see them as *our* future? Maybe the project of fatherhood can be understood through the immortality project.

Why does Plato think this approach is likely to be unsuccessful? For one, the child isn't identical to you, so you're not really becoming immortal. Sure, your child takes on a part of you, and if they have children of their own, that part will still be there, although less and less so with each generation. In the end, your line might die out. But in any case, although your kids will certainly remember you and your grandkids might, your great-grandkids probably won't. After that, forget about it.

And don't forget that children die, too. Sometimes they die before you. This is another problem with seeking immortality through parenthood. So while parenthood might be a possible project, and one that philosophers have taken seriously, there are considerable problems with pursuing it as the meaning of life.

I am employing Plato here as an example. No doubt we could describe how fatherhood could figure in any of the other "big" projects I mentioned above. In each case, we would discover the same thing: fatherhood can describe a strategy for accomplishing what we take as the highest purpose of life, but it is a strategy replete with dangers and might end in failure. And the possibility of the death of the child looms as the clearest expression of that failure, even if it is not the only shape such a failure might take. The reason that I dwell on Plato's example is because it exposes that possibility most clearly.

Plato's example also highlights another important consideration in Heidegger's account of worlds and projects. Whether we talk about small projects or big projects, we always have to deal with the possibility of failure. When hammering a nail, I might accidentally hit my thumb instead. This possibility is built into my project as part of what my world means. Built into trying to be a good father is the fear that I'll fail. Even if Plato is right that we all want immortality, built into that desire is the possibility of death. For Heidegger, death is the clearest way to understand what the possibility of failure means for any project. Whatever other projects I have, one thing is certain: those projects will come to an end when I die. And I *will* die. But rather than seeing mortality as wholly negative, Heidegger sees it as a productive part of what it means to be alive. Although death means the end of my projects, the possibility of death makes it possible to have projects at all. The fact that I will die means that I have a limited amount of time. And that makes the time that I have meaningful to me. I will return to this point later.

The World of the Man-Child

Even if fatherhood represents a particularly masculine project or strategy for some larger project (such as immortality), it isn't the only possible masculine project. There is another example that our society provides us, even though it's designed to avoid the cares and responsibilities associated with fatherhood and by extension with the traditional notion of masculinity. This is the world of the man-child. If fatherhood gives me a new way of understanding the world and things in it, then man-childhood should too.

We are inundated with simplistic claims that men are naturally more attuned to things and projects while women are more attuned to people and relationships. I doubt that this is true, but regardless, people often internalize it as though it were true. While the distinction between masculinity as project-oriented and femininity as relationship-oriented is simplistic, the myriad ways in which this distinction is broadcast to us is

AMMON ALLRED

not. We hear it from pop psychologists and pop evolutionists, magazines, and music, to name a few.

Heidegger's hammer is a good example of an internalized conception of manhood. Heidegger was a man of the people. He taught his lectures with his skis propped against the wall and prided himself on his competence and know-how. No doubt one of the reasons he chose the hammer as an example was that it fed into a macho image he found appealing (and that many of us might find appealing too).

My generation, Gen X, has been happy to contest this conception of masculinity. In this, we have followed the hipsters, ironists, and slackers who people the mythology of the post-World War II world. We like to think that we have reinvented masculinity along with the world. And we sometimes think that in doing so, we have done away with a world that involves any projects at all. We like to think that we have found a way of being men different from the way our dads were. And we certainly don't want to have anything to do with hammers, busy work, and other nonsense.

Consider a Seth Rogan character in almost any Judd Apatow movie. His aimless life lacks any real significance. He doesn't undertake any project more serious than deciding when to get high. The biggest project in his life is to remain project-free. Although such a life is presented as being particularly attractive to a certain kind of man or boy, it is a life that avoids the very project oriented conception of masculinity (and masculine responsibility) that Heidegger implicitly relies on in discussing what worlds mean. It also involves shirking those duties that our cultural imagination associates with fatherhood, like steady employment, skill with tools, or emotional stability.

Nonetheless, it would be wrong to say that Rogan's character doesn't have any projects at all. One of the primary reasons his life is attractive is that it entails a freedom from relationships that allows one to do whatever one wants whenever one wants and takes seriously things that mature, responsible grownups aren't supposed to care about. The man-child avoids what the world takes to be valuable projects so that he can focus on what he cares about: doing stand-up comedy, collecting action figures, perfecting his drumming technique, and laboriously documenting the precise moment in a movie when an actress disrobes. These are projects, even if they are insignificant, irresponsible projects, chosen as a way of saying "no" to a world that demands more meaningful endeavors. We might speculate they are projects designed to avoid the possibility of failure, the fragility of all projects. They are activities chosen precisely to give no significance to things. But they are significant nonetheless.

And this is a crucial point of Heidegger's exposition of the meaning of the world. There is no eternally fixed, proper meaning of things, nor is there a stable, proper sense of the world. The world of the macho man is no more or less a world than the world of the man-child. Society might call some life projects better or more useful, but that begs the question. Better for what? More useful for what? And the answer we give to these questions will depend upon the sort of world we inhabit.

I imagined that I was being quite responsible by finishing my dissertation before our first daughter was born. My grandfather begged to differ. After asking me what it was about (philosophy and poetry and crap like that), and listening to an answer that was way too long, he slowly said, "There's only one problem." He pointed at my wife, who is an attorney, and said, "She'll be making more than you." He was, of course, right that she would make more money than me. But it was only a problem from his conception of masculinity, which is different than mine. As alike as we are in some respects, my grandfather and I inhabit different worlds. Grandpa may say that masculinity is defined by hammers and spreadsheets, responsibility, and handiness. He may imagine an adult world empty of childish things. But the man-child will not put childish things behind him. Grandpa may regard action figures as childish and 1970s cartoons as moronic, but the man-child doesn't care. They matter to him. When I look at someone else's projects, they may seem useless and meaningless. They aren't my thing. But they are someone else's thing.

Knocked Up

So we have to acknowledge that what seems meaningful or useful depends upon a whole conception of the world, and this depends upon the projects that structure that world. Earlier, I said those projects were embedded in other projects and limited by the possibility that any project might fail. From this perspective, we could see how fatherhood and man-childhood presented different strategies for coping with life's biggest projects and problems, different strategies for "being a man." But we still need to see how both of these worlds answer the same basic life questions and respond to the same limits of being human. We still have not pushed our conception of projects far enough. To see how these two strategies speak to the same questions about meaning, consider the movie *Knocked Up*.[3]

This particular iteration of the Apatow/Rogan shtick shows us a man-child whose world is turned upside down after he "knocks up" an accomplished, beautiful woman far out of his league, played by Katherine Heigl. He ultimately has to prove himself worthy of her by evolving from a slovenly but charming man-child into a somewhat more sophisticated but still charming fellow, someone worthy not just of her but of being her baby's father. The aims of becoming a worthwhile mate and father prove to be world-changing events. They reorder what matters to Rogan's character. So far, so good. He discovers a new world, but what kind of world is it? Does he simply discover that new things matter now more than what they once mattered? No, he discovers the old things don't mean much and many of the new things don't really matter much either.

It is important to notice that Rogan doesn't give up the life of the man-child simply because he decides he wants to start a new kind of project. Rather, something happens to him as a result of his current projects that forces him to start new projects. He scores with a woman way too good for him, but gets her pregnant. He fails in his life project precisely because he succeeded in one of the smaller projects that made up that life.

So now he has to become responsible, because he's a good guy. Every project has risks and things may not go according to plan. Trying to get lucky is no exception. In fact, in Heidegger's thought, the significance of a thing is often most clearly revealed when it fails to fulfill its function, because then this forces us to see what it already meant. In the case of *Knocked Up*, Rogan's impending fatherhood forces him to consider the meaning of his shiftless life. And once he throws himself into the role of being a dad, the stakes of the world shift. What would risk or loss entail now? I hope I won't be seen as either too morbid or too flippant if I insist that it would now involve the death of the child. It may seem too morbid because it's a lightweight Hollywood flick. And too flippant because it may seem to equate the "failure" of remaining a bachelor with the "failure" of a dead child. To see what I mean, we might benefit by turning from feel-good Hollywood comedies to a dark poem by one of the darkest poets of the twentieth century. But I promise we'll get back to *Knocked Up*.

Stillbirth

Paul Celan's poetry is marked by loss. The deepest of which corresponds to the real-life destruction of the German-Jewish world of Bukovina where he grew up. This tragedy is organized in his poetry around the death of his mother, who died in the Holocaust. But this is not the only loss that inhabits Celan's poetry. There is also François, his first son, who died soon after being born. Here is Celan's poem, "Epitaph for François:"

> Both doors of the world
> Stand open
> Opened by you
> At twilight
> We hear the doors slamming and slamming
> And we bear what can't be known
> And we bear what's green in your always[4]

The two doors refer to birth and death. And the fact that they both stand open is an indication of the fact that, for François Celan, these are not two events that occur at different times, but are one and the same event. Considered from the perspective of his brief life, the world of François is utterly empty of any significance. "Dumb, what climbed into life, dumb,"[5] Celan says elsewhere. François' world is dumb. It cannot speak. It is empty. Because he dies so soon after being born, he never has any projects, he never encounters anything. François' world might not be a world at all.

But the worlds of his parents are real. They are the "we" who continually hear the doors opening and shutting without remaining permanently open or shut. François' birth already had a certain meaning for them. He occupied a position in their world before he was born, and his stillbirth shattered their sense of what that meaning was. They had to find a way to cope with this loss, to adjust their lives to accommodate the reality of their absent son. Although I have not gone through such an experience, I can imagine it would be unbearable. But it has to be endured. How? Perhaps Celan is saying that it must be borne without knowing how it can be borne. The word I've translated here as "what can't be known" is *das Ungewisse*, which means "that which is uncertain." "We" don't know if or how we will endure this unendurable loss. But we do know one thing for certain: although the stillbirth only happens once, the memory of it continues. The doors remain open. We bear an "evergreen" wound, a rawness that never grows old. Something about the memory will therefore preserve what is often covered over. The stillborn child remains stillborn. This also means that he remains a baby even as François' younger brother Eric grows up.

When I said earlier that the possibility of the death of the child played the same role in the project of fatherhood that the possibility of fatherhood played in the project of man-childhood, what I meant was that both represent a certain failure of a project that shows what that project meant all along. The man-child is always haunted by the possibility of growing up. And the father is always haunted by the possibility of his child dying.

But, of course, the death of a child is something infinitely different than the prospect of inadvertently getting a casual sexual partner pregnant. And this means that the worlds are infinitely different. They aren't just different instances of the same sort of world.

After You, the World Will Always Be Empty

I come from a family where melancholia is endemic. My uncle says that once you have children, you are a hostage to fate. This was the first thing my father told me after I was in a car accident that should have killed me. I was no longer a child by then. My own daughter, Elena, had been born seven weeks earlier. I remember coming to in the ICU with no idea of where I was (my last memory was driving to work), but insisting that someone call my wife and let her know I wouldn't be home to help care for Elena, who was just beginning to show signs of the high-intensity personality that we now know well. At the time, an idea was fresh that five full years have covered over: what our children need more from us than anything is time. What I was worried about wasn't anything immediately about myself. What I worried about most was how little time I'd had with Elena, and how much more time there was to have. When Elena was born, my world began to change. It was still changing. I wasn't ready to leave.

The reason that I dwell on this experience is that it gets at the crucial notion of what shapes the world for both Heidegger and Celan. Beyond the significance of particular things we encounter, the full significance in our lives is found in the bare fact of time. Time is always with us in our projects, but for both Heidegger and Celan, it reveals itself in its most bare form in death. Death, the ultimate figure of the possibility of failure, looms as a possibility in any project. While we may not know when this failure will come, we know it is inevitable.

And no one else can die for me. Each person's death is unique. The easiest way of understanding that is to think about the unique meaning one's own death has. What Celan is saying is that the death of *any* human being is the irreversible loss of a whole world of meaning. This is true for ourselves, but it is even truer for those we would be happy to die in the place of. Because once a child is born, we cannot imagine bearing the world without them. This is true in a life that is full of other things that obscure this fundamental fact, but it is also true in the world of the stillborn child. The empty world of the stillborn child preserves this insight most clearly. But the possibility of the death of our children and our awareness and concern over that possibility make this a feature of parenthood generally.

This is the case even for a parent like Rogan's character in *Knocked Up*. In the movies, a reformed man-child is presented as suddenly caring passionately about things he never cared about before: pushing strollers in the park, rocking his baby late at night, and changing diapers. We know that Rogan has reformed when he finds out that Heigl's character has gone into labor and asks if she's had her "bloody show." This isn't the first question that a red-blooded man thinks to ask, so he must have reformed, right? And yes, all fathers know that things that seem unbearably gross, like labor and diapers, suddenly become valuable (a friend of mine said that when his wife was giving birth, he thought, "That thing is *functional*"). But if it turns out that reformed man-children are principally interested in labor and diapers, then they are in for a sore disappointment as their kids get older and these things disappear right when most of us are breathing a sigh of relief (only before taking another deep, concerned breath as our kids head to school).

The main thing that is required of a parent is the flexibility to care about different things as the occasion demands. This flexibility is possible because as being a father reveals, apart from the child, nothing else matters. This is also because the child is not a thing about which we can ask its purpose, but is a thing whose being is like ours but not us. And because everything that matters only matters in the fleeting itinerary of the growing child, nothing matters as much as the possibility of having time to be with our children and of our children having time of their own. After all, ultimately, what will be significant to them is not necessarily what is significant to us (otherwise I wouldn't have spent so much time doing "guys parades";

don't ask). And what we want more than anything, more than even our own immortality, is for our children to have a rich world of their own.

This realization marks Celan's deeply tragic poems addressed to his stillborn son François. But it also marks the poems he wrote about his other son, Eric. The death of François showed that both doors of the world were open. But they remain open as Celan watches Eric grow up, when Eric says his first word, and when he holds Eric's hand and walks through the streets of Paris, seeing scenes differently than when he was a young boy.

When I look at you, I see that both doors of the world are open. You have been born and someday you will die. But as long as I am alive, I will do what I can so you do not. I will die too, and I hope that it will be before you. Because the doors of my world are open also. You opened a door for me when you were born and everything that I thought I had control of, my time most of all, has been flying out that door ever since. Everything that once mattered no longer matters. And so I know that what seems to matter now will not always matter. I hope that some of what is in my life reaches you before my world is fully empty. Ever since you were born, my world has been emptying out. Once I might have been scared by that, but because I have discovered that I love you more than myself, I fear the emptiness of my world much less than I love the increasing fullness of yours.

After you, my world will always be empty.

NOTES

1   Martin Heidegger, *Being and Time*, trans. John Macquarrie and Edward Robinson (New York: Harper, 2008).
2   Ibid., H69ff.
3   *Knocked Up*, directed by Judd Apatow (Universal Pictures, 2007).
4   Paul Celan, *Gesammelte Werke* (Frankfurt: Suhrkamp, 2002), 1:105; my translation.
5   Ibid., 1:108; my translation.

CHAPTER 3

THE BORN IDENTITY

Becoming Daddy

It's exciting to be on the cusp of change. Over the past few decades there has been a shift in the activities that accompany a man's transition to "father." The clichéd picture of becoming a father used to include nervous pacing in green-walled hospital waiting rooms and passing out cigars with a pink or blue ribbon. Now, over 90 percent of fathers (at least in North America) are present at the birth of their child, massaging their laboring partner through contractions and even catching the baby and cutting the umbilical cord.

In the summer of 2008 I began collecting stories from couples as they began their journey into parenthood. It was a privilege to hear their tales, both before and after the birth of their first child, and to join them in their prenatal classes and reunions. This project was undertaken not only because I love to hear about birth, but to discover the other half of the story. Being pregnant and giving birth is a transformative experience for women, and most birth stories are told from a woman's perspective. But what does participating in these experiences mean for men?

In anthropology, narrative analysis (the study of stories) examines the context, content, and form of narratives in order to discover why and how a story is told. Narrative analysis recognizes that the stories we tell are important cultural and social clues to social status and identity.[1] Put more simply, the stories that we choose to tell say a lot about who we are and what we think. The stories mothers and fathers tell offer insights as to what "counts" toward their identities of "mom" or "dad."

When you put a bunch of mothers in the same room, they love to share their accounts of being pregnant and giving birth. It's partly entertainment, but it's also an important way for them to connect and pass on knowledge. Moms exchange humorous anecdotes, personal experiences (good and bad), and practical tips on coping with labor and the trials of early and later parenthood. By our stories we mark ourselves as someone who knows through experience and reinforce our identities as a "mom." But when you put a bunch of dads in the same room, even new dads, chances are they won't be regaling each other with stories about morning sickness, mucus plugs, or even how they felt upon first holding their child. The ease with which women recount their birth stories, and the disinclination of men to share theirs, points to a difference worth examining. It's not that birth isn't as important to fathers as to mothers or that they don't want to share their experiences of birth (they are more than willing to do so when asked). Men just talk about different things. But if stories are how we reinforce who we are, what *makes* a man a father?

Questioning one's identity is among the most complex and deeply personal philosophical issues anyone can tackle. Who am I? What makes me who I am? Am I a son, a man, a father? Am I my career? Am I all of these or none of these? Perhaps that is why most of us simplify our identities by using labels. We introduce ourselves with our name and perhaps a job title or other signifier. And while labels might orient others to where we are from or what we do, they usually don't convey who we really are or what we care about. So, as we get to know someone, we tell them stories. We tell stories to create who we are, to put some flesh on the identity labels we claim. Then we listen to others as they tell stories. Together, the stories a culture or society tells form a fluid definition for what it is that makes us who we are. These shared definitions of what various labels mean become particularly important when identities are in transition, such as when a man becomes a father.

Identity Transitions

It's a shift into a new stage of life for me. That's what it is. A life shift from being primarily a self-centered individual into being a parent and the reality that I will never not be a parent again.

Marc

It's like a tidal wave, a massive tidal wave. I wouldn't trade it for the world, but still, it's like whoa, my old life is over and I chose this.

Jim[2]

My husband is outside playing with our two children, watering the forest behind our house with water from the kiddie pool, bucket by bucket. Watching this scene, I am reminded of something he once told me: he said that the moment our daughter was born everyone started calling him "daddy," but that it took a while for him to really feel that this was who he was. He said, "There isn't one single moment when suddenly you feel you're a dad. It's a gradual becoming. It's something that's still happening." As far as society is concerned, acquiring the external or social identity of "father" is instantaneous. Like tipping the pool out all at once, the moment your child is born you are suddenly a parent. There are clues to this in the language we use. When the child is not yet born, you are *going to be* a father, but after birth you *are* a father, regardless of how you feel. The *internal* identity of father, the feeling of fatherhood to which my partner referred, is something which takes time to develop, bucket by bucket. Socially, it is a tidal wave of change that can leave a sense of disorientation and chaos. Suddenly, you are expected to be a "father," with all its implied traits and qualities. But fatherhood doesn't really happen overnight. Finding equilibrium and settling into a new identity takes time, and this is where it is helpful to be given a map to follow.

Socially (or externally), transitions are marked by rites of passage, both formally and informally, which serve to orient and guide the process of change. Familiar rites include graduations, birthday celebrations, and weddings, to name a few. These rites celebrate transitions and acknowledge changes in identity. In anthropology, rituals that accompany changes in social identity are often divided into three stages:[3]

1   A person (or group) is separated from their former identity. This can be accomplished through a change in costume or a change in location, such as the donning of a cap and gown or entering a ceremonial space.

KIMBERLEY FINK-JENSEN

2   Once separated from the "everyday self," there follows a time of transition (known as liminal time) during which a person is neither their former identity, nor their new identity. This phase is accompanied by ritual activities which publicly signify a change in status, such as a wedding or graduation ceremony.

3   The period of ritual ends by reincorporating the individual(s) into society, connecting them to a new or expanded identity (e.g., "I present to you the Class of 2010").

But what about the *internal* transition of identity, that feeling that you *are* what you have become? This is where storytelling re-enters the picture.

People tell stories for two main reasons. The first is to work out the *meaning* of their experience to their identity, to understand how their life has changed and what it means to who they are. The second is to externally *legitimize* their new identity status. Repetition of their story deepens the internal and external recognition of change, and makes the steps that need to be followed clearer for those that come after.[4] Anthropologists Cheryl Mattingly and Linda Garro state that "narrative mediates between an inner world of thought-feeling and an outer world of observable action and states of affairs."[5] In this way, stories and rites of passage reinforce one another in the internal and external worlds of transformation. Telling the story allows one to integrate the tidal wave of change, bucket by bucket.

Connection or Alienation?

Before we get lost in theory and metaphor, let's return to how a man becomes a dad. We all know the biology of this transformation, and can accept that you start being *called* a father once your baby is born. But does having a biological role in conception *make* you a father or are there some rites of passage which men must pass through in order to legitimately claim the title? Unlike graduating or getting married, the ritual behaviors and rites of passage which help to cement the identity of dad or father are less readily recognizable. That, and men don't talk about it much.

For women, it's mostly taken for granted that becoming pregnant begins the transition to motherhood. Pregnancy is a biological separation from the "everyday self" and there are constant physical and social reminders (baby showers, maternity clothes, prenatal appointments, and unsolicited advice from strangers) that underscore the state of transition. Birth completes the transformation, and suddenly a woman is also a mom. If you listen to mothers, these are the events that are at the center of their stories of transition, followed by the inevitable period of adjustment to life with a newborn. The story of birth is repeated frequently, especially in the early days when everyone wants to hear both the pleasant and sordid details of the event. This continual retelling serves to solidify a woman's new identity as she connects more deeply to her experience. (Wow! I gave birth? I must be different!).

For men, the rites of passage to fatherhood are less clearly defined. Because men do not biologically experience pregnancy, the time of transition remains largely unrecognized. It is not at all uncommon for men to defer to their partner to describe the events of pregnancy and birth. Pregnancy and birth are, after all, female experiences – at least, biologically. Instead of "Wow, I gave birth," it's more like "I didn't do much; all I did was feed her ice chips and tell her she was doing great." That just doesn't have the same impact. In fact, many fathers I spoke to described a feeling of separation from the process, an alienation which limits the event's power to connect them to their new identity as fathers.

"I want to be involved"

> I think most ... or many, many more fathers that I know want to be more involved in things. You know, of course, there's only so much you can do from the guy's side of things. But what I think is important is for fathers to have the opportunity and feel supported in their explorations of how to be involved in the process as much as they like, so that there are no barriers. If someone says "I want to do this," then no one will say, "No you can't do that; you're just the dad.
>
> Craig

> My involvement in prenatal care? Well yeah, actually I would like to be – even though I know that with most of the midwife stuff the focus is on the mother – I would like to be, just a little more acknowledged as a part of the process.
>
> Marc

Many expectant dads have a strong desire to be involved, to participate in, and experience pregnancy and birth. I remember addressing the first prenatal class I observed, with couples ranging from scared, to excited, to waiting for that first post-birth beer. The reaction to my study was immediate: "Finally, something for the dads! Someone *is* on our side!" As Craig pointed out above, there is "only so much" that men are able to do during the prenatal period and birth, and even that bit of involvement seems under-acknowledged. The modest attention that my study focused on their experiences was enough to draw comment. There was palpable excitement that they would finally be able to tell *somebody* stories about pregnancy and birth from the male perspective.

Over and over, expectant fathers expressed a desire to be more involved and recognized for their role in pregnancy and birth, something that promotes them above a member of the supporting cast. To put it another way, perhaps somewhat radically, men need to experience a kind of pregnancy too, a time in which coming changes are anticipated and their impacts sewn into the fabric of self-identity. It goes without saying that some women would be only too pleased if men also had to endure morning sickness, large weight gain, and the agony of giving birth. But given biological absolutes, there needs to be some other experience of a transitioning identity. Perhaps for men the period of gestation for a human baby should also be recognized as a period of gestation for fathers.

In many cultures outside the Western world, ritual involvement of men in birthing activities is well recognized. These activities ensure a safe pregnancy and delivery and play an important role individually and socially in the transformation of men into fathers.[6] Collectively, these rituals are referred to as "couvades." By having a clear ritual roadmap, it is perhaps easier for men in these cultures to make the transition into fatherhood. A few anthropologists[7] have concluded that although it is not widely recognized, "couvade" also exists in Western societies. Richard K. Reed argues that "couvade" in the West is any activity which increases the subjective experience of pregnancy for men.[8] And what I heard over the course of numerous interviews is that feeling involved and recognized as part of the process (the subjective experience) is what men want. Perhaps men need to be ritually pregnant, or to have a recognized period of "couvade" to reduce the sense of alienation from their experiences, to help them connect more deeply to their identities as fathers. The more they talk about it, the clearer the roadmap of transition will become.

Rites of Passage

It's an experience unlike anything else. It's very primitive; it's the only real thing that we're here to do, to procreate, right? And to see it all happen ... it's just ... amazing.

Steve

There really wasn't much that I could do ... I think that for me it was just being part of the experience – that was my little selfishness – just being a part of it.

Marc

At the moment that he was born, there was complete sheer joy – it seems odd to try and describe it further – just joy. I was completely blissed-out by having him and by having Tanis and to be able to be part of that whole experience.

Craig

By the "whole experience," these brand new fathers were talking about more than just being in the room for the birth of their child. But what forms the "whole experience" of pregnancy and birth for a man? If you were to ask a dad to list them, I doubt that any of them could. But ask them to tell you a story about what it means to be "pregnant," what were the highlights of birth, and the similarity of their answers may surprise you. Each of the fathers I interviewed mentioned the *same* key activities. These were:

- *Learning about pregnancy, birth, and early parenting through reading and talking to others.* Information allows fathers to build a sense of connection with the events their partner is experiencing and to feel prepared for their role in birth. Reading and talking to others also exposes expectant fathers to culturally shared ideas about fatherhood, pregnancy, and birth, and helps socialize them in their new identities as fathers.
- *Ensuring their partner is healthy physically and emotionally.* Expectant fathers quickly learn how important it is to help ensure their partner is healthy throughout their pregnancy. Given the physiological challenges of being pregnant, fathers-to-be discover that they have a key role in supporting their partner to maintain good nutrition, to balance rest and activity, and to manage stress. It also allows fathers involvement in providing the best start for their baby, and to develop a supportive connection with

their partner. Taking on greater responsibilities in the house, preparing food and caring for the welfare of their partner also accomplishes a shift to a more nurturing role which is required in fatherhood.

- *Attending prenatal appointments.* Making the time to attend prenatal appointments with the doctor or midwife gives fathers the opportunity to experience one of the key activities of pregnancy for women. This helps dads to feel closer to the process, and they are also there to ask questions and learn the same things as their partner. When it comes time to make decisions, they have the information and can easily be included.

- *Developing a connection to their baby.* Attending prenatal appointments also allows fathers to develop a sense of connection to their baby prior to birth, by hearing the child's heartbeat or seeing him or her on ultrasound. Since they don't have the mother's internal experience of the baby's movements, hearing the heartbeat, seeing ultrasound images, and externally feeling their baby's movement helps fathers to experience the reality of pregnancy. Connecting with their baby while still *in utero* is important in helping men to feel that they are fathers.

- *Supporting their partner to make decisions throughout pregnancy and birth.* There are many decisions that are made during the course of pregnancy and birth, including whether or not to undergo prenatal testing, type of care-provider and planned birth location, and other elements of the birth plan. Overall, the fathers I spoke to told me they felt "absolutely" included in decision-making, helping them to feel involved in the pregnancy and birth.

- *Attending prenatal classes.* In prenatal classes, men learn what to expect and what they can do during birth. It also provides them with the opportunity to connect with other expectant fathers. The research of anthropologist Richard K. Reed finds that prenatal education helps to develop men's identities as fathers.[9] Attending prenatal classes is a powerful way for men to focus on impending fatherhood, to further developing a connection to the baby, redefine their relationship with their partner as parents, and to define their relationship with members of the birthing team.

Although the men I interviewed did not agree on a defining moment that started them on the road to fatherhood, they did share a *feeling* of when it began. The feeling that they were actually a father-to-be came when there was a sense that their partner's pregnancy was a reality. This feeling might have come from a positive pregnancy test, hearing the baby's heartbeat, seeing an image on ultrasound, or feeling the baby's first kicks, but whatever the event was, it signified a separation from their "everyday self." Suddenly, financial and job security took on new importance, and expectant fathers felt inclined to start behaving differently.

After the birth of their child, all of the fathers placed importance on having "just been there" for the birth of their child, regardless of what their role in that actual birth ended up being. In that way they were truly present for the moment they "became" fathers.

Having said all this, let's return for a moment to the role of storytelling. If, as was stated earlier, people tell stories to develop a sense of meaning for their experiences and to legitimize their claims to a certain identity, then stories are a way of simultaneously connecting people to their experiences (to make them seem more "real") and to their identity. Rites of passage (a particular set of experiences) are a way to publicly and legitimately connect a person to a particular identity. Therefore, if a person completes the rites of passage required for an identity and then tells stories about that experience, they are both internally and externally reinforcing their connection to their newly acquired identity. The story of *My wife and I had a baby and this is what it was like* is a kind of ritual that signifies and legitimizes a new father. By contrast, if fathers feel disconnected or alienated from the experiences of pregnancy and birth, they will be more likely to feel a lack of security in their identity as fathers.

If we review the list of activities that new fathers had in common, you'll spot something interesting. All of them serve the function of enhancing a sense of connection to the experience of transition (pregnancy and birth), to their partner, to the baby, or to the identity of "father." They also perform the function of birth rituals mentioned in our discussion of "couvade" in other cultures: they safeguard pregnancy and delivery and play an important role individually and socially in forming the identities of fathers. Although these activities are not consciously recognized as such, being involved in the ways mentioned above may easily be viewed as nascent rites of passage to fatherhood.

Daddy at Last

I asked one new father if he had told the guys at work about his birth experiences. He laughed and answered, "No, no, no, not really. No. They don't need to know all that stuff." He continued, "I hadn't thought about it much, to be honest with you. I *should* repeat it more and more and more because it will help me to remember it." Another father emailed me later saying, "I enjoyed talking with you and found it an important part of my own mental preparing and then post-birth internal processing. Thank you for that."

When a woman tells her story of giving birth, it connects her to the experience and to her child. That sense of connection deepens the feeling that she *is* a mom. If to be a father is to be connected to the elements of transition, to the mother of their child, and to their baby, then anything which serves to increase the feeling of connection will also serve to increase the sense that you are a father. Perhaps most importantly, though, a reinforced feeling of fatherhood increases your satisfaction with that as an aspect of your identity. Telling stories about how you developed a connection, and how you are maintaining that connection, also serves to reinforce that identity. Since being there for birth and being involved in pregnancy are important aspects of developing that connection, it follows that getting men to tell these stories will help reinforce their identities as dads. And the more they tell their stories, the clearer the road ahead for fathers of the future.

Postscript

At the conclusion of my series of interviews with dads, I asked them to share the advice they would give to other men about to become fathers. Two answers stuck out, and I am going to give the last word – the last stories – to these men:

> Be as prepared and as educated as you can and be open to simply having an experience. I think your experience depends on whether you're preparing for something that you are going to do or whether you're preparing for an experience that you're going to have. Because if you're preparing for something that you are going to do and it goes differently, then you are not prepared for it, but if you're prepared to have an experience then you just accept what comes along and deal with it with the tools that you have at your disposal. If all you have is duct tape, then you make it work with duct tape; if you have more sophisticated tools, then you make it happen with more sophisticated tools. But at the end of the day you have the experience of having a wonderful baby come into your world … I'm liking fatherhood very much and I'm recommending it highly to others. (Craig)

Everyone seems to focus on the delivery, those few short hours, and a lot less on how to be a parent after. Be mentally prepared for the demands of having a baby. That's probably the biggest thing. Make sure that you are prepared and accept that things are going to change and it's going to be different. But daddyhood's good. Yeah, it's all good. (Marc)

NOTES

1 Dorothy C. Holland and Naomi Quinn, "Culture and Cognition," in Dorothy C. Holland and Naomi Quinn (eds.) *Cultural Models in Language and Thought* (Cambridge: Cambridge University Press, 1987).
2 Unless otherwise noted, quotations throughout this chapter are excerpts from interviews I conducted with first-time parents. They have been edited for clarity. Out of respect for their privacy, all names have been changed.
3 See Arthur Van Gennep, *The Rites of Passage*, revd. edn. (New York: Routledge, 2004); Victor Witter Turner, *The Ritual Process: Structure and Anti-Structure*, illustrated edn. (Chicago: Aldine Transaction, 1995).
4 Arthur Frank, quoted in Judy Segal, *Health and the Rhetoric of Medicine* (Carbondale: Southern Illinois University Press, 2005).
5 Cheryl Mattingly and Linda C. Garro (eds.) *Narrative and the Cultural Construction of Illness and Healing* (Berkeley: University of California Press, 2000).
6 Van Gennep, *The Rites of Passage*.
7 For example, Robbie E. Davis-Floyd, *Birth as an American Rite of Passage* (Berkeley: University of California Press, 1992); Richard K. Reed, *Birthing Fathers: The Transformation of Men in American Rites of Birth* (New Brunswick: Rutgers University Press, 2005).
8 Reed, *Birthing Fathers*.
9 Ibid.

CHAPTER 4

FATHERHOOD AND THE MEANING OF LIFE

Some men have claimed that, though they did not realize it at the time, they were incomplete before becoming fathers. Their lives were missing some component necessary for them to experience ultimately meaningful lives, and fatherhood was that component. Prior to becoming a father myself, I was always suspicious about such claims. First, many philosophers deny there is a meaning to life at all. And secondly, even if there is a meaning to life, it certainly seemed a stretch to think that some men must wait until fatherhood to fully experience it. After all, a man's life (both before and after fatherhood) is much more than being a father: there is his career, his friends, his significant other, his hobbies, and so on. How could it be that among so many varied aspects of a man's life, some men are able to find ultimate meaning only in being a father? After becoming a father myself, I quit asking this question. Instead, I became one who likewise claims that fatherhood is what gives my life a meaningfulness that was, unbeknownst to me, previously lacking.

In this chapter, I will offer some general philosophical reasons why this may be the case. Before doing so, however, I want to clarify a few points. First, I am not saying that all men do, or even should, finally find their life's meaning in being a father. There are many men who do not, and I am in no position to judge them. Furthermore, I am not even claiming that all fathers *should* find their life's meaning in fatherhood. Instead, I am speaking only to those men who, like me, believe fatherhood provided *them* a component they were previously missing so as to have ultimately meaningful lives. Finally, saying that fatherhood gives some men's lives their ultimate meaning is not to claim that other aspects of those men's lives are completely meaningless or unimportant. There are degrees of meaning, and certain aspects of a man's life can be, in some sense, meaningful without thereby providing ultimate "meaning" to his life in the way fatherhood does.

Let me begin by discussing some problems with claiming that father-hood can constitute a man's life's meaning. If I can show that these problems are not as difficult as they seem, then I will have gone a long way toward demonstrating that some of us can confidently claim what we already know inside of ourselves: that we found our lives' ultimate meaning in fatherhood. The first problem with claiming this lies in a certain paradox. To say that being a father is my life's meaning is the same as saying that the meaning of *my* life is found in the process of tak-ing care of *another* life. After all, that's what being a parent is all about – doing things for those to whom we're parents. It is ultimately an activity that is directed not to us, but to others, our children. One of my friends (who also claims to have found his life's meaning in fatherhood) expressed this sentiment exactly when he wrote to me, in capital letters, that his life "IS ALL ABOUT THE KIDS!" But herein lies the paradox: if a father's life is all about the kids, then it seems that the father's life can't be about the father! How can something that is not about the father constitute his ultimate life's meaning? While people do indeed find some meaning in devoting themselves to others, isn't it still (so the objection goes) somewhat contradictory to say that the ultimate mean-ing of one's life could be constituted by doing something that is not directed toward oneself, but to *somebody else*? Isn't that the same as say-ing that fundamentally one's own life, in and of itself, isn't ultimately important or meaningful?

Although this paradox also faces mothers who want to claim that moth-erhood is the meaning of their lives,[1] I think it causes special problems in the case of fathers. Fathers lack the intimate biological connection to their children that exists between children and their birth mothers. Our chil-dren aren't ever a "part of us" as they are of the mother while being carried in the womb. Nor do we fathers have any special role in giving physical

MICHAEL BARNWELL

birth (other than boiling water, letting the mothers squeeze our hands, and trying not to faint ourselves!). Indeed, the very act by which we become biological fathers is very distinct, both temporally and physically, from the end result of a child being born. As a result, our children are, so to speak, very separate from us, separate in a way that they aren't from their mothers. Given this complete "otherness" of our children, it seems as if an activity oriented toward *them* cannot give *us* our life's meaning.

While this paradox may at first seem especially problematic, I think it can be easily resolved by looking at what being a father is. Fatherhood is comprised of various activities, which range from changing diapers, making funny faces to make a child laugh, listening to and advising your children about issues they have in their lives, playing a game with them, or simply spending quiet, peaceful time in their presence. And while it is true that those activities are *directed* toward somebody else, if we do them they are nonetheless *our* activities – they are things that *we* are doing. Moreover, they are activities that are a result of *our* choices. Nobody has to be a father in the first place – and sometimes even those who are fathers do not, for various reasons, choose to engage in the types of activities I have just mentioned. If you do those activities I have mentioned, then they are activities that you have chosen.

This realization helps solve the paradox mentioned above. Although being a father is comprised of activities directed toward others, it is still about *us* to an extent because it is comprised of *our* activities that are a result of *our* choices. We are not totally irrelevant to the process. We ourselves, by virtue of our choices and activities, are intimately involved in the process of fatherhood.

What I have just tried to do is resolve the paradox mentioned above by observing that fatherhood's being directed toward others need not disqualify it from constituting our own life's meaning. But I believe this resolution not only shows that fatherhood is not disqualified from constituting life's meaning, but also provides some positive reasons to think that fatherhood can indeed constitute a man's life's meaning.

First, many philosophers claim that the meaning of one's life cannot be found solely within or with reference to oneself anyway. A life that truly has meaning, they say, reaches out beyond itself to affect others and make an impact that is, in some sense, significant and positive.[2] Although some disagree with this assessment, at the very least it is relatively uncontroversial that making such an impact *can* be a component in an ultimately meaningful life. And all other things being equal, a life that does create a positive impact does seem to be more meaningful than a similar life that doesn't. Given this, the other-directedness of fatherhood may actually be regarded not as a problem, but rather as a possible reason why fatherhood can provide ultimate meaningfulness to some men.

This point, in fact, reminds me of the moment I became convinced that fatherhood constituted the meaning of my life. It was when my son was only about six months old and I was home watching him. I remember being very stressed about various things in my life at the time: finances, career, relationships, and so on. I realized he needed a diaper change and took him up to his room. While changing him, I started making funny faces and noises in an attempt to make him laugh. (Luckily, I had always possessed this particular skill with reference to him.) And laugh he did! He kept laughing and laughing to the point where he was beside himself. It was at that moment that I realized this was ultimately all that really mattered – making this kind of positive impact on my son. And no matter how bad things were in the rest of my life, I knew that at that moment there was nothing else I could have been doing that would have been making a bigger impact in the world. Even if I were solving all the other stresses and problems in my life, doing so would not have been as important to me as what I was doing at that moment: causing my son to be as happy as he could be. Indeed, no other person in the world could be any happier than he was at that time, and it was because of what I was able to do for my son. Although it may have been something as silly as me making funny faces, my doing so was having infinite impact so far as my son was concerned. I realized that I, and my attention, mattered infinitely to my son regardless of what else may be occurring in my life.

Now, I don't mean to paint any sort of Pollyanna picture that if you make your children happy while changing their diapers then nothing else matters and every other problem in your life goes away. Far from it! Those other problems were still there, and I still have to deal with those and other problems daily. Nor do I mean to imply that a father can always make their children happy – very often they will not. Instead, I think what affected me so much at that moment was that I was able to have some positive impact on my son, and that my making that positive impact was more important to me than other things that were going on in my life. Sure, any particular moment in which I'm making my son laugh would pass and he would then no longer be laughing. But the moment will hopefully never pass in which I'm able to have some sort of positive impact on my son – whether it be by listening to him, correcting him, helping him, or doing something else. And as long as that's the case, then my life will have meaning.

If this is correct, then the problem with which we started this chapter isn't really a problem at all but instead provides a way in which to understand how fatherhood can provide ultimate meaning for some men's lives. It can do so exactly because fatherhood is an activity that is directed toward another.

I had also mentioned, while responding to the paradox with which we began, that in many cases fatherhood consists of certain *activities* that are a result of our *choices*. What I now want to do is to show that these two characteristics of fatherhood – activities and choices – provide further reason to think that one can find one's meaning in life by being a father. Indeed, both of these characteristics have been variously mentioned by philosophers as components that help provide a life its meaning.

Let's start with the *activities* aspect. Although some may deny that activities of some sort are absolutely required for a meaningful life, it again seems uncontroversial that engaging in certain activities can help provide one's life with ultimate meaning. Interestingly, even some of those who deny there is any meaning to life at all (called "nihilists") often counsel activity since it at least helps one not think about what they take to be a meaningless life. Both sides seem to agree, therefore, that there is some value to activity. And if you believe that fatherhood provides meaning to life, then you will think that fatherly activities help provide that meaning.

I presume this idea of fatherly activity providing meaning to life is what makes the "empty nest syndrome" so difficult for some parents. Although there are still fatherly activities that a father can do for a child once he or she has left home, the number of those activities is no doubt drastically decreased. Furthermore, many of the activities that remain are really not all that "activity-like" anyway, such as providing financial assistance. This explains many fathers' insistence on actually doing things for their children whenever they visit home. It also helps to explain why parents typically want their children living close to them – the farther away they live, the harder it would be to actively do things for them.

If fatherhood does provide a meaning to life, therefore, it may do so partly in virtue of the fatherly activities one performs. If a father receives his meaning in life from performing those activities, it is because he himself has *chosen* to perform those activities. As I mentioned above, many fathers (for various reasons) do not perform fatherly activities. If you are, it is because at some level you freely chose to perform those activities. This idea of freely choosing to do something, moreover, is an idea with a long history of being associated with a meaningful life. Your very choosing to do something means that the thing you chose to do must provide value to you. Otherwise, you wouldn't have chosen it. In fact, some philosophers, called existentialists, go so far as to say that it is our very choice itself which creates the value in the chosen activity – a chosen option becomes meaningful to me because I chose it.[3]

Perhaps a quick anecdote, unrelated to my being a father, would help explain this last point. I once spent a summer taking a language class in a foreign country. There was a girl in that class, let's call her Sally, who loved oatmeal but couldn't find it where we lived. At the time, Sally and I were just friends, and neither of us was interested in our being anything beyond that. One day on a lark, however, I decided that I was going to find and buy oatmeal for Sally. I did. Now, you might think that, if anything, this would have caused Sally to become romantically attracted to me. To the contrary, it wasn't Sally's feeling that subsequently changed – it was mine! After buying the oatmeal, I immediately became very romantically attracted to Sally. Neither her looks nor her personality nor her attitude toward me had changed to cause this conversion in me. Instead, it seemed that my *choosing* to do some activity for Sally caused me to value her more; Sally now *meant* more to me because I had chosen to perform some action for her. (As the reader has probably guessed, Sally never seemed to have similar feelings toward me; perhaps if I could have convinced her to buy me some bacon and eggs things would have been different!)

Now, I realize this anecdote does not prove the existentialist claim that choices actually create value, nor do I have any interest in doing so here. The main point I want to make is that a person's choices are intimately bound up with what that person finds valuable and thus are meaningful to him. And if you have chosen to do fatherly activities – and especially if you have chosen to regard fatherhood as the primary aspect of your life – then it does indeed make sense for you to claim that fatherhood is the meaning of your life. Note, furthermore, that this doesn't mean other aspects of your life (marriage, career, being a son to your own parents) need be meaningless to you or non-valuable. Instead, I'm simply trying to say that if, like me, you have realized that being a father is what ultimately gives your life meaning, it probably results in some sense from your having chosen to be a father and perform fatherly activities.

This emphasis on choosing to perform fatherly activities, however, brings us to another problem with claiming that fatherhood is the meaning of life. Indeed, this problem is a version of one of the most famous arguments against there being any meaning of life at all! To explain this problem, we need to consider the ancient Greek myth of a man named

MICHAEL BARNWELL

Sisyphus. According to the myth, Sisyphus' misdeeds earned him a particularly harsh punishment. He was forced by the Greek gods to roll a heavy boulder up a hill, an activity requiring considerable effort, strength, and sweat. After Sisyphus finally pushed the boulder to the top of the hill, the gods would make it roll all the way back down, forcing Sisyphus to start the process again. The especially brutal part of his punishment is that this scenario would happen over and over forever.

Sisyphus' existence is thought to be a paradigmatic case of a meaningless life.[4] It is filled with endless and repetitive activity (pushing a rock) that is all for naught. Nothing ever comes from his pushing that rock except for his having to push it yet again. His life seems pointless. Analogously, it is thought that trying to construct life's meaning out of activities is similarly pointless. Any time we complete some activity, there is just another activity that we undertake – and on and on until we die. Constructing the meaning of our lives from fatherly activities faces a similar challenge. Every time one fatherly activity is accomplished, another arises. It seems never ending. We, as fathers, seem to be incessantly pushing that fatherly rock up the hill, just like Sisyphus. Is such a Sisyphean struggle really the way to find life's meaning?

Sisyphus' situation does indeed sound dire. But I don't think that we fathers need to identify too much with his pointlessness, as there is a big difference between Sisyphus and us. The object of Sisyphus' actions is a rock, whereas ours is our children! Part of the reason Sisyphus' existence sounds so awful to us is that he is forced to expend so much energy on something as inconsequential and base as a rock. Who cares about rocks? But our children aren't rocks (though they do seem to have quite a predilection in their toddler years to throw them!). We *do* care about our children in a way that we don't care about rocks. Moreover, our children grow, change, and mature as a result of our efforts, unlike rocks. So, our lives of children oriented activities need not seem as meaningless to us as Sisyphus' life of rock oriented activities seems to him. We're not just simply rolling an inanimate stone up a hill, but rather doing things that matter to another sentient, living human being. Our children have value to us in a way that rocks do not.

This last point, though, raises a further concern. Is it really true that our children have value in a way a rock does not so as to help us avoid Sisyphus' fate? While it may seem ridiculous to most readers that I dare even ask this question, allow me to explain why the answer is not necessarily as obvious as it no doubt seems. Recall that we are trying to defend the claim that, for some of us men, the meaning of our lives consists in being a father. But suppose this pattern holds for our children. In that case, the meaning of their lives would likewise consist in being a father (or mother) to their children. And the meaning of their children's (our grandchildren's) lives would be in being fathers (and mothers) to their children, and so on. In philosopher's terms, this sets up a chain of seeming instrumental goods without any actual intrinsic goods at the end of the chain; there appears to be no independent, self-standing "value" anchoring the chain of meaning, so to speak.

Let me make this point a little differently. Usually, some activity has value in that it produces something distinct from itself. For example, baking has value in that it produces a cake that can be eaten. If, however, the only point of baking were to perform more baking, so that more baking could be done and so on, then you would think I was crazy to say that baking has value since all it does is enable more baking! But doesn't what I have been saying in these last two paragraphs ultimately amount to the same thing – that the point of being a father is so that our children can be fathers, so their children can be fathers, and so on? And if so, then how can being a father be ultimately meaningful? Sure, being a father may *feel* meaningful to us, but feeling isn't necessarily the same as reality. As one famous philosopher has pointed out, it is possible that even Sisyphus could *feel* like his life was meaningful if the gods were to have implanted in him a love to roll rocks up hills. This feeling, though, wouldn't change the *actuality* of the meaninglessness of his situation.[5] Likewise, when we fathers step back and look at the big picture I have just sketched, the feeling of meaningfulness that we get from being a father may not match the reality. It appears that the challenge posed by the myth of Sisyphus remains, except now it's spread out over successive generations: I'm a father, so my son can be a father, so he can be a father, and so on without end.

Sisyphus' challenge is indeed a formidable one, and it's often hard to know what to say in response to it. Its intractability is most likely the reason most philosophers don't broach the problem of the meaning of life in the first place: it's too difficult! But I think we can at least say a few things in response. The first thing to note is that some activities are valuable just insofar as they are activities that someone enjoys. For example, some chefs value baking not just because it necessarily yields a sweet tasting dessert, but because the activity of baking itself brings them joy. Likewise, the very activity of being a father could be valuable to one regardless of whether the child turns out to be a parent or not.

I also think we can challenge the assumption that our children have no value independent of their being fathers and mothers themselves.

MICHAEL BARNWELL

First, nothing I have said entails that *every* person has to find their meaning in life in being a parent. I have simply said that *I* do (and I suspect some of you do, too). So, the putative value-less "chain" I mentioned above need not begin. Second, value need not be the same thing as meaning.[6] Even if our children had no meaning in their lives (which we hope is not the case), that still would not mean that they lack value – far from it. In fact, it is because we are already confident they are valuable that we hope, for their sake, that they too find meaning in their lives. It is outside the scope of this chapter to go through all the possible things that can make a person valuable (the history of philosophy has listed various things, such as a person's rationality and a person's status as being the creation of a divine being). And if our children are indeed valuable in and of themselves, then being fathers to them can provide meaning to our lives.

Some, no doubt, may believe that I have still missed the point of Sisyphus' challenge. How, they will ask, can fatherhood or anything else matter given that we're all going to die one day anyway? In fact, the whole human race will supposedly cease to exist once our sun burns out. Given this, isn't all of our and our children's metaphorical rock-pushing still fated to come to naught? And even if we weren't to die out, it is still hard to believe anything we do in this life is meaningful given that we and our lives are so tiny when compared to the vast expanses of the universe. Can our pushing this little rock of fatherhood in our small corner of the universe be truly meaningful?

These latter worries persistently vex philosophers dealing with the meaning of life. While I do not pretend to address them adequately here, a few things ought to be noted. First, those with particular religious beliefs in an afterlife may not, for various reasons, be bothered by the shortness or minuteness of our earthly life.[7] Second, the brevity of our lives may not be an issue anyway. If *my* life is to have meaning for *me*, I don't want that meaning shoved off into thousands of years from now – I want that meaning *now* during my life. The fact that my life won't have meaning thousands of years from now is, in some senses, irrelevant to me because I won't be around thousands of years from now anyway! A similar point can be said with regard to our minuteness. I don't care if my life has meaning on Pluto or in some distant galaxy. I don't live in those places! If my life is to have any meaning at all, it *better* have meaning here in this little corner of the universe. And since this tiny corner of the universe is the only place where my life will ever be, then the only things that matter to me are the things that happen in it, such as being a father.

As indicated at the beginning of this chapter, I have not argued that all fathers ought to find the ultimate meaning of their lives in fatherhood. Similarly, I have not claimed that other aspects of a father's life are meaningless and incapable of providing ultimate meaning to some men's lives. What I have instead tried to do is offer some philosophical reflections that can be appealed to by those who already know, without any prior need of philosophical argument, that fatherhood is what ultimately gave meaning to their lives. And although these arguments would not necessarily convince professional philosophers who are skeptical of life having meaning, they may nonetheless be helpful to men who want to explain why "Daddy" is their *true* first name.

NOTES

1   This paradox was pointed out in Sarah Conly, "Can a Life of Child-Rearing Be Meaningful?" *Philosophy Now* 24 (1999): 24.
2   Many philosophers have made this point, including Robert Nozick, Susan Wolf, and David Schmidtz. Please note that making this claim is not the same as saying that for a person to be happy or experience joy, his life must reach out beyond itself and affect others. Joy and meaningfulness are two different concepts, neither of which is necessarily implied by the other. Moreover, claiming that having an impact is part of a meaningful life does not imply that *any* impact one has on others contributes toward one's life being meaningful. Which impacts do and do not count toward making a life meaningful is a separate question that cannot be explored here.
3   Perhaps the most famous example is that of a young French man having to decide whether to stay with his mother or join the Free French Forces in England during World War II. See Jean-Paul Sartre, *Existentialism and Human Emotions*, trans. Bernard Fechtman (New York: Philosophical Library, 1948).
4   The most famous discussion of Sisyphus' relation to the meaning of life is Albert Camus, *The Myth of Sisyphus and Other Essays*, trans. Justin O'Brien (New York: Vintage, 1991).
5   Richard Taylor, "The Meaning of Life," in *Good and Evil* (New York: Macmillan, 1970), pp. 256–68.
6   Robert Nozick makes this point in "Value and Meaning," in *Philosophical Explanations* (Cambridge, MA: Harvard University Press, 1981), pp. 162–9.
7   It should be noted that some philosophers argue that *simply* appealing to an afterlife or a particular religious tradition does not necessarily solve all questions with regard to life's meaning. To address these issues, though, is outside the scope of this essay.

MICHAEL BARNWELL

PART II

ETHICS AND PARENTING STYLES

CHAPTER 5

IN VIRTUE OF UPBRINGING

The Art of Raising a Good Person

If you've visited an elementary school during the last ten years or so, you've probably seen posters on classroom walls proclaiming that "character counts." I think I first saw one about nine years ago. Aside from my initial shock that posters had to be put up to remind people of such obvious things (are these kids all set to become monsters if some visual sound bite doesn't remind them every day?), I couldn't help but wonder at the time what goes into making a child ethical. Perhaps it's something that happens naturally on its own as they mature. Maybe ethics is just an archaic byproduct of the spankings dads used to give their kids. Maybe it's something society takes care of when a kid gets to school and all those rules and posters are awaiting them. Then again, maybe not.

Given how many unethical actions seem to take place daily in our world, it's safe to say these matters don't entirely take care of themselves, or at least not with everyone. You can call me a skeptic, but something tells me it takes a lot more than a handful of reminders and rules to produce an ethical person.

No doubt parents are very important in this process. And historically, fathers have been expected to make strong contributions. I contend that if we as fathers don't get the job done right early in a child's formative years, it just gets more difficult as time goes on to get them back on the right path. It all compounds over time: their repeated choices produce tendencies which become habits which make similar future choices very likely and taken collectively form what we call character. And yes, character definitely counts. But if we ignore our role in this process and leave it to institutions to later try and overturn five to ten years of bad habits using a few signs and speeches, well, good luck with that. Hopefully, they can help keep a good kid on the right path that way, but it's up to us to deliver children to the world that are already on the right path.

On Ethical Choices

So we've decided we want our children to have good character, since otherwise they might bite other kids and steal their toys when they get to daycare. Sounds good. After all, those discussions with the teachers about Johnny's tantrums can get pretty embarrassing. But our reasons include more than that. Adult life provides us with an abundance of opportunities to dump on each other, and I for one don't want to add more jerks to the general population. As we said, we want our kids to make ethically good choices. We want them to consistently do the right thing.

But is making ethical choices the same thing as having good character? Of course, as philosophers love to point out, it all depends on what you mean by those words. But for the sake of discussion, character focuses on the quality of *habits*, while being ethical is an aspect of our *choices*: whether they are morally right or wrong choices. Tommy's telling a lie is a choice he made. The impulse he might have to tell lies when facing problems is a habit. But repeatedly making ethically bad choices produces certain bad habits, so you can see they are related.

One important difference though is how we judge habits versus how we critique actions. While habits are thought of as being good or bad by how they further or inhibit our goals, in philosophy, an action can be considered ethical or unethical based on a number of things: the specifics of the act itself, how it compares to other choices that could have been made, the consequences of the action, and even the motive of the action. So if Tommy tells a lie, we might need to look at what he said, how it impacted someone, what his other options were, and what motivated him to lie.

On this last note, why would we care *why* Tommy chose to lie? Isn't a lie unethical regardless of why someone did it? Granted, sometimes things can be that simple. But consider a situation in which Tommy chooses to visit his grandmother in the hospital instead of playing ball with his friends. At first blush, this sounds like an ethically commendable act. Way to go, Tommy! But think of how important the following possible motives would be in determining that: he wants a bigger stake in her will; he thinks it's his duty; he knows there's an awesome Xbox 360 set up in her hospital room; he doesn't want his mother yelling at him about it anymore; he feels for her being alone in the hospital. It's hard to ignore the impact motive has on our thinking about whether someone's actions are ethical.

Would we be satisfied that we have raised ethical children if their actions appear to be ethical but their motives are impure or even cold? The philosopher Immanuel Kant felt the most important motive was acting out of a sense of duty, doing something simply because it is the right thing to do. Some of us today would prefer to see our children act out of a combination of a respect for justice *and* concern for others. Your mileage may vary. But the point is we don't simply want to raise ethical robots ("Danger! Danger! Chronologically advanced human approaching sidewalk!"). We want them to do the right thing, but do it for genuinely good reasons, ideally out of love and concern for people.

What does this mean specifically for our goal of raising ethical kids? Well, as fathers, we have to recognize that promoting good habits is in the end not enough. As adults, they might do ethical things for higher reasons or simply out of habit. No one can control this. We can only hope for the best on that count. Maybe they will develop a love of goodness and empathy for others along the way, but maybe they won't. In our role as dads, we provide them with opportunities for growth. The rest is up to them.

Aristotle on Character

So now we realize that trying to build character can only help our children become ethical so much. But what exactly is good character and how do we promote it in our kids? In Aristotle's *Nichomachean Ethics*, the great philosopher lays out in detail what character traits we need to cultivate in children and how to achieve this. Some of this detail is only relevant if you happen to be an Athenian citizen living during the fourth century BCE, but many of his insights on character still stand today.

First of all, according to Aristotle, people seek happiness, which hardly sounds profound. However, when you realize by happiness he means a *flourishing life*, one in which we continually act virtuous over a long period of time, it starts to sound interesting. Happiness, for Aristotle, is not just a momentary smile after eating some ice cream. Whereas today we tend to think of happiness as a passing feeling of joy ("I was happy at the party"), Aristotle understood it primarily as a long-term quality of life ("he lived a happy life").

As people, we strive to be all that we can be, so to speak – or more accurately, do all we are capable of doing given that we have certain basic human needs and desires and of course individual talents. To achieve this is to flourish in one's life, to be happy in a full and rich sense. And, for Aristotle, this requires starting down the right path as a child. We need to develop the proper habits during childhood or we will go down paths that can make it very difficult for us to achieve a happy, satisfying life.

For instance, a child that becomes adept at manipulating his parents and friends to get what he wants will likely continue that behavior in his adult relationships. Obviously, he can change later, but the odds of that happening decrease as the habit gains strength over years of repetition (which is why usually the best advice for a victim of domestic abuse is to quit trying to change him – just get the heck out of there). And as we all know habits of procrastination can be very difficult to overcome.

Of course, not all habits are bad. Good habits carry us through much of our lives and we all have our share of them (thank goodness!). Virtues like kindness, patience, humility, and gratitude are learned by us over the years. For Aristotle, happiness in life lies in exemplifying such virtues in our actions, and we are typically rewarded by the degree to which we can do this. Humans are social beings, so it's no surprise that a rewarding life involves not only excellence in our chosen endeavors, but excellence in how we interact with others. Taken together, these good and bad habits we have – our virtues and vices – can be said to constitute our character.

But if we are to cultivate virtues in our children so they can live happy lives, how do we know a good habit when we see one? Is it just a matter of imitating successful, smiling people like the ones we see in TV commercials? Sometimes I wonder. But Aristotle had a better idea: a virtue is the middle ground between two extremes. So courage, for example, would be the midpoint between the extremes of hiding under a table (cowardice) and rushing at the enemy without a plan (foolhardiness). I think he was on to something here. For most every virtue, there does appear to be two vices that lie on each side of it in which we get too much (excess) or too little (deficiency) of what is needed. Modesty is surrounded by bashfulness and shamelessness. Generosity is the mean between stinginess and excessive extravagance. And so on.

But there's no magical formula for figuring out where that point is in each case. For Aristotle, determining that proper middle ground varies by situation and is a developed skill itself. Hopefully, a parent already has a good sense of it and children will learn the skill along the way through osmosis.

There's room for variation, too. The virtue of charity as it exists in the West looks excessive to many people from Asia. Where Aristotle places the mean for pride seems too boastful to some people today. It's going to vary to some extent by individuals, cultures, and the times. But as we are all human beings who need certain things in order to thrive, such as achievements, recognition and acceptance from others, friendships, self-respect, and so on, these will only vary so much.

This leads us to two very important character traits that are not exactly virtues for Aristotle but in a sense are more important than the virtues: *practical wisdom* and *self-control*. Practical wisdom is that skill that enables us to successfully find the virtuous middle in a situation, while self-control is the will power to follow the conclusion reached by wisdom. Obviously, we're not going to get very far if we can't figure out where the virtuous action lies and if we can't bring ourselves to do the right thing once we figure it out! After all, nobody's perfect. We've all got competing desires and impulses within us that often make it difficult to do what we know we should. (In fact, I'm currently on the lookout for a pitch-fork wielding mob of neighbors angry about my tall grass.) And thanks to the efforts of commercial television and the various media, we've got to contend with more competing desires and impulses now than ever before.

Lacking experience, children have to develop both of these traits to become virtuous, thriving adults, and the sooner they do so, the better. But achieving practical wisdom seems to require a lot of life experience, often into the adult years – if ever. Think of how much you learned from your first job and your first serious relationship (even if they both stunk in hindsight!). That's why we as fathers have to strategically substitute our wisdom (assuming we have some) in place of the children's until they have acquired enough judgment to consistently make good decisions without our guidance. We do this already of course. As dads, we're paying the rent, so they only get so many choices of where to go to school or what to eat for dinner.

Additionally, it's important that children do as we say when it counts. If they learn to comply consistently and effortlessly, they develop self-control, the ability to follow their own good judgment in the future. We're not talking about dictating what flavor of candy they eat. We're talking about expecting them to go to bed when you tell them to go to bed, to study when it's time to do homework, and so on.

If this sounds too paternalistic to you, keep in mind the goal is not controlling your child. *Au contraire*. The goal is *freeing* your child ASAP.

Freeing them to do what? Whatever they want to do without nagging or coercion from us, just *trust*. Instinctively, we can't place much trust in someone who's not in control of himself (likewise most cats get visibly nervous around small children – they can sense when kids lack self-control). We tend to coerce a child precisely when we give them some freedom but can't trust them to act responsibly in that situation.

Freeing them from what? From having their emotions, impulses, and desires override good sense. Infants are born with no control over their emotions, and that's part of what makes them so endearing (and loud). But as they become capable of obeying us and likewise disobeying us, our work begins. There's a reason it's called *raising* a child. They need their father's assistance and guidance to become adults in the full sense of the term: emotionally mature, joyful, and able to take on responsibilities.

Nobody gives a four-year-old the keys to a car, and that's because it doesn't make sense to give a child opportunities she can't handle (and not just because she can't see over the wheel). Likewise, we don't put loaded pistols in the hands of small children; the power is more than they can reasonably control.

These extreme examples point out that making choices includes an element of *wielding power*. Our actions often affect others, whether it's having the self-discipline to stop drinking long before getting behind the wheel of a car, helping clean the dishes after dinner, refusing to gossip about someone behind his back, or just lending an ear to a friend with a problem even though we're tired. Freedom is a privilege that comes with a price in society: acting responsibly (if you don't believe me, ask the guys serving time in your local prison). Raise children to act responsibly and you can hand them the keys to the kingdom far earlier than most children get to even think about controlling their own lives. And by doing so you foster self-discipline and practical wisdom, the two conditions necessary for developing virtues and in turn living a happy and fulfilling life.

Will-to-Power

Let's look at this from another angle, from the perspective of power. As Janet Jackson made clear in her 1986 musical treatise *Control*, we all want to have autonomy over our own lives. This control, it could be argued, is critical to achieving a satisfying life (Ms. Jackson certainly felt anything less was decidedly nasty). Control entails wielding power over yourself and your environment and to some extent over others, at least in so far as their actions can affect you. Call it Nietzsche's will-to-power if you like, but people want to achieve something, to make an impact in the world, and it starts with mastering oneself.

A child wants nothing more than to esteem herself, to actualize her potential, and regardless of whether that's playing piano, soccer, or becoming a rock star, it requires self-control. And as a child grows up, we give her more and more power over her life and the degree to which she can affect others – who she will have as friends, if and where she will go to college, what jobs to take, getting to drive a car, rocking the vote, and so on.

All too often we don't think of ethics or morality when we talk about teenagers gaining privileges or joining the ranks of adults. Instead, the words "ethics" and "morality" tend to conjure up images of saints, politicians, and criminals, of whether we're doing enough charity to help the poor, resisting the telling of bold-face lies, stealing, or deciding the fate of masses of people. This is because the primary focus in philosophy has typically been on our ethical decision-making, the grounds of our decisions. And that's no small matter.

But ethics for most of us is primarily about how we use the power we have as average Joes. The relationships we have in our daily lives often include a good deal of power over others by virtue of people being *vulnerable* in various ways. Teenagers, because of their strong need to be accepted by their peers, are highly susceptible to what other kids say about them. Romantic involvement involves making yourself emotionally very vulnerable to another person's actions and words. Employees are typically at the mercy of their managers because they need employment to live and to support a family. Children need the esteem and loving attention of their parents and so are highly vulnerable as well.

These are some of the arenas in our lives in which we are most likely to help or harm ourselves and others and in very deep ways. One or both sides of each of these relationships has the ability to easily do harm to the other because of the power being granted him to meet some basic human need. Notice we even have terms for the abuse of such power in many of these relationships: bullying, management abuse, spouse abuse, child abuse, and so on.

What's the point of this? That ethics and good character are mostly about how we wield the power we have over the people close to us in our everyday lives. We can't help but engage in these relationships, and how we handle the power and trust they grant us is absolutely critical to the wellbeing of the people involved. Don't get me wrong, whether to volunteer at a food drive is important too. But unless you are working full time in the Peace Corps, most of your impact on others is probably taking place elsewhere. At minimum, we should hope to have our own house in order before we start knocking on other doors.

So applying this to kids, developing good character in children first and foremost amounts to teaching them how to skillfully and justly handle power, to become worthy of trust. The wheels of society and our personal relationships depend on trusting each other. Children must be taught how to act responsibly, and that is not achieved through a few noble speeches here and there or from seeing some posters at school. It's a *skill set* attained through experiential learning. They need OJT (on-the job training) with the "job" in this case being everyday life. And they need this training before they reach puberty, when they memorize every lyric to the rap songs, and you begin to wonder if aliens recently kidnapped them.

Of course, children face challenges before the teenage years. Whether to share her toys or not can be an ethical dilemma for little Sheila. But the stakes are much lower for small children (and they quickly find other toys to play with anyway). We typically don't give them much power early on. But by the time they become teenagers, they need to have solid, good habits that can enable them to responsibly wield the new-found power they will encounter. They have to ethically navigate through the *Lord of the Flies* years, and then the stakes get even higher as they enter the workplace, take a partner, and start a family, if they so choose.

But if we teach them responsibility early, then we can also grant them significant freedoms early while there's less at stake. That gives them much more experience and confidence in making their own decisions before they reach the trials awaiting them as a teenager. Fathers can do more harm by failing to impose their will at this early stage and ironically they often do this because of a fear to do harm. A child lacking in self-control will have infinitely more problems along the way and be ill-prepared for the life challenges ahead. There are of course no guarantees, but as fathers we can stack the deck in our favor. That's what dads do best: give kids their best chance to thrive and build a success history as they go through life. In fact, that's all anyone can do when dealing with a free human being.

Caring and Justice

Up to this point, the focus of our discussion of character has been on self-control and practical wisdom. But being ethical also requires caring about others. Unfortunately, we cannot simply inject caring into our children ("Hold still, this will only hurt for a moment!"). In fact, nothing we do can make the child concerned about the wellbeing of those around her. On top of this, it's hard to tell if they really do care. While we can see the actions they take, the feelings they have can be much more difficult to uncover, and we don't usually expect depth of emotion until later anyway.

Empathy, as we sometimes call this feeling of caring, is different than sympathy. When sympathizing, one understands and consoles someone suffering an unfortunate event, but when we empathize, we *co-experience* someone else's pain or joy. Parents typically feel this way when their children undergo pain. I swear it really hurts us more than it does them! This distinction is probably one of degree rather than of kind, but you get the point. To feel someone else's anxieties along with that person is a serious step beyond just acknowledging them through kind words.

While philosophers haven't reached a consensus on a conception of empathy, Theodor Lipps' notion of "inner imitation" is fruitful. In empathy, we see the other person as our self. When we see joy on his face, we immediately imitate this joy within us. Recent brain research backs this up: during empathy with another person we stimulate areas of the brain that overlap the same areas that we stimulate when we experience the same emotion ourselves.

The power of empathy is tremendous. Throughout life we confide in others to share our emotions, and people who can empathize with us are invaluable for validating those feelings and helping us cope with the stresses of life. Perhaps most importantly, without empathy a guy is in for a really long, boring night when his wife makes him watch a chick flick.

Thankfully, empathy can be learned. It is a skill of sorts. We can move from apathy to sympathy to empathy in our interactions, and when we reach that level, we cannot easily ignore the needs of others. Children of course learn a lot through their interactions with us, so modeling empathy in how as fathers we respond to people's feelings goes a long way toward teaching them this skill. Something as simple as being good listeners to our children is very important. Being new to the world, they have a lot of discoveries to share.

Two related skills help make empathy possible and shouldn't be overlooked: *self-awareness*, the ability to abstract from the immediacy of one's sensations or activities and see your self so to speak, and *concentration*, the ability to focus thought for extended periods of time. If a child has very low self-awareness, then real awareness of others is not possible. Enjoying a cola, for example, is not the same thing as being aware of *oneself* enjoying a cola. Notice yourself reading these words for instance – it's different than simply reading. By abstracting even a little bit, a child learns to step outside herself, see herself as others do, and thereby more fully realize that others are "out there." Basically, putting yourself in someone else's shoes requires the ability to first step out of your own (and of course making sure their shoe size is at least as big as yours, but that goes without saying).

Being able to focus her attention enables a child to be observant and sensitive to the many aspects of her environment. Flitting about rapidly from one interesting object of her awareness to another conditions a child over time and prevents awareness of the more subtle aspects of her environment. As the philosopher Edmund Husserl would have put it, they can't notice the *background* because their attention is stuck in the *foreground*. Other people's feelings often lie in the background of what we directly experience (unless you've been ignoring them so much they get really pissed off; then their feelings become obvious!). If Julie doesn't notice the feelings of her friends or if she can't distinguish their envy from their anger, then her ability to ever empathize becomes doubtful.

Self-awareness and concentration skills can be developed by reading regularly with your child, by minimizing exposure to popular forms of entertainment (as they often use rapid video cuts, which fosters Attention Deficit Disorder), and by teaching self-discipline. Also, exposure to philosophy, which can require a lot of abstraction and concentration, is a great way to enhance these skills as they get older.

That brings us to the final piece of our puzzle: developing a respect for justice. Being ethical, as we said, ideally involves not just concern for others but also a love of fairness, the just. After all, some ethical issues we face go beyond our caring about people. Sometimes they're about how to ensure fairness *among* people, and that can mean we have to accept receiving a smaller piece of the pie. Without a strong respect for fairness, people rarely go along with that idea.

As with empathy, there's a lot of disagreement among philosophers concerning the nature of justice. For Aristotle, it is a virtue. I would agree, but add that justice is also a principle of distributing something according to each person's efforts, merits, or needs. Children can be taught to appreciate this principle by playing sports and games with friends. Their respect for fairness increases with their ability to follow the rules of a game and the ability to curb their disappointment at getting less than they would like. The easier they can abide by such limitations, the easier their acceptance of fairness can in turn become a habit, a virtue of justice. Thus, respect for justice also depends upon the acquired skill of self-discipline.

Stacking the Deck

So it appears that a lot more than seeing posters goes into making a child ethical. It's about developing good character, as Aristotle said. And we need to foster certain underlying skills to make virtues and empathy possible: practical wisdom, will-power, self-awareness, and concentration. As with the virtues, such skills are *not* taught primarily through words. Stories, poems, and expressions might help, but only because they make explicit what we already feel in the body as habit. Small children especially are not in a position to get much out of words – you might as well be *asking* your dog to quit barking.

No, skills require a lot of experience and practice to perfect. Excellence doesn't happen overnight. We know if we want our sons to become successful football players, we have to start training them while they are young. Likewise, if we are serious about our children becoming excellent people, we need to take seriously the opportunities for their moral education, namely, the days of their childhood. People fully understand that higher education and their child's future career will require them handling pressure and an unwieldy hierarchy, and yet some fathers choose to raise children in an environment completely lacking in expectations. How they can expect those same kids to suddenly sprout the skills necessary for coping with the real world upon graduation is beyond me.

Expect responsible behavior from your children and you will receive responsible behavior. Sure, they'll let you down occasionally. That's to be expected. And those are learning moments too. As with everything in life there are no guarantees. As dads, all we can do is stack the odds in our favor. That's what we do best.

CHAPTER 6

DOES MY FATHER *CARE?*

Paternalism, Care Ethics, and Fatherhood

It could be his Norwegian upbringing, but it's hard to get an emotional reaction out of my dad. At least one that doesn't involve a poorly wielded hammer, another heartbreaker by the Mets, or that one damn bulb in the string of Christmas lights. If we do try and hug, it can be pretty awkward – like trying to give the German chancellor a neck massage at the G-8. We don't have many shared interests: he's very much into sports, me not so much. We don't talk as often as we should, and when we do it's mostly about the weather and finances. And he's still waiting for me to get a "real" job. Even so, I have no doubt that he cares about me very much. That might seem a strange thing to say, given the way we normally think about caring, but that says more about our narrow view of caring than it does about my dad.

Caring About Caring

In the history of ethics there have been a few figures who have cast long shadows. Their arguments are still being scrutinized today and the concepts they introduced have become part of our vocabulary: virtue, the social contract, the categorical imperative, the greatest happiness principle and so on. Things were moving along smoothly until the psychologist Lawrence Kohlberg tried to synthesize all of those ideas into a comprehensive theory of moral development. Kohlberg tested his subjects with moral dilemmas and scored their answers according to a scale that ranged from the purely selfish to people who do things according to universal principles.[1] The real interesting part occurred when psychologists started to apply his methodology to female subjects. Generally speaking, women scored lower than men and almost no women could be found at the highest level of moral development (to be fair, not a lot of men made it either, but proportionally speaking women were underrepresented). Instead, women tended to score on the third and fourth levels (the so-called "conventional levels"), which meant that they based their moral decisions on what other people in society would think or a desire for social consensus.

Here's an example of one of those dilemmas: Heinz's wife is very sick and the pharmacist has the medicine she needs. The pharmacist is charging ten times what the drug costs to make, and Heinz only has half that amount. He asks the pharmacist to sell him the drug at a cheaper price or let him pay later. The pharmacist refuses. In desperation, Heinz breaks into the pharmacy and steals the drug. Should Heinz have done that? Some male subjects said he should steal because saving a human life trumps all other concerns. Many female subjects agreed that Heinz should steal the drug, but the reasons given appealed to his attachment to his wife or the poor behavior of the pharmacist. In addition, there were some female subjects who condemned the theft because Heinz could go to jail and something might happen to his wife while he was in prison. Instead, Heinz should talk to the pharmacist more or find another way to get the money.

No women gave an answer that scored at the highest level, post-conventional reasoning. If Kohlberg's theory was correct, women were morally less developed than men – there was a glass ceiling on moral judgment. These studies provoked a defense of the moral maturity of women. In 1982 Carol Gilligan published a book that presented the results of her studies of moral judgment in females.[2] Her central thesis was that ethics had been dominated by a "male" voice which emphasized individualism, abstraction, and the public sphere. However, this was not the only voice that could be used to speak about moral concerns. From her work was born care ethics.

Care ethics refers to any moral theory that puts a premium on attachment and relationship in determining what to do in a moral situation, which is what Gilligan argued the women were doing in the studies. Kohlberg's highest level requires abstracting from all social contexts, whereas care ethics holds that judgments without any social context lack the full force of morality. Similarly, almost all of the traditional theories of ethics hold that reason is how we discover right and wrong, whereas care ethics points to our emotions as the best way to figure out the right thing to do.

Gilligan argued that two different perspectives need to be considered when discussing morality: the justice orientation and the care orientation. In turn, two different kinds of care ethicists have sprouted up. One takes the distinction between a justice orientation and a care orientation to be the result of *biology*. On this view, men make moral judgments based upon principles of justice and women make moral judgments based upon their relationships and roles and never the twain shall meet. Such a view makes it biologically impossible for fathers to be practitioners of care ethics. A competing view is that the justice orientation has been favored by men because of their *experiences*, just as the care orientation was a product of women's experiences. On this view, the two moral orientations complement each other, and it is possible for a person to learn both orientations.

On the nature view, men think in terms of abstract principles because they are naturally more competitive than women, and so they are concerned with making sure the playing field is level. The socialization view would argue that until recently men have wielded the majority of the power in the public sphere and as a result they are in a situation where abstract rules are necessary. Trying to settle the debate between nature and nurture when it comes to sex differences seems almost impossible. However, I think we can err on the side of nurture if we consider that (1) men do seem to exhibit some of the traits that are associated with care ethics – for example, fathers will do things for the sake of their family that they would not think permissible for anyone else to do (even for their own family), and (2) if the nature view was correct, then there would be nothing further to say about the idea that fathers could care.

A Face Only a *Mother* Could Love?

One of the earliest advocates of care ethics is Nel Noddings.[3] She ascribes to the nurture view of care ethics, holding open the possibility that men could adopt a care orientation. But once you begin to unpack what caring means for Noddings, it seems less likely that caring could be something that the average father would practice.

Noddings defines caring as a relationship between the one caring and the one cared for, but all that matters for our purposes is the one caring. As she explains in *Caring*, "the one-caring is engrossed in the other. But this engrossment is not completely characterized as emotional feeling. There is a characteristic and appropriate mode of consciousness in caring." Caring involves understanding the wants and needs of the person you're caring for – although not so much that you lose yourself in it – and as a result you will be moved to help the person satisfy those needs.

Noddings' vision of care ethics is biased towards the model of maternal love in our society. Putting aside the question of whether fathers could learn to behave according to that model, I imagine that many fathers are like my own and do not currently do anything that entails the kind of engrossment she describes.[4] In fact, the kind of things my father does – pushing me to achieve my best, modeling values for me to emulate, and so on – are not compatible with the model of caring that Noddings provides. My dad often stood apart and, especially when I was younger, acted as an authority who was not going to let his personal feelings get in the way of making sure I was punished when I did wrong.

While there are still some care ethicists who agree with her ideal of caring as something with a distinctly maternal bent, a number of care ethicists were critical of what they perceived as an overemphasis on mothering. Virginia Held argues that caring must be found in all contexts that we think are moral. So it must include friends, strangers, government organizations, and so on.[5]

However, even Held's discussion of caring seems to exclude what I would identify as the most important aspects of the way my dad cares about me. In Held's discussion of caring, she focuses on the caring relationship as being between the caregiver and someone who is dependent on the caregiver. This dependence means that the caregiver has to attend to the needs of the person they are caring for. In her example, a mother who cooks for her child is caring for that child, but that same mother when cooking for her husband, who could make a meal himself, is doing him a service, hopefully out of love. Even when care ethics broadens the model of caring, it still leans in the direction of the kind of caring we associate with being a maternal figure.

ANDREW TERJESEN

Tough Love: Paternalism as a Form of Caring

Based on the definition of caring that Noddings and other care ethicists offer it appears that, at least in regards to my dad (and I strongly suspect many others), the answer to our original question "Does my father care?" would be: not much. It's possible that my father could learn to care that way. But I have to be honest. I don't think he'd want to. In fact, if he did, I think something would be lost from my life. It seems somewhat skewed that all caring seems to be analogous to a mother's love. I do think that my dad cares, but not by becoming engrossed in who I am.

Care ethics came about because of dissatisfaction with a model of morality that diminished the moral value of what women did. However, in coming up with a notion of caring that is modeled on women's experiences as mothers, an important form of caring was neglected: *paternal caring*, or as I will call it, *paternalism*. If you think about the verbs "to mother" and "to father," some interesting things are suggested about the caring attitudes of mothers and fathers. In our society, mothering is not always a good thing. As many people would point out, it's only one letter away from "smothering." There are times when it is positive, especially when we find ourselves feeling vulnerable, but too much mothering is a bad thing, as it leaves us afraid to act on our own.

Yet, the kind of engrossment that Noddings associates with caring seems a lot like mothering. In contrast, to father something is to serve as the originator of something and implies a certain bit of responsibility for one's creation insofar as you had a hand in making it what it is. It's interesting that the biological act on the part of the male in creating a child is called "fathering," but we don't refer to what the female does in creating and giving birth to a child "mothering." To father something is to be there at the start, but not so much to nurture. However, when we talk about someone fathering legislation or fathering a new program we usually include the idea that they were responsible for shaping what it became. Fathering carries the connotation of passing on your rights and responsibilities. When a king fathers a child, that child becomes heir to the throne. And being the father of an idea or a movement puts you in a position of authority that allows you to have some influence over its future development.

A stereotypical father is Bambi's dad, who shows up when Bambi needs him and teaches Bambi to become a young buck. Otherwise, he's not heavily involved in Bambi's life. Paternalism is a word that is derived from *pater*, the Latin word for "father," and so it suggests that being paternalistic is like being a father. A paternalist intervenes in your life in order to do what they think is best for you. A paternalist is not engrossed in who you are now; instead, the paternalist will often do things that will force you to become someone else. When you act paternalistically towards someone you are not accepting their view of the world. Instead, you are judging the values they choose to hold.

Behaving paternalistically – under the right conditions – is a form of caring. Maternal models of caring focus on care as a way to understand and comfort someone based on their own way of looking at the world. On this model, the only way to get people to recognize their moral responsibilities to others is to get them to care about those people. The assumption is that if everyone cared about everyone else then they would be moved to do the right thing. Our moral standards are supposed to change spontaneously.

The paternalist recognizes that sometimes we need to be pushed out of our old values. This is not compatible with mothering because it opposes engrossment – it refuses to accept all of our beliefs about the world. Instead of focusing on how someone feels now, the attention is on how they should feel in the future. My dad was always worried about the man I would become and the choices I made that would contribute to who I would become. When needed he has stepped in for correction and he has done it in a "tough love" fashion, which is a form of love.

Paternalism is Not Justice by Another Name

Someone reading this might object to my claim – that there is a paternal form of caring which complements the maternal form – by pointing out that this sounds like a new name for the justice orientation. The justice orientation is concerned with adhering to an impersonal standard, which is what it sounds like the paternalist does. Let's look at how justice might be different from paternalism.

The justice orientation is meant to refer to the whole of Western ethics from Plato and Aristotle to John Stuart Mill's greatest happiness principle and Kant's categorical imperative. Much ink has been spilled arguing that one of those theories is better than all the others. What they all have in

ANDREW TERJESEN

common is pretty minimal, but it is important from a philosophical point of view. All of these moral philosophies emphasize using reason to discover abstract principles of right and wrong. For example, someone practicing the justice orientation might say that it is rational for everyone to respect their father. From a caring perspective, how I treat my father depends on our relationship. Instead of using some set of rules to determine what it means to respect fathers, the caring orientation considers the needs of my father in order to decide how to show respect towards him. My relationship to him is the starting point for my moral obligations.

Another difference is that the justice orientation is concerned with justifying our judgments about right and wrong through abstract rational principles. Someone who believes in the greatest happiness principle does not simply say, "It feels right"; they appeal to abstract rational principles. Noddings is very clear that she thinks asking for a justification of one's feelings and one's relationships is a wrong-headed approach. Paternalism is closer to Noddings on this issue. A father who cares that his children adopt certain values may not feel the need to justify those values to anyone, even the children. Holding a child to a certain standard or exercising authority over them for "their own good" may not be defensible. Although he is probably not the first person you would think of, Darth Vader was a misguided but caring father. He wanted his children to join him in what he thought was the right way to live. Unfortunately, that meant embracing the "Dark Side." In the end, Vader saw that his values were not the best for his children and saved them from the very thing he was originally trying to force upon them.

When Gilligan was describing the difference between justice and care, she said that the two orientations focused on different problems. Justice was concerned with ensuring equality, while care was about paying attention to the people involved and their emotional and social needs. Paternalism fits better with the care orientation in this case. Fathers are concerned with certain needs that people have, both emotionally and socially, that are related to the kind of life they'll lead and the kind of person they'll become. Maternal caring addresses certain emotional needs in the here and now, while paternal caring is focused on more long-term issues such as whether you'll be satisfied with the life you led and whether you'll be able to hold your head high in light of the choices you've made.

One distinction that Gilligan makes that might seem to work against paternalism is that she says that the care orientation is concerned to rectify problems of detachment and abandonment. Paternalism is about keeping one's distance, and so it would seem that it fails to address those issues. But paternalism is also about trying to make sure someone is developing a set of values and the skills needed to live according to those values, and not abandoning the idea of "who you are." The justice orientation isn't concerned about whether you identify with its values or principles, merely that you abide by them. It's really not the same as paternalism.[6]

Can My Dad Care Too Much?

Paternalism, or more precisely paternalistic caring, is related to other forms of paternalism, such as legal paternalism. What unites both paternalistic caring and legal paternalism is the focus on getting someone to do something – or keeping someone from doing something – for their own good. The difference is that legal paternalism is simply an action: making someone do or not do something for their own good. And it might be motivated by different reasons. Look at seatbelt laws. One argument for seatbelt laws is that they make everyone else safer (a body that is not buckled up can hit a car or someone). Another is that when people don't wear seatbelts, they increase the risk of major injuries and could end up paralyzed. Such accidents would drive up the cost of healthcare. Paternalistic caring is more than an action; it's an attitude of concern. From the perspective of paternalistic caring, seatbelts are necessary to help people protect themselves from injury. Also, the intent is to change the person's attitude and behaviors as opposed to just stopping their behavior. Despite these differences, paternalistic caring and legal paternalism are similar enough on the face of it that we can derive insights from philosophical discussions of legal paternalism.

There has been much debate over how paternalistic the government should be. Such a debate reminds us that just because you think someone will benefit from something doesn't mean you should always force them to do it. Paternalism has its limits. The tricky part is coming up with a good reason as to why it should be limited in some cases, but not others. Someone who argues that we should prohibit people from doing things that are bad for them (or requiring them to do things that are good for them) is called a *hard paternalist*. A father who locks his daughter in her room so she can't go out with a kid he thinks is a bad influence would be a hard paternalist. When maternal caring goes too far, it smothers the child and inhibits his independence. In the same vein, paternal caring that is so authoritarian that it doesn't let a child make any decisions for himself is unhealthy.

You might be thinking, "Who lets a two-year-old make decisions about anything?" Here we see an important difference between legal paternalism and paternalistic caring.[7] Legal paternalism is a part of the justice orientation and is based on abstract principles pertaining to adult citizenship. Laws regulating the behavior of children are not legally paternalistic because children do not have the rights, responsibilities, or capacity for reason that adults are supposed to have. Laws regulating how parents can raise their children are paternalistic. Paternalistic caring as a part of the care orientation is based on the details of the relationship. The age of the child, as well as other factors relevant to decision-making, would be a part of the process of deciding how much to intervene to stop a child from making a mistake. And unlike legal paternalism, paternalistic caring is interested in imparting to one's children a sense of responsibility and the tools needed for them to be responsible for themselves. Paternalistic caring wants to make itself obsolete.

A better approach would be what is called *soft paternalism,* a view that is outlined by the philosopher Gerald Dworkin.[8] Soft paternalism is a compromise between a completely hands-off approach (if your kid wants to spend a night with a known serial killer, who are you to interfere?) and the tyranny of hard paternalism. Dworkin points out that we all recognize the need for some level of paternalism because some actions can have severe and irreversible consequences. Letting a baby have access to a loaded gun is just asking for trouble. Even a teenager should at least be supervised to make sure they are serious about the responsibilities of gun ownership. For Dworkin, the kind of paternalistic intervention that is morally permissible depends upon both the rational capacities of the individual affected and the consequences of not intervening. The more likely that an action is to lead to a bad result that cannot be fixed, the more reason we have to intervene. Death is a permanent condition, so anything that endangers someone's life is a candidate for paternalist intervention. So is a severe injury that would make someone a paraplegic. Getting sick or getting your heart broken is not the kind of thing that would warrant serious action.

If one is dealing with someone with a diminished capacity to appreciate the consequences of their actions (and this includes young children), it is important to limit their actions. Soft paternalism recommends seeking out the least restrictive forms of intervention. So, if an adult is doing something dangerous, you try and explain the consequences to them. If it's really dangerous, the government might require some training before engaging in the activity. But you shouldn't do anything that takes away their freedom of action or dramatically alters the nature of the activity.

It would be unjustifiable paternalism to require that everyone who skydives do it while the plane is on the ground.

The least restrictive principle is too abstract for paternalistic caring, as the amount of intervention needed is quite high when dealing with young children. Still, Dworkin's soft paternalism can serve as an inspiration. Paternalistic caring should always be sensitive to the capacities of those involved to make decisions that can take into account all the consequences. In a nod to the least restrictive principle, all interventions by parents should be aimed at developing the child's sense of responsibility so that more restrictive interventions can be abandoned as soon as it is reasonable to do so.

Paternalistic caring works best when it follows such a principle. Although we might argue about the exact age, everyone would agree that children need to be supervised until they get to a certain age. And it would be appropriate to forbid a young girl (up until maybe 11 years?) from dating and punishing her if she disobeys. On the other hand, if a 16-year-old girl wants to date someone that you think has no future and might interfere with her plans, it is worth sitting her down and making sure she understands the consequences. And if you foresee some really, really bad consequences, it might even be acceptable to use incentives like cutting off her allowance or taking away her car keys. However, once she is old enough, there is nothing you can nor should do to stop her other than trying to talk her out of it. The only exception would be if you thought that she was "not in her right mind" and by that I mean really suffering from mental illness. When pushing someone to aim at certain goals or to accept certain values, there must be limits. Otherwise you don't really care about the person involved, you only care about getting your way. And you should always be thinking about how to help the child develop to the point where they are making sound decisions and your intervention is no longer required.

The Importance of Tough Love

Paternalistic caring is an important complement to maternalistic caring. It's important that we have relationships in which we are uncritically accepted and nurtured *and* that we have relationships in which we are challenged and guided. When it comes to caring, I favor a nurture view. Due to the way that social roles had been divided in the past, it ended up being the case that fathers were more often taking up the demands of paternalistic caring. In fact, I suspect that nowadays one is more likely to find parents who embody elements of both kinds of caring (as we have begun to redistribute the different aspects of childrearing and caregiving in general) and certainly mothers who are more about tough love than engrossment. Of course, it's hard to consistently exercise both forms of caring, which is why we'll probably continue to see a paternal parent and a maternal parent, even if it is not a biological category.

The cynics among you might think that this is all an elaborate attempt to cover up a neglectful or absentee father. After all, the simplistic explanation for paternalism might be that men are not particularly interested in childrearing and the actions they do take are more self-interested. Disciplining their children is a means of keeping the home quiet, and pushing them to succeed is merely about enhancing the father's reputation (and keeping the kids from leeching off of him till the day he dies). Such a father would actually be emotionally detached from his children, and that's why he keeps his distance.

I can't accept the cynical view (and not because I'm in denial). The cynical view is premised on the idea that such fathers don't really care, in any sense, for their children. At least, no more than they do for an old friend. I actually can see that paternalistic care in my father, but even if I couldn't, there would be evidence of it all around. As all too many deadbeat dads have proven, a father doesn't have to stick around or deal with the stresses of your average corporate job to take care of his family. When your dad brings work home at night or spends evenings refereeing some basketball games to earn a little more for your school clothes (as my dad did, and maybe yours did similar things), you can see the conflict. There's a lot they would rather do, but by getting their work done they end up providing more for their family. Whether he intended it or not, my father's example taught me a lot about the importance of work and the tough decisions one sometimes has to make in order to care for others. It takes a real passion to do those things; something that a truly distant father (as opposed to one who sometimes sees the importance of creating a little distance) would never be able to muster.

I'm not saying my dad is perfect. There are certainly things he wanted for me that I didn't agree with, and I'm sure even now he is concerned about the career I've chosen. Now that I've grown up, his paternalism has to be softer than ever, to the point where I don't even notice it much anymore (except when he insists on paying for dinner – as if I don't earn enough). Still, I know he cares – not the way my mother does, but in his own equally deep and far-reaching way. And I'm the better for it.

NOTES

1 An overview of Kohlberg's research can be found in his *Essays on Moral Development, Vol. 1: The Philosophy of Moral Development* (San Francisco: Harper and Row, 1981) and *Vol. 2: The Psychology of Moral Development* (San Francisco: Harper and Row, 1984).
2 Carol Gilligan, *In a Different Voice: Psychological Theory and Women's Development* (Cambridge, MA: Harvard University Press, 1982).
3 Nel Noddings, *Caring: A Feminine Approach to Ethics and Moral Education* (Berkeley: University of California Press, 2003).
4 There is no denying that traditional parental roles have been changing in the last few decades. However, if the model of all parental love moves too much towards an engrossment model, I think something will have been lost.
5 Virginia Held, *The Ethics of Care: Personal, Political and Global* (New York: Oxford University Press, 2007).
6 Michael Slote, *The Ethics of Care and Empathy* (New York: Routledge, 2007), is among those who argue that caring can include ideas associated with the justice orientation.
7 I am thankful to my editor for bringing this distinction to my attention.
8 Gerald Dworkin, "Paternalism," *The Monist* 56 (1972): 64–84.

CHAPTER 7

HOW SHOULD I PARENT?

Fathering That's Fun and Effective

That magical day has arrived when a father's first child has been born. It is a day that is excitedly anticipated and yet coupled with a sense of fear of the unknown. All of those days spent with your partner talking about what to name the child, reading self-help parenting books, and making sure you have the right baby equipment such as rockers, strollers, and cribs seem inconsequential now as you gaze at your newborn. How will you ensure that you set your child on the proper path to becoming a happy and productive adult?

Father as Protector and the Baby Product Industry

The safety aspect of the baby industry is a particularly strong selling point for fathers, as historically one of the primary roles of a father is to serve as a protector. Anyone who has had to make multiple stops to baby stores can appreciate the endless number of safety product choices, with each product claiming to be vitally important to your baby's health. Baby product marketers have brilliantly capitalized upon parents' sense of duty to protect the wellbeing of their child, as well as our insecurity regarding how to do this in our complex and ever-changing world. As a new father, you will swear that no harm will befall your children on your watch. You will study every baby product and go to excruciating pains to baby-proof the house. It will quickly become apparent, however, that the true utility of electric socket protectors is preventing any person from using the electric socket! Similarly, toilet seat clamps are quite effective in doubling time in the restroom, as unlocking and re-locking such devices can be particularly cumbersome. The first hurdle of parenthood, therefore, is overcoming the onslaught of come-ons in the baby products market. If one can successfully navigate this minefield, then surely one can survive and even thrive being a father.

Fatherhood During Infancy

During the early stages in your child's life it can be difficult to determine the father's role in the care and parenting of an infant. Over the course of pregnancy the mother has become familiar with the child's rhythms and movements. The baby can recognize the mother's voice at birth. If the mother is breastfeeding, the father is further cut off from the bonding that occurs between mother and baby during nursing. Unfortunately, there remains a stigma against stay-at-home fathers, and few employers offer paternity leave following the birth of the baby. Thus, the inclination for the father may be to return to work as usual and consider the care of the baby to be the role of the mother. However, the wise father will look past the current norms in our culture for new fathers and take it upon himself to become an active participant in the care and nurturance of his new baby.

There are a number of different ways that a new father can participate in the life of his newborn. A new father can take as much vacation time or unpaid leave as is allowed and possible for the family and spend the time getting to know his newborn. This has the secondary benefit of allowing the new father to spend time with his spouse if the mother is also at home. If the mother must return to work, such time could be taken after the mother's maternity leave has expired. This will allow the father one-on-one bonding time with his new child. The father of a nursing infant can ask the mother to pump milk so that he can periodically feed the infant with a bottle. A father who has to continue to work can also give the mother the "evening off" and handle all changing, bathing, swaddling, rocking, and playing duties. This should be done with minimal questions regarding how to complete such tasks. This is the grand adventure of fatherhood, figuring out how your child works and relating to him or her. We challenge any father to find a video game that requires more dexterity than feeding an infant baby food! If you are the competitive type, you can keep score by the amount of stains on the bib, food on the floor, and in all likelihood on yourself. These types of activities are how you get to know your child's nature and become a confident and empowered parent.

Fathers should also never forget that both you and your mate will be in "survival mode" through much of the first year of the baby's life! Mothers don't have all the answers and can be as overwhelmed as you. By being a true participant in your baby's early life, a father can support his spouse, get to know his child, and begin to learn the true joys of fatherhood.

Father as Gender Enforcer

One of the unwritten rules of fatherhood is making sure that your child will fit in with his or her appropriate gender. A father typically takes this role very seriously. Many fathers start their gender enforcement behavior after the first ultrasound when they learn the sex of the child. This means decorating the boy's room with a basketball goal and sports team memorabilia; and painting the girl's room pink with a wall of flowers and butterflies. As the children get older and daddy brings presents home, the girl gets a doll and the boy gets a truck. Gender enforcement is particularly strong for a father with boys, as gender violations are frowned upon much more when it comes to boys than girls. This results in silly things such as a boy having his first pair of high performance sports shoes before he can walk!

A father needs to be assured that providing such gender appropriate items will neither harm nor necessarily help his child. It is true that there are different behavioral expectations for boys and girls even in our post-feminism culture, and parents need to help their children navigate these norms and expectations. However, it is also the case that steering children towards gender appropriate activities and items and away from gender inappropriate ones will not ensure that boys' behavior is always masculine and girls' behavior is always feminine; and such an outcome is not in the best interest of children anyway. The wise father will understand that both boys and girls benefit from having both masculine and feminine qualities. He will therefore help his children develop the appropriate combination of both traits.

The Role of the Father in Developing the Moral Child

There have been a multitude of takes on the innate nature of infants as they relate to being either good, evil, or neutral, and the stance that a father takes on this issue has far-reaching consequences for how he chooses to parent his child. Two contemporary psychologists explored the nature of children's understanding of right and wrong. Jean Piaget proposed that a child is born without morals. This makes sense, as infants and toddlers tend to do what they want whenever they want. There is not a thought of obeying rules. For example, if a very young child wants to scream in the middle of church services, they do so with gusto! Lawrence Kohlberg recognized that children in general do not remember rules by themselves, but rather have to be acted on by their environment, mainly through parents and peers, before they become moral beings. This brings us to the two main experiences that children must have while growing up if they are to become moral adults: negative reactions from caregivers when rules are violated and the development of impulse control.

The first experience needed for the development of moral behavior is for children to face negative reactions from caregivers when they violate the rules. For example, a parent might bellow at a child to stop before they put their hand on a hot stove or run into the street. The child may not be used to such a tone from his parents, and this makes the child have negative feelings. These bad feelings become internalized by the child and make him think twice before repeating the action. Over time, children begin to modify their behaviors so as to avoid feeling the negative emotions. So, the bottom line is that discipline is important. Parents *must* discipline their children if they are to develop into moral adults. We will discuss the best ways to discipline your child in the next section.

The second experience needed for the development of morality is for children to control their impulses to engage in prohibited behaviors. The classic experiment that illustrates this concept is the marshmallow experiment by Walter Michel. In this experiment, young children were given a big marshmallow that they were told they could eat as soon as the experimenter

DAN FLORELL AND STEFFEN WILSON

left the room. Children were also told that if they were able to wait until the experimenter came back in the room, they could have two marshmallows. Some children were unable to resist and ate the marshmallow as soon as the experimenter left the room. Who can really blame them? The sweet treat of a marshmallow is hard to resist! However, there were other children who were able to hold out. They used a variety of techniques to resist the allure of the marshmallow. Some children closed their eyes, others sat on their hands, some sang to themselves, and others engaged in self-talk about the benefit of waiting until the adult returned. In the end, those children who were able to wait were awarded the additional marshmallow.

The experimenters then tracked the children during their initial elementary school years and found that the children who were able to resist the impulse to eat the marshmallow right away performed better academically, were able to cope with frustration, and had higher self-esteem than their more impulsive classmates. The marshmallow experiment illustrates the importance of encouraging children to inhibit their impulses, as children who are able to do this develop qualities that facilitate success in the adult world. Thus, impulse control is a skill that a father should consciously develop in his children in order to facilitate their development into mature and high-functioning adults.

Fatherhood and Parenting Styles

So, what is the best way for a father to discipline his children and promote the development of impulse control? It all comes down to parenting style. There are four primary parenting styles. The four styles are combinations of two characteristics: responsiveness and control. Responsive fathers are fathers who show love and care for their children. They interact with their children in positive and enjoyable ways: playing games, talking about the day, and giving hugs and kisses. They comfort their children when they are hurt or upset. They are excited to see their children after an absence such as work, school, or daycare, and they enjoy being reunited as a family at the end of the day. On the other end of the spectrum are fathers who are unresponsive and uninvolved with their children. These fathers are more focused on their own needs than the needs of their children. They do not enjoy spending time with their children, nor are they affectionate towards their children. They are not concerned about their children's emotional states, and they do not try to alleviate their children's distress.

As you can probably surmise, children thrive with responsive and involved fathers (and mothers). Children with responsive and involved fathers feel good about themselves and they know that they have a place that they can turn when they are in distress.

The other dimension of parenting style is control. Fathers who are high in control regulate virtually every aspect of their children's lives. These children are told what to eat, what to wear, and even the types of activities and friends with which they can be involved. When rules are broken, punishments are usually quite harsh. Fathers who are high in control often resort to physical punishments or yelling and degrading their children. On the other extreme are fathers who are low in control. These fathers place few boundaries on their children, allowing even young children choice in all areas of their life. These children can eat, sleep, and play whenever and wherever they want. They can break "rules" with few, if any, consequences. They pretty much rule the household.

As you can probably imagine, the best approach regarding control is somewhere in between these extremes. That is, children thrive when fathers (and mothers) exert intermediate control over their lives. After all, they are children and they do not always know what is best for themselves. Fathers need to set age appropriate boundaries on children's behavior. However, children also need to be allowed to make age appropriate choices and experience the consequences of their actions in order to develop self-esteem and morality, learn their individual preferences, and feel competent and empowered.

There are four ways to combine these dimensions into parenting style. Each style occurs within an age appropriate developmental context. This means that fathers whose parenting is considered strict with a six-year-old will still display what is considered strict behaviors when dealing with a 16–year-old, even though the father's exact behaviors towards their child will differ based on the child's age.

The authoritarian father is high in control, but low in responsiveness. These children are frequently either rebellious against their fathers or become dependent upon their fathers. Why does this occur? The rebellious child figures, "What's the point in behaving correctly if my father is not going to be nice to me?" Unfortunately, rebellion can be quite dangerous and destructive. Rebellious children may turn to behaviors such as flunking out of school or abusing dangerous substances in order to rise up against their harsh fathers. On the other hand, children fathered in an authoritarian fashion can also become dependent upon their father. This occurs because they are never allowed to make their own choices and experience both the satisfaction of success and learn from their mistakes. This is also quite detrimental to the child, as he or she is never able to move fully into the adult world and live up to his or her potential.

The permissive father is responsive, but does little to control his children. These children are frequently immature. This occurs because indulged children have not been taught to control their behavior and they feel entitled because of their fathers' indulgent behavior towards them! Other adults may point to these children and use words like "spoiled" and "brat." This style of parenting becomes particularly problematic for children when they interact with the outside world. The children move into the world feeling entitled, but without the ability to work diligently and delay gratification – skills that are needed for success in our achievement-oriented culture.

The uninvolved father is neither responsive, nor controlling. Usually, such fathers are experiencing a crisis such as a difficult divorce, job responsibilities, or are simply overwhelmed by the responsibilities of fatherhood. Children parented in this manner often resort to delinquent and seriously maladaptive behavior, including stealing and vandalism. This occurs because these children do not feel cared for by their father, nor is their behavior monitored. These children have been rejected by the adult world, and they are lashing back at adults with their extremely destructive and often illegal behavior. These children are at a high risk of being arrested and finding themselves in our juvenile justice system.

Finally, the optimum fathering (and mothering) style is authoritative parenting. These fathers are both responsive with their children and moderately controlling. They love to spend time with their children and they enjoy their children. There are also rules and regulations in the household, and there are consequences for breaking rules which are consistently enforced. Consequences, however, are developmentally appropriate, do not involve physical punishments or harsh words, are given consistently after each transgression, and explanations for consequences are clearly given so that children understand why they are being punished. Children parented in this manner grow up to be competent, well liked, and industrious. They feel good about themselves because they are loved, but they have also been taught what is appropriate and what is inappropriate through appropriate discipline.

Unfortunately, our culture is not likely to teach or model an authoritative parenting style to men. Few men had a warm and responsive role-model in their own father, as the father has traditionally been considered the disciplinarian of the home. Because of the emphasis on career success in male culture, a father may focus more on his career aspirations and leave meeting the needs of his children to his spouse. Fathers should be especially aware of the utility of parental warmth and responsiveness, and if this is not a behavior that comes naturally, fathers should look to their spouses and perhaps their own mothers or friends for modeling and guidance on how to respond warmly to and enjoy their children. Fathers should also develop a grab bag of discipline strategies that are developmentally appropriate and do not involve physical punishment or harsh words or tones. Examples of such discipline strategies include distraction and redirection for toddlers, time-outs for preschoolers and young children, and groundings and restrictions for older children and adolescents. A background of warmth, support, and enjoyable activities will make children responsive to their father's displeasure with their behavior and motivated to improve in order to return to good standing in their father's eyes.

Child Temperament and Fathering Style

Speculation on the nature of children and the optimal conditions for positive development outcomes was recorded as early as the third century BCE by Plato and Aristotle. However, it was philosophers John Locke and Jean-Jacques Rousseau who brought this discussion into the modern era. John Locke proposed that infants and children were *tabula rasa* or "blank slates." This implied that children were neither innately good nor evil, but rather that children were products of their environment. According to this view, the quality of parenting was of the utmost importance to the ultimate outcome of the child. A half century later, Jean-Jacques Rousseau proposed that infants and children were *noble savages*. These savages were naturally endowed with a sense of right and wrong. If infants and children were allowed to develop naturally with little intervention or manipulation from the environment, then they would become high-functioning adults. Their caregivers simply needed to meet their children's physical and emotional needs.

Rousseau and Locke hit upon a classic conundrum in development: the concept of *nature vs. nurture*. The nature approach takes the stance that children's genetics is the major driving force in development. The nurture approach proposes that children develop based on their environmental experiences. What we now know is that both nature and nurture are essential to child development, with each contributing roughly half to child outcome. So, while high quality parenting is a key to positive child outcomes, children also bring innate characteristics including personality, talents, and intellectual skills to the parenting arena. These innate traits will undoubtedly affect how a father will approach his child.

The skilled father will recognize that while he is choosing to be a responsive and moderately controlling parent, his children are unique human beings with different strengths, weaknesses, and needs. Therefore, he will adjust his parenting to each of his children's individual differences while maintaining his overall philosophy and style of parenting with all of his children. Thus, the more outgoing and defiant child may need a bit more discipline, although it should never be harsh or punitive. The more inhibited child may need more warmth and reassurance in order to thrive. Read each of your children. Look at them as individuals. Learn about their innate interests and skills, and modify your parenting style to best address the needs of each child. A father that takes this individualistic approach should not worry about playing favorites or seeming to give one child more than another. If each child's individual needs are met, he or she will feel loved and cared for and be competent to face the world as a mature and well-rounded adult.

Teaching Our Boys to Be Fathers

From a very young age, girls are taught to consider motherhood to be the most noble, giving, and fulfilling role of a lifetime. Boys and young men, however, receive different messages and images of fatherhood. Boys are told that they should not play with dolls. If they play house, they are to be the "father" who goes to work while the girl is the mother who stays home and cares for the children. Young men are told that having a child will "tie them down." The wise father helps the next generation of boys embrace the joys of fatherhood by teaching his sons about the rewards of caring for and nurturing a child. This can be done by being an active father, who spends time with and enjoys his own children. A father should feel comfortable displaying physical affection for his sons, as well as his daughters. And a father should tell his sons, as well as his daughters, how happy he is to have his children in his life. All children will then learn that *parenthood* is the most noble, giving, and fulfilling activity of a lifetime.

CHAPTER 8

FATHERING FOR FREEDOM

For Jake and Andy

Every known human society rests firmly on the learned nurturing behavior of men.

Margaret Mead[1]

Why a Philosophy of Fatherhood?

What can philosophy contribute to our understanding of fatherhood? Social science has discovered many important general facts about family life. As a rule, kids raised by their biological fathers and mothers together turn out "better," with less drug abuse, more stable personal relationships, more productive careers, etc. But social science describes how things are and does not tell us how to live. In fact, it often seems that social science revels in the aberrant, the deficient, and the abnormal – not to say sensational.

By contrast, philosophy asks not only how things *are* with us, but how they *ought* to be. As Plato, who invented the subject, teaches, philosophy directs us to the ideal. Since social science aims to be non-directive about ideals and norms, it cannot pursue the philosophical goal. Exploring the ideal enables us to see not just how we are doing but how we might do better. Like other social roles, fatherhood can be fully defined only by including ideals or norms of the practice. My aim here is to argue that the ideal of fatherhood is to enable children to achieve lives worth living, ones that involve considerable *independence* while maintaining mutual relationships or *interdependence*. I call this ideal engendering *autonomy*.

I think fatherhood means constant willingness and effort – with joy and pride and humor – to maintain the unity and wellbeing of his family in its material and social context. This in turn entails a variety of more specific virtues that respond to kids' needs. These virtues all have to do with protecting, nurturing, guiding, and educating children, especially during their formative, vulnerable years. They all have to do with producing adults able to guide their own conduct and the conduct of society responsibly.

Fatherhood means dependability in the face of temptations. It means fair and informed leadership that is sensitive to the good of the family and of its individual members. It means readiness to share and execute legitimate parental authority. It means willingness to reflect on both experience and some basic concepts in order to develop material and social wisdom. And it means sharing all this with our children. Most of all fatherhood means cultivating in children that special human combination of independence and interdependence we call autonomy, and in this, as we will see, the father or father figure has a special role.

Practicing fatherhood mindful of such an ideal sustains not only the family but fatherhood itself. For loss of the ideal leaves us without the perspective to diagnose and remedy dysfunctional cases, which may only increase their number. Like other social practices, we have to think about it carefully to do it right.

As Aristotle says, we are social creatures. The most obvious proof of this is that we are all born into families of one sort or another and, of course, there are many kinds of families encompassing an enormous variety of relationships. Still, it is not unreasonable to take the root family – and therefore social – relationship to be a shared commitment to raise children to lead worthwhile lives of their own. Unlike other creatures whose character and behavior are more genetically fixed, our individual character is largely up to us, even if it is constrained by social influences. Our family is the most powerful part of our social context, especially during the earliest years. Some have imagined that the family is dispensable, but it is not an accident that it remains the core social structure of human life. No other social arrangement provides both the intimate attention and the personal respect children need.

Role Responsibilities

We are all quite familiar with social roles, since we all occupy many of them. Each of us is a son or daughter, a member of a religious group, a co-worker, a citizen, and so on. Since there may be many others filling each of these roles, a role is, in philosophical language, *abstract*. By contrast, the persons filling the roles are said to be *concrete*. In professional baseball, a starting pitcher is commonly replaced by a relief pitcher. So the role of pitcher is abstract while the men who pitch are concrete individuals. The role is defined by something like a job description: an open slot that many suitably qualified individuals may fill. Such interchangeability is characteristic of social roles.

Fatherhood is a social role in this sense. Fatherhood, like starting pitcher, is an abstraction. It is concrete when individual fathers take up the role. Games like baseball and practices like fatherhood are *systems* of such roles. The practices in which we live out our individual and collective lives are systems of roles filled by concrete persons.

Pitchers' performances vary widely and different performances may be appropriate or even inevitable in different contexts. We should not expect a Roger Clemens performance from almost anyone else, but pitchers everywhere emulate him. They try to pitch as well as he does in their own contexts.

Similarly, there have been perhaps 50 billion human fathers and each has made the role uniquely his own. One father will be authoritarian, another will be a teacher, another will be a nurturer, and some will abdicate altogether. Others, too, may serve as fathers, for instance grandfathers, uncles, stepfathers, and guardians. It is only because the fatherhood role is abstract that each way of living out the role counts as fatherhood. For this same reason, each way of being a father may come to serve as a model for a family or community.

Some social roles like fatherhood may be thought to be natural. But the concrete expression of a role is practically always a combination of social forces and the choices of the individual, making it a kind of construct or artifact. While the practices of individual fathers may be pretty uniform throughout a given society, there is room for variation among local norms. Nevertheless, the basic role remains the same throughout the enormous range of its concrete expressions, since it is defined in terms of its function. The philosophical task is to account for what remains constant or ought to.

But wherever there is a norm there is the possibility of failing to satisfy it, making mistakes, being in error. This means that there will be some rational basis, at least in the norms of the local community, for evaluating the performance of any given father. One father may be judged to be unforgiving towards his children and another may be seen as so demanding as to be abusive. Local standards, sometimes codified into law, typically impose broad limitations on such behavior.

But what does it mean to engage in a practice that sets standards of conduct for that very practice? How does a father become subject to the standards of fatherhood? Clearly, it's not like signing a contract or making a promise, for no such document may ever be present and no such words may ever be spoken. (Wedding vows are typically directed toward spouses.)

It's more like learning to speak a language. The meanings of words aren't one's own. They come from the intentions people have when speaking with each other. I intend such and such by what I say and you intend to understand me and we have to meet each other half way. When our intentions coincide, they are properly *collective*: we achieve mutual understanding and each get what the other says.

Similarly, fatherhood is a matter of *intending* to share in rearing children. The role springs from the intentions fathers express in their conduct. Just as saying what we mean both takes advantage of what words mean in the group *and* gives words their meaning, performing the activities of fatherhood *constitutes* the standards of fatherhood. Standards of fatherhood are, in this sense, a social construct.

It may seem almost magical, almost a conjuring trick. The standards are not imposed from outside. Instead, we impose them on ourselves. The practice sets standards for those engaged in the practice. Thus fathers, in constructing collective standards for themselves, are *autonomous*, for autonomy is just self-governance. We may think of these standards as the obligations (and rights) of fatherhood: if one engages in the practice, this is the way it should go.

Some have held that autonomy is merely endorsing one's passing desires or feelings. But there is a more important side to it. Fathers frequently have to do what they would personally rather not do. But we are able to act for desire-independent reasons.

If an action is morally acceptable in one circumstance for one person, it should be acceptable in comparable circumstances for anyone. To be reasonable, we have to be able to generalize our intentions. This is the collective side of autonomy. A man who abuses his child or his wife today should be willing to suffer as they do were the shoe on the other foot. We each have to think what it would be like if everyone did as we want to do. Without such reflection, we would be making exceptions for ourselves constantly, at the expense of the vulnerable, even those closest to us. Without such reflection, we are governed by our desires and feelings. And when our desires run our lives instead of consistent judgment, we are not free. We lose our autonomy.

Autonomy

Autonomy is self-rule. It is literally giving laws or norms to ourselves. Personal autonomy means acting consistently from good intentions. We can take away our children's chances of becoming autonomous by creating adverse conditions. Allowing them to cheat at games, for example, can lead them to think the rules don't apply to them. Expecting them to play by the same rules as others won't make them autonomous, but it's a start. No one can literally make anyone else autonomous.

So, where does autonomy come from? It takes two steps. Standards of conduct entail *accountability*. And accountability in turn entails autonomy. If I am subject to a norm like feeding my children, I am accountable for satisfying it. But only if I am autonomous can I be accountable. Kant's famous slogan holds: *ought implies can*. Whatever I am accountable for, I must have the power to do. If I don't have the power to do it, I am not accountable. Normally, I would have an obligation to provide needed medicine for my children. But if I have no means of providing it – if I am down and out – my accountability is reduced and finally defeated. As bad as I may feel, another remedy would have to be found or the situation would turn tragic.

Thus, accountability *confers* autonomy. By holding myself accountable for clothing my children, I become to that extent autonomous. We are autonomous when we accept our responsibilities. And what we are accountable for is not just ours alone. The same norms apply to everyone in a similar situation.

Whoever obligates himself by imposing a norm on himself must be able to satisfy its demands. Lack of this ability defeats the obligation. This is why we often accept excuses for ignorance, accidents, addiction, coercion, and the like. Autonomy, I take to be this remarkable capacity to satisfy or to fail to satisfy self-imposed norms.

Far from a private feeling, this makes autonomy a thoroughly social affair. By expressing the intention to conform to rules that are equally applicable to all, autonomy expresses both independence and interdependence. I can coherently claim to be my own highest authority only by accepting accountability for my actions under norms that apply to others. Making exceptions for myself – spending the rent money for drugs or defrauding a naïve customer at work – exposes a mere hodge-podge of desires rather than a coherent character fit to be emulated by my children. Lack of accountability in parents is easy for children to imitate, but ones who do are likely to develop confused character of their own and fail to develop personal autonomy. In this respect, as we will see, fathers have a special burden.

However, as role models, we need to do more than slavishly follow rules. We need to show our children how to reflect on the norms that constitute *their* practices. Some rules, as philosophers say, are merely *regulative* while others are *constitutive*. In the US I drive on the right hand side of the road, but in Britain I drive on the left. The side of the road we drive on is merely regulative: locally, we have to pick one or other and it is enough to conform.

Most relations with children are not so simple. If I want to know whether to keep my promise to take my son fishing on Saturday, I have to recognize that the promise is believed only because it is part of the practice of promising. The practice of promising is partly *constituted* by the obligation to do as one promises. Not keeping my promise not only undermines my example to my son, but it also weakens his respect for the practice of making and keeping promises and thereby weakens the practice itself. As Kant says, to avoid merely blind rule following, we have to do something uniquely human. We have to constitute our practice by conforming not merely to the rule but to the *concept* of the rule. In keeping my promise to my son, we not only enjoy fishing together, I begin to teach him to evaluate his own practices in light of understanding them.

Most philosophers have thought of action in individual terms, as the doings of *individual persons*. But organized endeavors like governments, games, and businesses have in the last couple of centuries led some to see social groups as a distinctive kind of *collective persons*. Thus, it may appear that, since parents or guardians form a group, the group, even if only a dyad, is itself a collective person. Fortunately, this classic debate between "collectivists" and "individualists"[2] has moderated. A substantial consensus now agrees that, since only individuals literally have intentions, there are no collective persons. Rather, it is the *content* of our intentions – what we intend – that constitutes collectives.

It is a remarkable fact about us that we are able to act on intentions of different kinds. Singular or *individual* intentions guide our own actions. These would normally be expressed by saying things like, "I intend to hang this picture of Emily." A *collective* intention would be expressed like this: "We aim to toilet train Ethan."

When we act collectively, we share our goals and knowledge and usually our feelings. These form the shared contents of our collective intentions. Parents are not like strangers on a train, what philosophers call an *aggregate*. Rather, they are bound together across many social and moral dimensions to form a genuine *collective*. The links that join parents into a collective are vital to successful childrearing. In this way, satisfactory family life springs from collective intentions. Because of men's competitive tendencies, it may be more difficult for them to share their intentions, but only in such relationships may fatherhood flourish.

But what goals should fathers pursue? Ideally, they would implement the norms that give the practice of fatherhood its meaning. We are subject to an immense variety of norms, many of which we hardly think about. When we speak to each other, we have to satisfy the basic norms of our language – word usage, pronunciation, and so on – just to be understood. When we argue with each other, we either respect basic, common norms of reasoning or fail to make any sense at all. Like a batter who refuses to leave the box after three strikes, if we ignore too many of the constitutive rules, we cease playing the game.

The statute law defines some important limits of relations with others for a community. But most of our social practice, including the practice of fatherhood, depends on norms that lie outside the reach of the law. Ignore moral norms and people get hurt. Ignoring the norms of fatherhood damages children. So, what are the norms of fatherhood? What are the standards to which all fathers ought to aspire in their relationships with their children? To turn the question around, when are we justified in criticizing fathers for failing to live up to the standards of fatherhood?

Part of the answer was given at the outset in terms of key personal virtues – like nurturing and dependability – that fathers need to achieve the goal of fatherhood. These suggest the actions and attitudes of successful fathers. But we should try to state the goals toward which a father ought to aspire to clarify these virtues. Without that our practice is blind. That goal, I believe, is our children's autonomy.

Autonomy and Fatherhood

Nature has suited us for family life. It brings many advantages, especially for a species like ours with such a long period to maturity. With two parents, many necessary tasks can be divided, although plenty are best done together. Competition with others outside the family is needed for some purposes, but most tasks require mainly cooperation. And most of the richness and meaning associated with family life comes from cooperation and collaboration among family members.

Nevertheless, evolution seems to dispose men and women differently towards childrearing, and these dispositions, like others, are typically exaggerated by culture. It is a chronic problem for us to change these dispositions and the cultural pressures we feel to the advantage of our children. In general, men are notoriously more competitive (aggressive, willing to take risks, independent). But such traits can make them uncooperative and can hurt their children as well as relations with their partners. Women, on the other hand, tend to be better at cooperation (relationship, connection, interdependence).

Since it is a distinct advantage for a child to be raised by both parents,[3] this difference creates a potential problem for fatherhood. How can fathers provide a model of task oriented independence without putting their children and partners at risk?

I have said that autonomy includes both independence and interdependence. Because men often seem disposed to be more independent than women, they have a better (though hardly exclusive) chance of engendering that aspect of autonomy in their children. But it can be overdone. The boy's independence becomes the man's aggression. How these characteristics develop is a matter of social and cultural circumstances.

But the point is for parents to direct the development of both independence and interdependence in their children towards autonomy. Autonomy is the most unique and essential characteristic of both a meaningful human life and a good society. Living a meaningful life in a good society requires autonomy. Adults demand it for themselves. Children long for it. So, fathers should aim to engender autonomy in their children. People, whether alone or in groups, flourish best when they govern themselves.

To develop autonomy it is necessary for a father to understand the ideal of fatherhood. The better a father understands the ideal, the better father he is likely to be. The key for him to engender autonomy is for him to practice and carefully enforce accountability. Like Socrates, he should guide without imposing, aiming to draw out the best in his child. As a child develops accountability for his actions, he learns to impose norms on himself. The aim is for children to gradually accept their accountability, as Aristotle says, because, on reflection, they understand that it is theirs. Thus, with responsible parenting, the child sets *himself* free. Thus is he socialized in a way that is uniquely human. Other conceptions of fatherhood – authoritarian, teacher, even hero – risk suppressing or deforming autonomy.

When we act, there are just these two possibilities: we act alone or together. Both are essential to a good life and a flourishing society. In general, mothers tend to be the role models for interdependence and the role modeling of independence tends to be the work of fathers. These are the two faces of autonomy. Both are essential.

Autonomous people are social products and remain socially engaged. But when they find themselves engaged in unacceptable social practices, they create and give themselves new norms to live by. A valued employee who discovers that his company has been misbehaving might risk his social status by acting independently and blow the whistle.

My assumption throughout has been that children are natural imitators. Both interdependence and independence are essential to child development and mothers and fathers can model both. But independence in particular runs counter to mere mimicry. So, in the nature of the case, more than slavishly following even good role models is necessary for the development of the child's autonomy. Children must gradually develop their own practices independently, but anchored within their social setting. A child might take a step towards autonomy by tattling on a school bully, thus risking his social standing in his class.

Thus, the delicate task of fatherhood is to balance his independence with his partner's interdependence. Fathers have to transcend the social exaggeration of their native competitiveness for the sake of their kids.

Autonomy is not gendered. Nevertheless, I have pointed out a key difference in the dispositions of men and women and suggested that these are aligned with our two basic kinds of intentions. I have also said that it is autonomy, as giving norms of conduct to oneself, that makes life meaningful. Thus, a meaningful life incorporates both aspects of autonomy. It follows that a father's special contribution to making his children's lives worth living is to engender independence within a cooperative context.

Exercising self-control while being dedicated to the wellbeing of his children and his partner is the first step in realizing the ideal of fatherhood. Perhaps the best example a father can set for his children is to respect and nurture his partner's autonomy. He must not be overwhelmed by fear of his responsibilities. He must resist temptations like flight or physical abuse and avoid false gratifications like unaffordable gambling, drug abuse, philandering, and so on. Traditionally, fathers have held most of the social power, which, sadly, they have often abused.

Conclusion

Developing autonomy is about finding oneself, a social process ideally driven by acceptance of accountability, which means holding oneself to the same standards as others. Parents should help their children find themselves. But beyond the personal development they themselves have achieved, they can point their children towards ideals they have aimed to live by. Although it is a hard row for him to hoe, while remaining interdependent with his partner, mindful of the moral limitations on his powers, a father's native independence positions him well to impart this essential element of identity to his children.

Autonomy is something to be achieved, and it cannot be maintained without reflective effort. It is a lifelong project serving as the cornerstone of a good life that fathers themselves can pursue along with their partners and jointly pass on to their children.

My wife and I have raised two fine sons. The older one is now married and, to us, his wife is like the daughter we never had. We are now eager to welcome grandchildren into our family. My immediate motive here has been to pass on to our sons some reflections on what it may mean to raise families of their own. But my hope is that they are of interest and use to fathers and would-be fathers generally.[4]

NOTES

1 Margaret Mead, *Male and Female* (New York: Harper Collins, 1967), p. 176.
2 See, for example, Margaret Gilbert, *On Social Facts* (Princeton: Princeton University Press, 1989); John Searle, *The Construction of Social Reality* (New York: Free Press, 1995); and Raimo Tuomela, *The Philosophy of Sociality* (Oxford: Oxford University Press, 2007). John Dewey foreshadowed much of the current consensus – insofar as there is one – in 1927, in *The Public and Its Problems* (Chicago: Henry Holt, 1927; Swallow Press, 1954), especially chapters 1 and 7.
3 Caitlin Flanagan writes, "Few things hamper a child as much as not having a father at home. 'As a feminist, I didn't want to believe it,' says Maria Kefalas, a sociologist who studies marriage and family issues and co-authored a seminal book on low-income mothers.... 'Women always tell me, "I can be a mother and a father to a child," but it's not true.' Growing up without a father has deep psychological effects on a child. 'The mom may not need that man,' Kefalas says, 'but her children do.'" *Time*, "Why Marriage Matters," July 13, 2009, p. 47.
4 Thanks go to Daniel Breyer and Lon Nease for their helpful comments on an earlier draft. I am especially grateful to my wife, Lauren, for her very insightful observations about both substance and style: *she without whom not.*

PART III

KEEPING IT REAL

Authentic Fatherhood

CHAPTER 9

REAL FATHERS BAKE COOKIES

For my father – he is what a father is; and for my son, Connor, who has given me the chance to be the father I want to be.

In Chris Rock's 2004 HBO special *Chris Rock: Never Scared*, the comedian notes that, if a child can't read because mom is at the club every night until 2 a.m., then it's the mom's fault. However, if the child can't read because there are no lights on in the house, then it's the dad's fault![1] I'm not sure we could find a better summary of the traditional role of the father. Dad's role is to make money to provide the family financial support. That's what a real father does.

Contrast this notion with the following from comedian and radio talk show host Pete Dominick: "The most manly thing you can do is read to your children every night."[2] The idea portrayed here is that Dad should be more emotionally involved in the lives of his children. He should be home more often. We might even go so far as to say that he should demonstrate that it's alright for men to cry, that he should make dinner – even bake cookies. This more recent notion (popularly speaking) makes a different claim: real dads are those who are there for their children emotionally, physically, spiritually, and in a variety of other ways. They take time off from work to go to games, to come to day-time school events. They might even take extended time to be primary caregivers.

It can be tempting to say that "real" in this sense is simply "the right way of being or doing something." If that were true, we could make our cases for each type of father portrayed above; we could argue for which is better, and then say that's what any father ought to do. Or we might say that either is fine, so long as the father in question is doing something positive for his family. It's certainly tempting to try to reduce our understanding of a "real" father to something like this, since once we know which of these options is better, we would have an easy plan to follow. We might even say that if both are equally fine, that would be a relief, because then we could do whichever we happened to be doing and feel quite good about it.

I think that when we use the world "real" when we say something like "he is a real father," however, we mean something a little different than "he is doing the right thing." I think we might start out meaning something like "the right way" or "the correct way" to be a father on the surface. If we dig down a bit deeper, however, I think we come across something else we mean by the word "real" when used in something like "real father." A "real" father isn't just someone who provides well for his family. He isn't someone who is a nurturer. He isn't even someone who does these things in a certain way.

Instead, a "real" father is more like this: he is someone who is a father because he truly chooses his fatherhood freely and in reference to the children of whom he is a father. He does this knowing that only he can make these choices, and that he must make them. He realizes that he can't know before he makes his choices whether they will really be the right ones or not – but he still makes them. And he does all of this with the needs and choices of his children in mind, whose choices provide a sounding-board for his choices in a way that establishes a reciprocal bond between him and his children. In other words, a "real" father is one who makes the right choices because he really wants them to be his choices.

This way of thinking about the "real" in "real father" brings up the philosophical notion of authenticity. Authenticity is an attempt to understand what makes the person or thing referred to as "real" different or truer than what it would be if it weren't authentic.

In what follows, I offer two views of authenticity. The first is something called *existentialist authenticity*. I think this style is best represented by Jean-Paul Sartre. The second is known as *dialogical authenticity*, whose best advocate is Charles Taylor. Although these two views seem opposed at first, I believe they can be reconciled in something like the experience

🚶‍♂️ DAN COLLINS-CAVANAUGH

of authentic fatherhood. In fact, in the final section, I will try to show that they should be reconciled in someone who wants to be an authentic, which is to say a "real," father.

Two Views of Authenticity

What's the difference between a "real" father in the authentic sense and some other kind of father? After all, a father who wasn't "real" in the sense of being authentic would still be a father. In fact, from an external point of view, we might say that there really isn't any way to tell the difference. This is why critics of the idea of authenticity have such a hard time with the concept. Those of us who aren't the particular father can't experience anything other than what he does. Either he does something praiseworthy or he doesn't. What does authenticity add to the mix?

Consider these two examples, though: a chocolate chip cookie and Derek Jeter. If we come across a particularly good chocolate chip cookie, we might say to ourselves, "That's a real cookie!" When we watch Derek Jeter play baseball, we might say to ourselves (or to the people around us): "That Derek Jeter – he's a real baseball player!" Our idea of the "real" here is about more than what we immediately experience.

Take the cookie. When we eat a particularly good cookie, we make certain assumptions about it. We assume that it was made with certain ingredients (flour, sugar, chocolate chips, butter, and so on). These are things that make a "real" cookie real. We could also say that these are things that make a cookie like this an "authentic" cookie. What if we found out that the cookie in question wasn't made the way we thought it was made, though? What if the sugar was Splenda (a sugar substitute)? What if the flour was cut with something meant to simulate flour? Or if, instead of all-purpose flour, something like rice or barley flour was included to make the cookie "healthier"? What if the butter was replaced by light butter (there is such a thing – it has half the calories and fat of real butter)? We might feel as if we were deceived by such a cookie – even if it tasted quite good. We might believe that the cookie wasn't "real" in the sense of being how a cookie should be (I believe my father holds this view!).

Of course, a cookie is just a thing – the actual deceiver here would be the baker. He should have told us before we ate the cookie that it wasn't "real" in this sense, that it wasn't an authentic cookie. With the Derek

Jeter example, it's a bit more obvious how the appearances we associate with "real," as in "authentic," could be misleading. We say that Jeter is a "real" baseball player because he is seen to play the game a certain way: he hustles, he cares about winning, he plays the game free of illicit or illegal substances (like steroids), he cares more about winning than his own fame and fortune, and he cares about the history and tradition of the game.

What if all of this was an act, though? What if Derek Jeter only appeared to be this way, but secretly, he really just wanted to be rich, and decided that his best route to wealth as a player was to appear to be a "real" player, when he couldn't really care less about winning or tradition or hustling? We might very well say that he isn't really a "real" or "authentic" baseball player – despite the fact that he might appear to be one, because he isn't choosing to be authentic, he is choosing to appear authentic. To be authentic, though, one must choose it for one's self – and for everyone else, too. If Jeter only chooses to appear authentic because he thinks that's the easiest way to accomplish his own goals, he isn't really choosing it at all.

This is how Sartre sees it. Authenticity is a matter of free choices. This is the existentialist view. Existentialism basically says that there is no overriding or preexisting essence to human existence. We exist first. We only become what we are through a series of choices that only we can make. There is no previous right answer to which we can turn. Sartre claims there is no essence that precedes our existence. He says, "Man being condemned to be free carries the weight of the whole world on his shoulders; he is responsible for the world and for himself as a way of being."[3] This freedom can produce a lot of anxiety, though. How can we know if the choice we make is the right choice? The answer is, we cannot – but we still must choose.

Some people find this a bit overwhelming. They prefer to try to give up their freedom and adopt a ready made formula that explains their existence, what they should do, how they should be, and so forth. Of course, even our choice to give up choice is still a choice, so we don't actually escape our freedom. Instead, we end up in a condition that Sartre calls "bad faith." Bad faith happens when we accept another plan as our own, without understanding that our choices are still always and only our own. And it happens even if the bad faith we adopt has good results.

If Derek Jeter chooses to appear to care about winning, hustling, and all the other things we associate with "real" or "authentic" baseball players, but does so because that's what others have told him is the best way rather than because that's what he freely wants to do, then he operates in bad faith – regardless of how many games his team wins, or how many of those wins seem directly linked to the things he does on the field. To be authentic, Jeter has to choose to be the way he is, without any assurance that his choices are correct. He has to make himself a model for all others, because that is what he wants to do. He must make these choices alone, and only he can make them.

The existentialist idea of authenticity claims that we exist first and then we create the essences that we use to define ourselves. There is another idea of authenticity we could turn to, though, one that might seem a bit less isolated. Existentialists like Sartre will claim that we are alone in our freedom. I can appeal to no one but myself in making my decisions.

As Charles Taylor points out, this doesn't match our experience. We live within certain "horizons of meaning" that determine what choices we can and do make. Sure, we have to freely make choices, but we always do so in relation to other people. This is what dialogical authenticity is about.[4] Taylor thought existentialist notions of authenticity could be dangerous. This was because the understanding of freedom was not in reference to others, which could lead to excessive self-love or even the mistaken view that I'm the only thing in the world that matters. By including others in our attempt to become authentic, dialogical forms of thinking are more likely to be morally grounded and historically informed. This doesn't mean that freedom disappears or isn't important. It just means that we don't consider ourselves as free choosers without any regard to others. We have to consider others. And this, Taylor thought, led to a preferable form of authenticity.

So, for Jeter, not only does he have to freely choose to be what he is, but he has to do so in reference to and in consideration of other players, the history of the sport, and other similar factors. After all, baseball players, by definition, are involved in an activity with others. They couldn't be baseball players otherwise. What other players do gives meaning to what Derek Jeter does as a baseball player, and vice versa. This forms the horizon of meaning that situates what he does as a baseball player within the context of baseball generally.

People who prefer the existentialist style of authenticity might think that so much consideration of others could lead to bad faith. How can we tell if we are really freely choosing what we choose if we have to base our choices, in part at least, on the needs and desires of others? Might those others not override our freedom somehow, or convince us to allow it to be overridden?

Conversely, people who prefer the dialogical style of authenticity could claim that without the horizon of meaning this view provides, we run the risk of "authentically" choosing things that are morally dubious, even morally reprehensible. A dialogical thinker could ask: What is to stop someone from "freely" and "authentically" choosing to be something undesirable? Couldn't the existentialist claim that because no essence precedes existence, he can freely choose to be rude, or cruel, or a thief? Dialogical thinkers believe that without due consideration of others, these things are all too risky. It's only through the horizon of meaning produced by our relationships to others that we can guarantee that the things we do will be good things.

Both objections might have a point, but I don't think these two views are necessarily incompatible. In fact, for certain things, like being a father, I think a genuine, authentic experience of fatherhood likely combines both the existentialist and dialogical styles of authenticity. In what follows, I try to sketch out what this combination might look like, particularly when it comes to fatherhood.

Being a Real Father

Every father probably remembers the moment he realized the following two things. The first is the full comprehension that he was going to be a father, that he would have a child in his life, that he would be responsible for that child. The second thing, which almost certainly followed very quickly on the first, was the realization that he had absolutely no idea whatsoever what he was going to be doing as a father.

I think the existentialist style of authenticity deals best with the second thought. For an existentialist, this realization of our ignorance is not surprising. It's just the way things are for us. We don't know what we are doing as fathers prior to being fathers because we can't possibly know how to be a father prior to actually being one. There is a frightening amount of uncertainty that comes with this – what the existentialist calls anxiety. And what makes this uncertainty particularly nerve-wracking is the fact that, as fathers, we don't know what we should do; but we know we have to know what to do. We know that it's important that we know what to do as fathers. Finally, and most importantly, we want to know what to do because we (presumably) want to be real fathers.

An existentialist like Sartre would say that an authentic, that is, "real" father would have to embrace this fear, this uncertainty and anxiety. He would have to embrace the fact that he couldn't know that the choices he makes as a father are the right choices prior to making them. He would still make his choices. And the choices he makes would be choices that he makes on behalf of fathers everywhere. That is, the choices the "real" father makes are choices that he thinks any father in a similar situation, fully embracing his freedom, could and should make, too. The father who chooses to work long hours chooses that style of fatherhood for all fathers. The father who chooses to forego the long work hours to be physically and emotionally available, the father who bakes cookies, chooses this style of fatherhood for all fathers.

Existentialists like Sartre claim that having to choose produces anxiety. It can be tempting, then, to let someone else do the choosing for us. When we realize for the first time that we are to be fathers, we might (and probably did) look for someone to tell us what to do, how to do it, and how things would likely turn out. Should we work more to get a better house? Should we take on an extra job to get enough money to move to where there are better schools? Or do we need to become well versed in children's stories, songs, and activities? Would it be a good idea to learn how to bake and cook? Would the right thing be to find ways to work less, so that we can be there for our children, both physically and emotionally? Do we have to find some way to be both kinds of father?

When it comes to the right way to be a father, there is no shortage of folks who will share their wisdom. There are many plans we could follow. If we simply adopt a plan in order to avoid having to make these choices ourselves, though, then we would be acting in bad faith, Sartre would say. There's nothing wrong with either version of fatherhood mentioned. Being the provider dad or the nurturer dad, or a combination, is great.

The question for someone who wants to be these things in an authentic way is this: How did I choose the way of being a dad I chose? Did I come to it through an embrace of my freedom and anxiety? Did I choose to be this kind of father because that's what I really wanted, knowing that I really didn't know the right answer? Or did I come to it because that's what others told me was right, and I just accepted it because I didn't want to be faced with the difficult task of having to decide for myself. The former, freely chosen type of fatherhood would be the real, authentic type, from an existentialist standpoint. The other type would not be authentic – even if everyone seemed to benefit.

For example, if I decide to embrace the provider dad style, and succeed at giving my family a nice house in a good neighborhood with good schools, so that my child grows up with every material advantage, that would seem to be beneficial. However, if I only adopted this role because that's what others told me was right and I would have rather spent less time working and more time as a nurturer dad, then the choice to be the provider dad wouldn't be authentic for me. To be an authentic father, the choice I make must be my own, and I must embrace it as my own.

I find Taylor's dialogical style of authenticity addresses the first concern I named: that we are going to be the father of a child, and be responsible for someone else. It's fine to talk about the uncertainty of our freedom. Of course we should make good choices for ourselves. What about the child, though? From Taylor's dialogical way of thinking about what something like a real father would be, the real, authentic father would have to make his choices within a horizon of meaning. That horizon of meaning would be formed by the child to whom he is a father. The needs, desires, and goods of the child would have to inform whatever choices the real father would make. What's more, these choices are also made within a certain historical and cultural framework. All of these things go into the choices we make, and all of them help define what a real father would be. Choices that don't include both couldn't be authentic choices.

So returning to the decision between provider dad and nurturer dad, the child's needs, desires, and choices need to form part of the decision-making process. If I don't recognize how my child needs to be provided for, even my free choice to be a provider dad won't be fully authentic. If I don't understand the kind of nurturing my child needs, my free choice to be nurturer dad won't be fully authentic either. This isn't about getting negative results from the choices. It's not about maximizing benefit. It's about recognizing in the other person what choices the other person wants to make, and working together to form choices that are real choices for both parties. Of course, this can be complicated when one party, the child, is still an infant, and can't really express their desires in any coherent way. Taylor would argue that we could make reasonable assumptions, though, and still work to make mutually authentic decisions.

From an existentialist perspective like Sartre's, this sort of thing risks bad faith. This is not because the others aren't important. It's only because we could let our understanding of the needs of the other overwhelm our experience of the freedom of our choices. I might feel constrained to be more of the provider dad than the nurturer dad, based on what I think my child's needs are, or vice versa. This would mean a less than totally free decision. From a dialogical perspective such as Taylor's, the existentialist risks ignoring the needs of the child. This might turn the child into an object that is only an extension of the father making the

DAN COLLINS-CAVANAUGH

choices. This risks the child's ability to be a free chooser, and such a risk doesn't strike someone like Taylor as authentic.

I think that these two styles aren't exclusive, though – particularly when it comes to something like fatherhood. I said in the first part of this chapter that being a "real" father isn't so much about what choice is made. Both provider dad and nurturer dad are fine choices. Being authentic is about how the choices we make are made. Being a real father is about how fatherhood choices are made.

There might be instances where the existentialist style is more appropriate. There might be instances where the dialogical style is more appropriate. When it comes to something like fatherhood, I think both are appropriate, and both can be combined coherently. This is because to be a father means to be the father of a child. So there is necessarily an "other" who needs to be there in order for me to be a father at all. This isn't an "essence preceding existence," as Sartre would say – it's just an empirical necessity. So my choices, even from an existentialist perspective, already involve another person, namely, the child. But even if that is the case, the actual choices themselves are still always and only my own. I can be, and should be, informed by what my child needs. That doesn't change the fact that only I can make the choices as a father. I still have to struggle with the freedom and uncertainty of being a father, even as I recognize the needs of the child of whom I am a father. And because I am making the choices I make for all fathers, as Sartre would say, it would seem unlikely that I would make choices that would seem harmful on the surface and really claim that those choices are what I thought any free-choosing father would choose. A real father would be one who understood his freedom as a father, and made his choices in line with that and with the free and uncertain needs of his child.

So what might an example of authentic fatherhood look like? Let's say I have a child with a talent, such as sports or music. Should I push the child to excel? Should I let the child develop the talent on his or her own? What would a "real" father do?

First, I would have to examine my own reasons. If I want to push the child, why do I want to do this? Is it because I truly and freely think this is what is best? Or am I afraid that not pushing him will lose him fame and fortune? If it's the latter, that would seem to be inauthentic – in bad faith, as Sartre would say. If it's the former, then I might be acting authentically to push the child to develop the talent.

Next, I have to consider the child's perspective. Does the child want to develop the talent in this way? Will pushing the child mean that she or he comes to hate the talent? Do I think my child will be grateful for the diligence? Or do I think my child will be resentful for taking the joy out of the sport or music the child had previously enjoyed? If I act without regard to what the child wants, then someone like Taylor would say I fail to act authentically. If I take the child's desires and freedom into account, then I might be acting authentically, from this point of view.

This is a hard decision to make. Both kinds of thinking seem appropriate – and I think both are. Taylor is right that to be a "real" father I have to try my best to figure out what it is my child really wants and needs, in terms of the talent in question. This is true even if my child isn't fully aware of what he or she wants – a circumstance that makes the choice very difficult. Here is where Sartre is helpful – sort of. I have to choose. I can't know which choice is right beforehand, if by "right" I mean produces the most benefit or is most in line with other notions of the good. I can ask what others would do. Maybe they would even offer helpful advice. In the end, though, only I can make the choice. If I choose to push the child's development of the talent, I can't abdicate my responsibility for that choice, because only I could make it. If I choose to let the child develop the talent on her or his own, the same thing applies – I'm still fully responsible for my choice, and I have no one to appeal to ultimately but myself. I don't choose in a vacuum when I make choices as a father, because I'm only a father if I'm the father of my child. At the same time, even though the needs and desires of my child form a horizon of meaning that informs my choices, they are still choices only I can make, since only I am the father, but they are choices which I also must make.

So either way I go can be authentic, or "real," if I make the choice freely in concert with as full as possible an understanding of what my child needs and wants. And this was why the choice between being provider dad and nurturer dad isn't a choice based on which way of being a father was better. It's a choice between which kind of father I really want to be. Since neither is a bad option (like being a hyper-parent or a dead beat dad), it's up to me to freely decide what kind of father I want to be, so long as I do so in full recognition of the fact that I am the father of my child, so my child needs to play a role in what it means for me to be a real father, too.

So since I freely choose to be the style of father who bakes cookies, and since I believe my son has expressed a freely chosen desire for cookies, I believe I'll go and bake some with him.[5]

DAN COLLINS-CAVANAUGH

NOTES

1 Chris Rock, *Chris Rock: Never Scared* (Los Angeles: HBO Productions, 2004).

2 Pete Dominick, *Stand Up With Pete Dominick* (New York: Sirius/XM Radio, 2009), February 12, 2009.

3 Jean Paul Sartre, "Freedom and Responsibility," in *Existentialism and Human Emotions*, trans. Hazel E. Barnes (New York: Citadel Press, 1985), p. 52.

4 Charles Taylor, *The Ethics of Authenticity* (Cambridge, MA: Harvard University Press, 1991), pp. 31–3.

5 I want to thank my wife Alethea, whose proofreading made this much more readable! I also want to thank the editors for many useful suggestions.

CHAPTER 10

MAYBE HAPPINESS IS LOVING OUR FATHER

Confucius and the Rituals of Dad

I think what Confucius says about fatherhood is even more applicable today than when he wrote it. In the fifth century BCE he said, "if the fathers would be fathers, the sons sons, and the governors governors," then there would be prosperity.[1] For Confucius, how people relate to each other is the key to happiness, and he thinks the most important relationships to master are the family relationships. Confucius had the deep-seated belief that if each father, son, mother, and daughter would choose to live according to their role in the family (father, son, mother, or daughter), then that person's life would go well.

For Confucius, all of these roles are important, but the most important relationship for living well is between fathers and sons. The model that Confucius suggests here is a *virtue ethic*, an idea I explain in more detail below. The passage above, while it sounds somewhat like a lament, is really a motivational speech with practical advice. In this chapter we'll look at some of Confucius' key thoughts and how they can help us understand happiness and fatherhood.

Unfortunately, to help us get his advice, I have to find ways to explain a culture that is 2,500 years old and nearly 7,000 miles away. There are two dangerous mistakes that we need to be careful to avoid. First, we have to remember that much in Confucius' picture of the world is foreign to us. Second, we have to recognize that the differences between cultures are more than just words with the same meaning in different languages. While an English-speaking audience might see Confucius' *Analects* as the esoteric scriptures of a foreign religion, I think we can understand his advice to fathers quite easily if we follow three key ideas: *ritual, excellence,* and *wisdom.*

Humanizing Ritual: Finding the Way to Say "I Love You"

The first key for understanding Confucius' advice is *ritual.* While the word "ritual" brings to mind few pleasant thoughts for me or for most contemporary readers, Confucius sees rituals as rich and valuable performances that are more important than governments or laws. Since what Confucius means by ritual is so different from what we might imagine, we might want to remember this different sense of the word "ritual" when we see it in Confucius' works. I think Confucius has good reasons for emphasizing ritual, which we can find by first thinking about grammar and then looking at a comparison with the ancient West in Plato's *Euthyphro.*

Grammar helps us to understand ritual. Li Chenyang, a contemporary expert on Chinese philosophy, identifies this notion of ritual with "cultural grammar."[2] In Li's interpretation, rituals play the same role for our social behaviors as grammar does in speech. While grammar might conjure up bad memories of boring English classes, the reality is that we use and *enjoy* using grammar every day. Without it, I would not be able to write this and you would not be able to read it.

In the same way that grammar enables speakers to communicate verbally with one another, the Confucian idea we translate as ritual enables individuals to communicate with each other through their actions. For Li and Confucius, these rituals are not boring or trite. Instead, rituals are ways to express ourselves clearly so our friends and family can understand.

For instance, the idea of a man dropping to one knee and offering a ring to a woman is well understood in our culture as "getting engaged" but could just as easily be called an "engagement ritual." I did this when

I became engaged, and most of the men I know did the same. Those few who did not follow this pattern had to spend hours calming their fiancées for not expressing their desire to get engaged the right way. Blowing out the candles at a birthday party is something else we might rightly call ritual. These practical examples help to make the word sound less strange and obtuse – even if it is foreign for us to call these rituals.

While practicing these rituals is important, the ritual itself is not the goal. Instead, a ritual provides a *means* to an end. Here, a good example is rising in a court room as the judge comes in. The purpose of this is to symbolize respect for the judge. Still, failing to stand does not necessarily mean disrespect. We all agree that if someone has a disability, they can still show respect to a judge without standing.

For the Confucian, what makes ritual right and important is that rituals provide really good ways for people to relate to each other. Thus, while saying "I love you," "please," and "thank you" are kinds of rituals, their value comes from their ability to clearly express feelings within our culture.[3] In this way, rituals really just provide patterns of being a good father or good friend *by doing* the things that fathers or friends *do* within our culture. Rituals are ways to express what a father should be: affectionate, providing for his children, protective, and supportive.

While some of the ways our culture enables people to express themselves only work in our culture, like walking a daughter down an aisle at her wedding, the basic feelings of love, pride, and affection are nearly universal in the relationship of a father to his children. In our culture there are many ways to express our feelings and we might not think of all of these as rituals. But ritual in the way Confucius uses it refers to any culturally given way of expressing ourselves in word or action to one another. Still, just like a word must be *meant* when said to have meaning, a ritual takes its meaning from the intention or feeling behind the person who does it.

Plato and Confucius: The Importance of the Father-Son Relationship

Confucius thought the most important relationship for building a good life was the father-son relationship and the rituals that go with it.[4] He also believed there were some elements that should define these rituals that go way beyond writing thank you notes for gifts. If a father finds the right rituals to relate to his sons, Confucius thought *everything in the world* would fall into its proper place. While this sounds outlandish, I think we can make better sense of it by looking at why he thinks this. In making his point, Confucius provocatively suggests that it is more important than the laws of his country:

> The Duke of She said to Confucius, "Among my people there is one we call 'Upright Gong.' When his father stole a sheep, he reported him to the authorities."
>
> Confucius replied, "Among my people, those who we consider 'upright' are different from this: fathers cover up for their sons, and sons cover up for their fathers. 'Uprightness' is to be found in this."

While Confucius has great praise for ritual, he often has disdain for governmental laws. We often think of the right thing to do and the legal thing to do as the same, so Confucius' denial of this highlights how much he values the father-son relationship. For him, the relationship between father and son is more important than obeying the laws. While this question does not often occur in our culture, it was very much alive in both Confucius' China and Plato's Greece.

In Plato's *Euthyphro*, Socrates encounters his friend Euthyphro, who is a prosecutor for the city of Athens, while he is awaiting his own trial for impiety. To pass the time, Socrates asks Euthyphro what brings him to court that day. When Euthyphro says he is there to prosecute his own father for murder, Socrates expresses his belief that there is something awry and impious in Euthyphro's actions, and so proceeds to argue with him about the nature of piety.

The question under discussion in both cases is *not* whether the respective father's actions were wrong. The astute reader will notice that neither Plato nor Confucius praises the morality of the father in question. I think it is important to emphasize that Confucius is not licensing fathers to kill and steal, but rather saying that the father-son relationship should be the focus of interaction between fathers and sons. Both discussions focus on what sort of behavior is appropriate for a son in relationship to his father. Similar questions arise in the ancient context for how a father should relate to his child. The point is that cultures like Confucius' spent a lot of effort evaluating the right ritual for the relationship they thought was the key: the father-son relationship.

The Guide of Excellence: Making Sense of the Master

> *The Master said, "If you try to guide the common people with coercive regulations ... and keep them in line with punishments, the people will become evasive and will have no sense of shame. If, however, you guide them with virtue, and keep them in line by means of ritual, then they will have a sense of shame and will rectify themselves."*

In the passage above, "the Master" is another name for Confucius. While he held that the father-son relationship had the highest importance, Confucius' followers thought the teacher-student relationship was important as well. As a result, they often called him "Master" to remind themselves to relate to him using the right ritual for this relationship. In particular, it reminded them that their views were not on an equal footing with his.

Even though this passage is about how a ruler should construct his society, it has interesting things to say about how fathers should raise their children, an area Confucius thought was even more important than how to govern: "if the fathers would be fathers, the sons sons, and the governors governors." Government plays second fiddle. In fact, Confucius sees family relationships as providing the basis of good government: "Being a good son and good brother one is already taking part in government [or ordered society]."

Thus, a question is common to both rulers and fathers: "How do I get obedience?" Confucius thinks there are two ways to get them to do what you want. First, you can *make* them do it by strictness. As bigger or more powerful, a ruler can force his subjects (or his children) to do what he says with the threat of punishment. Confucius does not think this way is best since he thinks it will merely make them "evasive." By this, he means that they will only be obedient when punishment is nearby and will not develop an internal sense of what is right and wrong. Punishment by itself will not produce maturity.

Second, Confucius suggests one could instead guide them with *virtue* and *ritual*. He thinks the obedience arises from them imitating the example of the one to be obeyed. We saw above that what Confucius means by ritual is both broader and more applicable than what we might have assumed based only on the word itself. Even though virtue still gets used in English, I think it is worthwhile for our purposes to explain what Confucius meant by it in the section that follows.

ANDREW KOMASINSKI

Confucius' writings do not make it clear if he refuses the use of punishment altogether. While this seems like what he might be trying to say, it's difficult to believe that Confucius, who was himself a father, would not have seen some uses for discipline. At the very least, he would have to say there are situations where obedience here and now is important enough to justify coercion – like stopping a child from touching a hot stove. Still, if you can set an example that your children will want to emulate in honesty or kindness, this has the best chance of staying with them into mature adulthood.

Making Sense of Virtue: Excelling at Relating

Our English word "virtue" derives from the Latin word for man. At the same time, it serves as the translation for a Greek word that means "excellence." Virtue theories understand ethics as *excelling* at the task of being human. This stands in contrast to seeing ethics as rule-following or trying to figure out what action will have the best consequences. Some translators of Confucius, fed up with misunderstandings that the word "virtue" can produce, have kept the word "excellence" and eschewed the use of the word "virtue" due to connotations they feel should not be applied to Confucius or Chinese culture in general.[5]

The connection between this idea of virtue ethics and fatherhood might not be apparent to us, and there are virtue theories that do not see it as important. For Confucius, however, the *excellence* he wants us to achieve is excellence at *relating to others*. Confucius states, "Virtue is never solitary; it always has neighbors." While this sounds like fortune cookie wisdom, the riddle can be easily deciphered. If we understand the answer to the question "What are we supposed to excel at?" to be "relating to others," then this statement is really saying that we can never excel if we do not relate to others. And for Confucius, the way we relate to others is going through the right rituals to show our feelings of love and respect.

While the passage at the beginning of this section was about governing, the two points he makes also apply to childrearing and education. First, setting an example will provide the children with the possibility of a sense of shame or pride; shame when they fail to pursue good relationships and a sense of fulfillment when they do. Second and consequently, they will "rectify" or straighten up their act themselves. Confucius' understanding of virtue for fathers can be summed up with the saying "fathers be fathers," meaning be someone that your children can look up to: "Be an example, not a disciplinarian." If you set the example in excellence and ritual, Confucius argues that "they will straighten up their own act!"

Confucius' advice seems a little one-sided at times. As in the "Upright Gong" story above, we need to be careful not to confuse our interest with his focus. We might jump to the conclusion that "Confucius believes we should never discipline," but this would be a misunderstanding on our part. In fact, Confucius is trying to dissuade fathers and leaders from thinking that punishment *alone* will produce maturity. Instead of deciding whether or not we should punish, he wants us to see virtue as the right mentality for us to pursue and thinks this will produce upright sons and daughters who are not merely obedient but genuinely moral.

From Theory to Practice: Wisely Applied

Since his advice is merely that "fathers are to be fathers" and "sons to be sons," the Confucian picture sounds idealistic as it supposes that if people acted appropriately in their roles this will somehow lead to a better society. In this case, it tells fathers to be affectionate fathers and sons and daughters to be respectful and obedient. It further suggests that the best way to raise your child is to practice the same behavior types you expect of him or her.

This advice seems incomplete and naïve by itself, so I think we should look at the sort of wisdom Confucius expects us to have in following this advice. First, I think there are good reasons to see his advice as working around an ideal with very practical psychological limits. Second, I think these limits help us to see how to relate even with a problem child by viewing the child through a "personality ideal."

I think Confucius' advice is at its sharpest when applied to a failed relationship. In fact, his advice to follow ritual leads to a better result than abandoning one's role and the practices appropriate to it when things go poorly or the other party to the relationship puts in little effort. Here, the well-known parable of the prodigal son in the Gospel of Luke provides an interesting thought experiment for the Confucian program of ritual and virtue. In this parable a son begins by acting in a very

ANDREW KOMASINSKI

improper way to his father. He asks his father for his inheritance while his father is still alive and well. Even though this is an affront, the father acts graciously and gives it to him, only to have the son leave and squander the money. When this disrespectful son finally loses everything, he decides to return to his father, whom he thinks would at least treat him better as a servant than his current master.

Upon his return, something surprising happens. Rather than merely accepting him as a servant, his father treats him far better than that: "And while [the son] was still a long way off, his father saw him coming. Filled with love and compassion, he ran to his son, embraced him, and kissed him." As the text continues, the father indicates that he still views this ungrateful one as his son: "This son of mine was dead and has now returned to life." For the father, this is a cause for celebration.

According to the parable, this celebration of the disrespectful son as a son angers his brother, who points out the disrespect his brother has shown their father: "This son of yours comes back after squandering your money on prostitutes." The older brother insists that the younger one should at the most be accepted – not celebrated.

While Luke and Confucius' writings have different audiences, this parable demonstrates striking thematic consistency with Confucius' position. First and foremost, the responses of the father and older brother to the younger son's return express the two different ways of getting obedience. The older brother thinks the younger should be punished for his disrespect and disobedience, but the father instead responds by being excellent in his own conduct. Surely the father could not have forgotten what his son had done to him, but he still chose to treat this situation as the return of a long-lost son.

By behaving this way, the father is not being naïve or idealistic. Instead, he is demonstrating a maturity that the older brother lacks. In particular, the father's response demonstrates an awareness that the time for corrective discipline has passed in this situation, while the older brother still wants retribution for the younger son's disrespect. Knowing this, the father treats this insolent child who has wasted what the father accumulated as if he were the dutiful son he should have been.

Tu Wei-Ming, a reader of Confucius presently teaching at Harvard, uses the phrase "personality ideal" to describe this way of thinking. To see the value of this way of thinking, I suggest we think of a really ornery teen. Even though she does not act like a daughter, as a father you should still treat her as one even when her behavior has not been very daughter-like.

Wisely Balancing Discipline

While Confucius focuses his advice and attention on the type of situation where he thinks the time for discipline has passed, I don't think this means we should conclude he has no place for discipline. Instead, I think the emphasis might instead reflect a corrective to a natural tendency in most fathers to want to force obedience. Confucius has a rather smart rule in his general advice:

> If someone is open to what you have to say, but you do not speak to them, this is letting the person go to waste. If, however, someone is not open to what you have to say, but you speak to them anyway, this is letting your words go to waste. The wise person does not let people go to waste, but also does not waste his words.

So while Confucius advocates having the proper behavior for your role as a father, son, brother, or friend, he does not mean for you to expend your efforts without purpose or direction. The Confucian insistence on continuing to be a father or son even in troubled relationships combines with the idea of wisely understanding the situation one faces.

While keeping an open heart in one's relationships should be the main policy, Confucius thinks it is also wise to know that there are times to behave differently to avoid abuse. Here, Tu's idea of a *personality ideal* takes on another dimension. To relate via a personality ideal is to consider how a good son would relate in this situation and avoid creating contexts where you know your son would not relate like a good son. Tu supplies an example of a son respecting his father by not letting him beat him in order to maintain their relationship:

> To run away from a severe beating, the argument goes, is not only to protect the body which has been entrusted to him by his parents but also to respect the fatherliness in his father that may have been temporarily obscured by rage.[6]

This personality ideal can help find a loving way to relate by not letting a son or daughter say things which could permanently harm the relationship. In the same way that the relationships are not to be abused, the limits of acceptable behavior should not be made into excuses. The argument is this: rather than let a father do something un-fatherly, avoid the situation so that he can thereby be a better father.

ANDREW KOMASINSKI

Conclusion: Building a Happy Family on Ritual, Excellence, and Wisdom

Confucius' advice for fathers is simple: love your sons and daughters as sons and daughters, express your love by using ritual expressions for it in your culture, set an example for them in virtue, and wisely discern how best to relate to them by knowing when to lavish love and when to avoid a manipulative situation. Confucius thinks that following the course of action he recommends has real practical benefits for the father who follows it.

The parable of the prodigal son can help us put all the pieces of his advice together. In it, we see the father use two rituals to express his love for his children. First, the division of the father's money to his sons occurs according to the pattern of his culture and so is a legitimate way for a father to show love to his children. Second, the father's ritual for celebrating his delight at his son's return occurs in a way that is normal for his culture in throwing a feast. While this may not be the first ritual that springs to mind for us in our culture, we too have many ritual ways for fathers to express love to their children: birthday parties, bedtime prayers and stories, dinner conversation, and teaching skills like riding a bicycle, training a dog together, and repairing a car, computer, or house as the father's skill allows.

A final point can be made. While I explained above that the word for virtue means excellence, Confucius and his followers also had a word for what this virtue would look like: "co-humanity."[7] For them, the most important way a human can excel is being good at relating to other people. Following the Confucian model might lead to a well-ordered society, but this does not mean there is no room for disagreement. Tu points out that relating to people according to their roles would allow for polite rather than cantankerous disagreement.[8] In fact, disagreement proves to be a part of healthy relationships since it enables growth.

The Confucian way can never guarantee the compliance of others, but can only work to encourage it. Even if relationships do not go well or according to plan, Confucius' advice remains the same: continue to love in the hope that those with whom one has relationships will also choose to love. Confucius expresses this focus by saying, "Once the roots are firmly established the way will grow." Rather than punishing those who do not live up to our ideals for them, Confucius encourages the individual to instead focus on self-cultivation and improvement as a means to a happier way of living.[9]

NOTES

1 Throughout this chapter, quotes from Confucius are from *Analects*, trans. Edward Slingerland (New York: Hackett, 2003).
2 Chenyang Li, "Li as Cultural Grammar: On the Relation Between Li and Ren in Confucius' Analects," *Philosophy East and West* 57: 311–29.
3 Ibid., p. 322.
4 Tu Wei-ming, "Selfhood and Otherness: The Father-Son Relationship in Confucian Thought," in *Confucian Thought: Selfhood as Creative Transformation* (Albany: State University of New York Press, 1985), p. 118. Quotes from Tu are from this text.
5 Here, I am referring to the series from the University of Hawaii Press from Hall and Ames. Some thinkers have called their interpretation postmodern since they are willing to dramatically rethink the text. See David Wong, "Rights and Community in Confucianism," in *Confucian Ethics* (New York: Cambridge University Press, 2004), p. 37.
6 Tu, "Selfhood and Otherness," p. 120.
7 Tu Wei-ming, "*Jen* as Living Metaphor in the Confucian *Analects*," in *Confucian Thought: Selfhood as Creative Transformation* (Albany: State University of New York Press, 1985), p. 84.
8 Ibid., p. 81.
9 Tu, "Selfhood and Otherness," p. 114.

ANDREW KOMASINSKI

ABIODUN OLADELE BALOGUN

CHAPTER 11

AUTHENTIC FATHERHOOD

A Traditional Yoruba-African Understanding

Being a father can be taxing, and not just because we fail sometimes. Rather, it has a lot to do with knowing what is involved in being a good father. Of course, having knowledge of the essential qualities of fatherhood is one thing; using such knowledge in daily living is another. But to become a good father, it is important to grasp the essentials of fatherhood. And this involves an understanding of the roles and responsibilities expected of a father more so than the rights and privileges of fatherhood.

There can be many possible interpretations of what is expected of a good father. One thing that is clear amid the diverse opinions is that many of them have ignored cultural and traditional understandings. This is because they incorrectly think that knowing and performing one's responsibilities as a father is a *personal* issue in which an individual's whims take privilege over cultural practices. In this age of liberal democracy in which freedoms and individual rights have been extended in every nook and cranny of society, it's common to hear fathers say, "This is my home, and no culture or tradition can tell me how to run my family affairs or dictate to me the way to raise my children." You also hear "I know what is good for my family and how best to be a father to them."

Remarks such as these demonstrate people's strong individual beliefs in themselves rather than reliance on cultural norms of fatherhood, which they often regard as traditional and outdated. Indeed, in this age in which science and technology influence everything, many now consider anything traditional as anachronistic. And as such, many despise such established ways of living. In short, traditional practices of fatherhood have been ignored in contemporary times.

Against this background, the aim of this chapter is to examine the idea of fatherhood within the context of a traditional culture and explore its relevance to contemporary ways of fatherhood. In this regard, I have chosen to use the Yoruba people as an illustrative example. The Yoruba is one of the major ethnic groups in Nigeria, West Africa. I intend to explore some of the essential attributes of a good father according to the traditional Yoruba culture and how such a conception can help contemporary fathers anywhere in the world be better fathers.

Authentic Fatherhood in Traditional Yoruba Thought

It is important to note from the outset that our use of the word "authentic" in this discussion refers to the indigenous Yoruban understanding of fatherhood in its pristine form, as opposed to the contemporary meaning of fatherhood in Nigeria, which is being influenced by many foreign values, concepts, and practices. To the traditional Yoruba, fatherhood is one of the major pillars of a flourishing family. Other critical components are motherhood, childhood, and the role of ancestors. Traditional Yoruba strongly believe that a happy home is made up of the father, mother, children, and the ancestors who oversee the affairs in the home.

A father, according to the traditional Yoruba, is not just a male parent who has brought children into the world. Rather, he is someone who is able to provide for, take care of, nurture, and instruct the children according to the dictates and norms of the culture. The traditional Yoruba despise any man who refuses to accept his responsibilities to his children and fails to bring them up according to the established standards of Yoruba culture.

Olu Daramola and A. Jeje tell us that fatherhood among the traditional Yoruba is a *holistic* concept. By this, they mean being a father among the Yoruba entails embracing the complete duties of the father role, which include spiritual, moral, metaphysical, physical, and material responsibilities. Any male parent who fails in one of these duties, according to Daramola

ABIODUN OLADELE BALOGUN

and Jeje, is a failed father and will not be treated as an honorable member of the Yoruba community.[1]

Because of this, the Yoruba hold that one does not become a father simply because one has helped bring a child into existence. There are failed fathers and there are authentic fathers. An authentic father is one who fulfills his responsibilities to the family. Family here is understood not in the nuclear sense predominant in Western culture and presently in Africa. Rather, it is defined for the Yoruba in broader terms to include the extended family.[2] This involves a family of extensive networks of kinship, which promotes a sense of belonging among the extended family members.

This understanding of family means that fatherhood for them is not seen as a mere biological relationship to children, which is individualistic in nature. Rather, fatherhood is seen in collective terms, in which children look to paternal uncles, aunts, and grandparents as fathers. Thus, the concept of authentic fatherhood includes not only the responsibilities of the male biological parent of the children, but also a collective responsibility of the paternal members of the family to the proper upbringing of the children.

In this conception, fatherhood is not necessarily a result of being a husband. If a biological father failed to provide for his children and nurture them in line with societal norms and standards, the disgrace would extend to the paternal lineage as a whole. In order to avoid dishonorable comments and the bad reputation the family would receive, serious efforts are usually made by the paternal members of the family to be responsible for the welfare of the children.

This is not to be misinterpreted as meaning the concept of biological fatherhood is absent among the Yoruba or that their emphasis is only on collective fatherhood. Both are considered complementary. And it is for this reason that after a child is born, the biological father together with the "collective fathers" assume some special roles and responsibilities. The former is expected to see to the healthy survival of the child, and this accounts for why he is the first person to be informed in the event of the child getting sick. He plays a major role in decision-making and in enforcing standards of behavior among the children. He is expected to be a good example of these behaviors, which the children are to take a cue from. Some of these are hard work, self-restraint, honesty, humility, and bravery, among others.

Additionally, this traditional Yoruba-African understanding of fatherhood dictates that a father must be actively involved in the moral and intellectual training of his children. He is someone who is well versed in the norms of society and is ready to teach them to his children. One way in which this is achieved is in the poetry game of *alo apamo* (riddles and folklores) and the moonlight folktales that are usually recited in the evenings after the day's work.

Yoruba Proverbs and Folktales

One such folktale is the story of the tortoise, his wife, and the priest. In this story, the tortoise and his wife Yonibo have been married for many years without any offspring. Worried about the situation, one day the tortoise decides to consult a priest in the hopes of ending his wife's barrenness. Once there, the priest promises him that his wife would have children soon if she drinks a soup the priest has prepared especially for her. When handing the soup to the tortoise, the priest warns him that the soup is only meant to be drunk by his wife. On his way home, however, the sweet aroma of the soup arouses the appetite of the tortoise, so much so that he can't resist eating it. After a while, instead of Yonibo becoming pregnant, the tortoise's glands become swollen. Worried about her husband, Yonibo suggests they both go and see the priest to report the development and hopefully get a cure to restore his health. As they leave home to visit the priest, the tortoise cries in pain for an antidote and laments in song:

> *Babalawo mo wa bebe, alugbinrin*
> (Here I am, priest, to seek forgiveness)
> *Ogun to se funmi lana, alugbinrin*
> (The soup given to me sometime ago)
> *Oni kin mama fowo benu, alugbinrin*
> (He instructed me not to taste of it)
> *Oni kin mama fi obe senu, alugbinrin*
> (He told me not to eat the soup)
> *Babalawo mo wa bebe, alugbinrin*
> (I seek your forgiveness, oh priest)
> *Mo fi ojukokoro towo bo obe, alugbinrin*
> (Greediness made me eat the soup)
> *Babalawo mo wa bebe, alugbinrin*
> (I beg you, priest, for forgiveness)

Upon hearing this confession song Yonibo knew what her husband had done. When they get to the priest's shed, the priest tells them there is no antidote for the soup intended for Yonibo, because what should have boosted her pregnancy is boosting the tortoise's glands. The priest asks furiously, "Didn't I warn you not to eat out of the soup?" But because of the tortoise's greed, he did not heed the priest's advice. The tortoise soon dies in pain in the arms of Yonibo on their way home.

This folktale is meant to teach children the value of heeding instructions. It is also meant to discourage them from coveting something that doesn't belong to them. Finally, the song in the folktale serves as entertainment for the listeners.

Fathers in traditional Yoruba societies see as their responsibilities the task of narrating such folktales and posing riddles to the children, who are organized to sit in a circle with the father at the center (though sometimes grown-ups join children in solving these riddles, as there is no social exclusion to the age, sex, or position of the participants).[3] Fathers believe that the practice of posing riddles and telling folktales in the light of the moon serves certain important functions in the socialization process of children. They have entertainment value as well as educational value because they shape the children's intellect and imagination.

This practice of sharing riddles, proverbs, and folktales by the father is seen as essential because it develops awareness of the values, beliefs, songs, and societal norms in the children. Some of these proverbs that fathers share with children include the following:

- *Ija o dola; oruko buruku ni o funi* (Joining gangs does not lead to success; it only earns one a bad reputation). In this proverb, children are urged not to involve themselves in violent activities. This is because violence and hanging out with hooligans will only hurt their reputation and mar their future prospects.
- *Iwa rere ni eso eniyan* (Good character is the adornment of a person). Fathers often say this to remind a child that nothing short of good behavior is required of them.
- *Aso fofo ko gba egba, ibi ope 'lomo* (Gossipers receive no financial reward, only a mere thank you). This is meant to keep children from gossiping.

Sharing proverbs like these creates a warm atmosphere of friendship, love, and togetherness between the father and the children, between the children and other adult participants, and among the children themselves.

The Yoruba believe that a father who fails to fulfill these responsibilities toward the socialization of the children in their formative years is not a good father. Interestingly, however, misbehavior of children is considered the fault of the mother, while a good child is praised as being a product of the father. This follows from the patriarchal nature of Yoruba society. But that is not to say that such transfer of blame to the mother is justified.

An authentic father, aside from being well versed in the norms of the society, is a person who must have a well-integrated personality. He must be hardworking, financially prudent, socially competent, morally acceptable, and culturally adept. By financial prudence, I mean having the skills necessary to provide for his entire household. To traditional Yoruba, while one must reach the age of puberty and then perform certain rites before one can become a father, a man must also be capable of providing for the needs of his family. A father is expected to be a socially and politically competent person, one who has the ability to participate in decisions affecting his life and that of his community.

The importance of good fathering in the development and growth of the child cannot be overemphasized. This is because a father provides material, physical, and emotional security for his family. While the Yoruba treat fathers and mothers differently, they believe that both parents are essential to the upbringing of the children. This is reflected in their saying that *iya ni wura, baba ni dingi* (mother is gold, father is mirror).[4] This proverb conveys an image of cooperative work by the two parents in childrearing. While our focus is not on motherhood, it is important to note that for the Yoruba only such an integrated effort can provide the proper moral and social upbringing for the children.

We need note at this point that the Yoruba-African concept of authentic fatherhood is a valued role for fathers to fill. That is, it is in the best interest of men to perform these duties. The Yoruba believe that fulfilling the responsibilities of the father entails a right of respect for men. Additionally, if a father is able do a good job raising his children and caring for the family as a whole, then in the long run, the caring, loving, and protection is reciprocated by the children and family to the father, especially when he gets old. Hence, the father becomes happier for having demonstrated authentic fatherhood when he ought to.

Yoruba Lessons for Contemporary Fathers

This notion of authentic fatherhood holds some lessons for contemporary fathers. In fact, many of the fatherly qualities emphasized by the

Yoruba are essential to being a good father anywhere and anytime. Irrespective of one's culture, color, class, or beliefs, integrating aspects of this concept of fatherhood into one's activities is important for being a good and responsible father. Of course, I do recognize that there are many differences between the conditions of the traditional Yoruba life-style and today's lifestyles, not the least of which include economic, social, political, and technological differences.

However, in spite of the sophistication in all these areas today, there are some notable lessons that can be learned from the Yoruba under-standing of fatherhood. For them, fatherhood must be total and not piecemeal as it is currently treated. Many contemporary fathers feel that being responsible for their children's welfare ends at meeting the eco-nomic needs of the children. But it does not.

To be an authentic father is to know and act on all of the responsibili-ties attached to fatherhood, which include spiritual, emotional, social, economic, and moral dimensions. Fathers today need to provide for their families in all of these areas. Additionally, in protecting the children and the family as a whole, fathers should provide protection and security for their family not only while they are alive, but also after they pass away. In order to provide this after death, fathers should strive to provide for their children when alive and have a will in place in order to posthumously ensure the wellbeing of the family.

Emotional protection is an aspect contemporary fathers cannot ignore. A father must show love to his children and wife and be faithful to them. Marital infidelity destroys the bond of emotional affection as well as the stability of the family. Thus it should be avoided, because a father's emo-tional support is the very basis of cooperation between husband and wife and the foundation upon which a healthy interpersonal relationship within the home is built.[5]

In providing for their children, fathers today should seek to protect their children from the undue negative influences of modern communi-cation and entertainment, on the one hand, and that of the children's peers on the other. There should be effective monitoring of the programs children are exposed to, especially in their formative years, through the media of television, radio, and magazines. Also, fathers should protect their kids from the undue influences of pornographic and other socially destructive materials spread via the Internet.

Authentic fatherhood of course still includes having some share of the economic responsibility for the family. While the father cannot exclusively provide for the financial needs of the family, especially in this period of global economic instability, fathers should strive to become more financially empowered to better meet their financial obligations to their family.

A vital component of the traditional Yoruba-African conception of fatherhood which the contemporary world can learn from greatly is the father's responsibility for teaching morals, norms, and values to his children. The actual teaching of folktales by fathers today (whether spoken or read) should complement the watching of cartoons, which today's children are so fond of. Achieving this requires a considerable sacrifice of time by the father so as to better raise his children. Contrary to the trend of excessive pursuit of money and status followed by many contemporary fathers, they should create time for showing affection to their children and teaching them the ideal ways of living.

Also, recall the roles played by paternal uncles and grandparents in raising children and building homes, both during their lifetimes and afterwards. This aspect of the Yoruba-African conception of fatherhood should not be dismissed as anachronistic. It is better to treat children as *ours* rather than as "mine." The Yoruba proverb *ojukan lon bi'mo, igba oju lon woo* (children are born individually, but raised collectively) expresses this well. Fathers should not limit the upbringing of their kids to their own nuclear family. Find ways to involve grandparents and extended family in the children's upbringing if possible. This in no way need entail a loss of parental autonomy.

Raising children through collective fatherhood is better because in cases where the father errs, the other paternal fathers can come to the rescue and fill the vacuum, preventing the children from fully bearing the brunt of the mistake. In the case of the biological father passing away or hitting hard times, the importance of collective fatherhood becomes more apparent as the other living elderly paternal members of the family can provide continuity of care. In addition to supporting the actual biological fathers in carrying out the expected roles and responsibilities of fatherhood, collective fatherhood avoids the breakdown of family ties and strengthens the father-children relationship.

Conclusion: An Intercultural Understanding of Fatherhood

So, in conclusion, I am not trying to say that the Yoruban conception of fatherhood is best, nor that African fathers have such a perfect understanding that non-African cultural interpretations of fatherhood become irrelevant. Rather, there is a need for an *intercultural understanding* of the essentials of fatherhood. Better insights into the ideal practices of good fathers can only be gained through this mutual borrowing of ideas between different cultures.

Many of the Yoruba fatherly qualities discussed are essential to being a good father no matter where in the world one lives and no matter what culture one belongs to. Granted, there are challenges to applying some of these principles today, but awareness of these practices leads us to be creative and to think in new ways about what it means to be a good father.

So long as being an excellent father is a virtue and skill worth improving upon, then it is important for all of us to learn and integrate many of the fatherly qualities practiced among the Yoruba, as well as those in other worthwhile conceptions of fatherhood. Anything short of this integration can only lead to a piecemeal and inauthentic fatherhood in the contemporary world.

NOTES

1   O. Daramola and A. Jeje, *Traditional Yoruba Culture and Modernity* (Ibadan: Exodus, 1995), p. 10.
2   Nhlanhla Mkhize, "Who is a Father?" *Children First*. Available online at www. hsrc.ac.za/Document-105-phtml.
3   O. O. Olatunji, *Features of Yoruba Oral Poetry* (Ibadan: University Press, 1984), p. 181.
4   T. Makinde, "Motherhood as a Source of Empowerment of Women in Yoruba Culture," *Nordic Journal of African Studies* 13, 2 (2004): 165.
5   S. O. Afolami, "Father: The Family Protector (An African Perspective)." Paper delivered at the first Congress of the Voice of the Family in Africa, Strathmore University, Nairobi, Kenya, August 19–21, 2005, p. 4.

CHAPTER 12

THE HEART OF THE MERCIFUL FATHER

I cannot think of any need in childhood as strong as the need for a father's protection.

Sigmund Freud[1]

In scripture, the word "heart" (lev or levan, kardia) *refers to the physical organ no more than perhaps ten times, whereas in the metaphorical sense it is used more than a thousand times, to indicate the seat of various psychological functions. It is the heart that thinks, reflects, conceives projects, makes resolutions and decisions, and assumes responsibilities.*

Cardinal Tomas Spidlik[2]

What is a Father?

I have wondered why dads can seem so remote, distant, and even cold when their children fail them not only in seemingly small matters, but especially in more significant situations. Growing up in the ethnic and cultural milieu of central Illinois in the 1970s I seldom saw a hostile or uncaring mother, but learned quickly that some dads were not emotionally safe to be around. Some did not seem to *like* being with their children or were distant and unavailable. They at times exuded harshness.

For example, there were the fathers who were exacting and compulsive: demanding to know how this or that pin-head sized nick occurred in the trim along the doorway, the fathers who yelled when their yard was entered, the fathers who seemed to dwell like dragons in their man-lairs, mesmerized and pleased by the luminous boxes into which they dreamily gazed year after year with legs elevated and soft drinks or canned beers perched within reach. There were dads who went to work quietly for years and arrived home as if knowingly and automatically carried by their metal and glass bubble of existential solitude, maybe or maybe not locating meaning within the everydayness of their existence at factory, boardroom, or cube.

Very early on I drew a few conclusions: dads were interested in order, laws, justice, and their rights. Dads worked hard outside the home and while home seemed to have given them permission to connect mainly to their own leisure interests, they could connect with their children through sports or other activities. Dads were powerful in some ways and weak in others. I knew that they could hurt my friends and I by what they said or did not say in ways that our mothers simply could not. As children, fathers impacted us more deeply, with much less effort.

This facilitated my lifelong philosophical reflection about patterns of good fatherly behavior. Fathers can unknowingly and unintentionally repeat what they observed in their own family growing up. They need to create, nourish, and sustain their own conscious and intentional vision of fatherhood. Fathers need a rich and authentic worldview in order to liberate themselves from unexamined and mechanical habits of fatherhood. Fathers do not have coursework in fatherhood in college.

My mind began to wonder constantly about fathers. I could not stop asking myself questions, even from the early ages of middle school, about what makes a dad a *good* dad. What is the essence of fatherhood? Where do fathers come from? What makes a good father and why try to be a good father? If fatherhood is like shooting arrows at targets, what are the targets?

What are the arrows? What is the bow? Do I exist? (Oh, that is another question entirely.) Some fathers appear happy enough adopting a maternal habit system and attitude and can seem to be more motherly than fatherly.

Let's willfully suspend our postmodern disbelief in knowable things for a while so that we can get close to the reality of fatherhood. It is perhaps more than legend and lore that a boy begins to really reflect about his father in his early teen years. A son thinks of this man in some way or another each day for the rest of his life. There is a profound impact of the father on the emotional and cognitive development of girls and boys. Father absence and father presence has been researched extensively in the past thirty years or more by sociologists, psychologists, and psychiatrists.

The bottom line: children wish to be loved by their fathers and *need to be*. Few are willing to propose that the impact of the father upon the child is negligible, regardless of their assumed anthropology of the human person. Children do not wish simply to live with a vague notion that their father loves them. They wish to be surrounded with consistent evidence of his compassionate love. They need to trust that the concrete responses of their father's love will continue. At a deeper level, they want to trust that the attitude of compassionate, self-giving love will persist. The attitude and vision of the father is the source of the concrete gestures. For the nineteenth-century Russian philosopher Vladimir Solovyov,

> The meaning and worth of love as a feeling is that it really forces us, with all our being, to acknowledge for another the same absolute significance which, because of the power of egoism, we are conscious of only in our own selves. Love is important not only as one of our feelings, but as the transfer of all our interest in life from ourselves to another, as the shifting of the very center of our lives.[3]

Fatherhood is about transferring an orientation from self to children. This transference requires attentiveness to the past and to any unresolved concerns which exist as barriers to love. It seems to me that each father carries a kind of matrushka doll with traces of his relationship with his father and grandfathers within himself, in the deep, quiet, vulnerable and dark center of himself. Fathers have memories of their fathers (and grandfathers) near their hearts and within reach at all times. Traces of the feelings and affective states are attached to these relationships and are stored in little containers. Men can, but usually do not, tell anyone where these are stored. We should resist any temptation to dismiss the male and his limbic system. The average male experiences approximately forty affective states each day (instead of the presumed two which are commonly attributed: anger and amorous states).

Many fathers quietly carry a wound of loss and grief when it comes to their father. They carry perhaps an image of a fantasy father, the father they never had: the father who did not put off telling them that he loved them, who went to their games, who listened to their music with them. Other dads assume that it is reasonable to over-commit to the relentless pursuit of careers, power, and competition. They may risk doing this to establish a felt sense of value or intrinsic purpose, especially if their father was not there to speak words of goodness, blessing, and healing directly into their situation in life. There are fathers who just mourn without full awareness of the cause, which is often the perception that their father was habitually remote, emotionally withholding, or distant.

So what is a father, anyway? What is a *good* father? I think we can accept at least that fatherhood is an intentional, sustained relationship of nurturance, protection, support, and compassion. The relationship between a father and his child has a specific, peculiar, and unique shape to it. Its primary orientation is one of loving, strong, and engaged presence to, for, and with the child. While a father can biologically become a "father" within the context of one act, a rich covenant orientation to fatherhood suggests that it is lived out in a life of creative and loving fidelity. The father is ever-willing to reflect upon and reorient his habits of response to his children for their ultimate good.

This "creative fidelity" was at the essence of fatherhood, according to the philosopher Gabriel Marcel.[4] His philosophy of fatherhood included consistent warmth, tenderness, and receptive silence. He taught that to truly listen to the child was to be *changed* by the child. He believed that a father *created* a better version of himself by practicing these habits of empathy.

The goal of this reflection is to communicate a vision of fatherhood which focuses on the benefits of cultivating an attitude of faithful, compassionate love: mercy. Merciful fatherhood involves thinking about one's children with an attitude of abiding faithfulness and responding with habits of empathy and compassion.

When the philosopher St. Thomas Aquinas spoke of habits (*habitus* in Latin) associated with virtue, he was speaking specifically about the human person's disposition of attitude and character. He was not recommending a mechanical repetition of superficial behaviors. For instance, he states: "Habitus is derived from habire (to have)."[5] The father can have a merciful attitude. It is a mode of being more than a set of tools or techniques to deploy. But what does this really mean? In the next section, we'll explore this virtue more closely.

Fatherly Mercy as Attitude

The ancient philosophers and writers seemed to have little use for the virtue (habit) of mercy. If virtue was a manly "power," manly men did not concern themselves with empathy, compassion, and sympathy. It was a better idea to either be stoic and distant or at least remote enough to take care of oneself and peer out at the suffering of others. One could help them tangibly, but should not show or feel empathy. See Aristotle's *Nichomachean Ethics* for a description of justice as favored over mercy. Aristotle also attempted to explore *pity* as a neutral type of passion which was either good or bad based on the virtue which it animated or sustained.[6] The ancient Romans at least recognized that some acts of mercy were as powerful as punishment, even if they at times used this power to manipulate.

The ancient Greeks preferred to use the term *eleos*, which has a root word similar to "oil" or "olive oil." It suggests that lived mercy connects one person in need or in pain to another person whose attitude and habits of mercy are a balm of healing. In Latin, the term used to describe this relational approach is *misericordia*: a loving, merciful heart.

The Hebrew word *rahamin* suggests and denotes a type of covenant bond between persons, which creates the environment in which mercifulness can occur. The Hebrew word *hesed* conveys the reality of lived *loving kindness* from the heart of the person – especially the father.

To be sure, some philosophers have written about mercy. But it is not so much a cognitive construct accessible only to intellectuals. Children naturally possess mercy. For instance, the great European philosopher Fr. Marie-Dominique Philippe wrote:

> A path of access, a special doorway to the mystery of God is given to little children, that of God's mercy. In light of mercy we can contemplate the whole mystery of God, and penetrate it very intimately. For this to occur, however, we must live this mercy. We must let ourselves be enveloped by it completely, which demands the attitude of great humility.[7]

The most concise and operative definition of mercy is "faithful compassionate love" and while the Hebrew word *hesed* is close to this, it still seems to

134   STEPHEN JOSEPH MATTERN

elude precise definition. For our purposes in this chapter, each use of the term "mercy" is meant to include each of these components: *fidelity, compassion,* and *love.* Fidelity is necessarily and naturally linked to mercy as it assures that habits of mercy occur across the long haul and with consistency. Mercy is therefore protected from episodic or inconsistent deployment. Compassion implies a certain amount of empathy and at times "suffering with" and "feeling with" the child. Love implies a consistent attitude (and not a mood) which responds creatively and concretely to the genuine needs of the child.

Mercy does not reside only in the brain of the father, but primarily within his heart, as an *attitude of compassionate love.* Within a father, then, it is a habit and attitude of faithful, compassionate love which is ready to respond to the child's needs with creativity, reverence, and warmth. It can be a noble goal for us as persons, but especially as fathers.

In fact, fathers who are habitually – or even occasionally – compassionate are known to effect neurochemical changes in their own brains. One may wish to research the neurochemistry of compassionate acts to see that fathers are hardwired to experience pleasure through conscious and free acts of kindness and compassion.

Mercy Enables Connection with Children

The habitually merciful father seeks to respond in order to connect deeply with his child. At the center of this connection between father and child is fidelity. Compassionate love and fidelity go together like hydrogen and oxygen. They cannot be naturally separated.

Let's pause for a moment of reflection. While we search our family histories and memories, we can now start the slide show playing while gazing at those slides which do or do not include mercy and fidelity on behalf of our fathers and grandfathers. How were these fathers faithful to their commitments, to their spouses and children? What if their habits of fidelity had more consistently showed love at key and meaningful points within their relationships? Go back as many generations as you can in your mind and envision placing your father, his father, his father, and so on in a room within a large circle and then pose the question of mercy. Ask if they consistently showed compassionate love. Might they have wished to have been more faithful and compassionate if they could be given a second chance? This narrative ethical encounter in our mind may yield some interesting reflections.

The merciful father locates himself directly within the "world" of his child. He chooses to be compassionate, tender, sensitive, and empathic, though he may wish to be perceived to be as strong as iron. Empathic fathers are competent at actively listening to their children's body language, words, and silence.

If you were to draw two sets of double circles on a large black chalk board with each set below the other, you could understand the meaning of empathy. The first circles would be side-by-side and non-overlapping. Father is in one circle. His daughter is in the other. They do not connect deeply. In the next set of circles there is a Venn diagram with a great deal of overlap. This occurs when the father works to actively listen to his child, to look at her, feed her snacks, dance and laugh with her. He listens to her actively. He touches, holds, and affirms her. Overlapping circles are the symbols of the ongoing, empathic, and connected relationship where faithful, compassionate love is practiced in day-to-day family life. There is the existential overlap of everydayness: smells, sights, sounds, and touch which are located in the shared worlds of father and daughter.

The philosopher St. Thomas Aquinas located mercy within and beneath the scope and action of reason. That is, mercy is not simply pity or attentiveness to the feelings of others. It is affective because one touches the brokenness or need of the other person with humanity and warmth. It is also effective because one responds with a gesture or act of some type to further the good for the person (and for each person in the relationship). Aquinas further taught that this virtue is one of the greatest attributes of God and of the human person:

> In itself, mercy takes precedence over other virtues, for it belongs to mercy to be bountiful to others, and, what is more, to succor others in their wants, which pertains chiefly to one who stands above. But of all the virtues which relate to our neighbor, mercy is the greatest, even as its act surpasses all others, since it belongs to one who is higher and better to supply the defect of another, in so far as the latter is deficient.[8]

Is there a larger meaning of mercy within our universe? I recall riding on a bitterly cold winter evening, as an 8-year-old passenger, in my father's 1972 Plymouth Fury III. It was dark and quiet in the car. We were driving over country roads in the darkness. I saw only the silhouette of my father's face, sometimes faintly illuminated by the red circle end of his unfiltered Camel cigarette during the inhale. For some reason I just needed to ask him if Adolf Hitler was in hell. There was a silence for the span of the red circle lighting up twice. A clearing of the throat and the surprisingly quiet answer: "If at the end he sought God's mercy, probably not." Then silence. The brief discussion seemed too significant to reopen later and I never did. I returned to my habits of playing war (fighting the bad guys), borrowing my father's US Marine uniform, and forgot all about mercy for a while. However, for a child at a developmental stage where justice mattered a great deal, I was comforted by the hope of living in a universe where mercy could have such ultimate significance. I later followed the golden thread of mercy in human relationships when I made a healthcare professional oath. However, it was my own fatherhood which allowed me to begin to understand the impact of faithful loving kindness.

Mercy can be seen as a type of "plea bargain," a request to be nice to someone who does not deserve it or who has no "right" to mercy from me at all. We can think of it as "clemency" or as a legal pardon. A father who seeks to orient himself more intentionally toward habits of compassionate love will find that this habit does not conflict with masculinity at all. This type of compassionate love is a source of strength. The cruelty, hatred, violence, and misery of the world can be engaged directly with the heart of the father, which invites the child into loving communion. The father is one who is given the privilege of strengthening the child and of making them feel safe. According to the philosopher Jean Vanier:

> When a child is loved, seen as precious, listened to, touched with reverence, then it is at peace. It knows it belongs. It is held, protected and safe. It opens up without fear. The deepest yearning of the child is to be in communion with its mother and father.[9]

Mercy Strengthens Relationships

Now we will turn our attention to how the father's mercy changes not only the relationship behaviors between the father and the child, but also their attitudes. The merciful father will inevitably find brokenness in the lives of his children, but habits of loving kindness attempt to draw good out of such pain and apparent meaninglessness. When the love of a father makes contact with the genuine needs, brokenness, and momentarily lost dignities of his child, this mercy has a strength and restorative power otherwise unknown in human relationships.

This power is something for which many men long for without even realizing it, far into their adult lives. Mercy changes the child who receives it and also transforms the father so that both are better persons. Ultimately, this can lead to a life of happiness. For the philosopher Karol Wojtyla,

> Love demands an affirmation of the value of a person. Basing itself on this affirmation, the will of the subject who loves, strives for the good of the person loved – for a full and total good. Such a good is identified with happiness.[10]

How can we *miss* compassionate love as a virtue for fathers? Maybe because there are few cultural icons of mercy. Maybe only men who over-connected with their mothers and who attempt to imitate them are the ones who *seem* to be merciful. But are they in fact any more empathic and compassionate than other men? A compassionate father does not risk losing his authentically male identity. He does not need to reinvent himself in a motherly role in order to creatively develop his capacity to exhibit loving kindness.

Let's give concrete examples of how such a father acts at home, on the road, and in the universe of parenting in general. Let's accept as true enough (even with an eye toward necessary further verification) that mercy matters, and that it means more than weakness or excusing someone. Being compassionate allows one to pause and become more responsive and empathic instead of being reactive and justice oriented. We need not over-use time-outs, sticker charts, and Skinnerian negative or positive reinforcement. The very notion of spanking gives me pause and cause for concern.

What Does Fatherly Mercy Look Like?

Of course, there seems to be an attraction to many of the parenting methodologies, and I confess I recommended some of these books as a therapist for years. There are good points within these books. As a professor I have for years impressed upon my students that as therapists or nurses they need to construct their practice models (which practically guide their treatment responses) and frames of reference (which provide a philosophical and anthropological basis to their practice models) from core philosophical assumptions about human nature. In other words, each professional needs a rigorously examined and sustained worldview. Without a vision, they risk becoming mere technicians. Fathers may need a worldview, frame of reference, and practice models more than anyone else in the world. However, we settle for books that are quick to diagnose our children and to see them as problems in need of our control and management.

This chapter has not been created to offer a how-to manual on parenting, but rather to craft a vision or framework of faithful, compassionate love. A merciful father strives daily (even commits) to grow in empathy for his children, spending more time playing with them, looking at their artwork, going on "dad dates" with them, and simply being attentively quiet around them and actively listening to their stories.

Such a father does discipline his children, but discipline is carried out specific to the needs of the child and not the needs of the parent. Here is an example. My 7-year-old son took a small toy stuffed rabbit from the grocery store without paying for it. My 5-year-old son reported this after the long drive home. What does he do? I can list some options: spank, ground, time out, give him a stern talking to, send him to speak with his mother, ignore the issue and go to bed, or congratulate him. He waits and reflects before responding. He invites his son into a space in which to present the concerns and to deeply listen. He will sit close to his son and look into his eyes. He will employ paraphrases (give back short phrases in his son's own words) and summaries (verbalizing what the main points of the conversation have been). He will actively reflect back the feelings and statements of the child. Loving kindness would be operative in the tone of voice of the father who would use "I" statements (for example, "I am very concerned about this") versus "You" statements ("What could you have been thinking?"). All of this goes deeper than justice. It allows the child to be lovingly accepted for who they are, but loved too compassionately to be allowed to stay the same.

A truly just, but ultimately merciful response will include returning the item and repairing the damage done (an apology to the storekeeper). The child will remember this type of encounter with his father longer than he would a simple punitive reaction. And finally, an empathic father in this case might find out that his son took the item to give as a gift for his mother. The fact that a father might create a quiet space to listen and talk, use a serious but loving tone, and utilize the moment to impart an understanding with the child actually illustrates how this attitude of love works. Justice should never be conceived as opposed to mercy, but as needing mercy for completeness.

Here are a few other concrete indicators of an attitude of mercy. Faithful and compassionate fathers apologize openly, expressing regret, and communicate their thoughts, feelings, and hopes. They avoid shame or guilt-producing phrases. Busy shopping trips and overwhelming vacations or holidays are evaluated in terms of their possible impact *upon the inner world of the child*. The child's behavioral concerns are not seen as a problem to be solved, but as a signal of what the child truly needs, emotionally, intellectually, and spiritually.

There is a range of creative options in each moment and mercy allows the father to more clearly *see* and choose from these options. Such a father avoids spanking, raising his voice, or threatening to remove privileges or things. He does not motivate through fear, nor does he habitually state that his child should do things because he "said so." He does not over-use sticker-charts or rewards for grades or accomplishments. He is empathically there with the child during tough moments and wonderful moments alike, communicating an attitude of love. Such a father reflects deeply and habitually about the developmental needs and make-up of his child, and meditates on what his children truly need most from him in that situation. He spends time in peaceful silence and plays with his child. Mercy is not a virtue which operates independently of justice, prudence, or temperance.

When habituated well, mercy counters inclinations toward self-absorption. These thought patterns can build up like lead-levels in the blood and are slowly and almost imperceptibly toxic to fathers. Fidelity as a key aspect of mercy motivates the father to wipe faces, go to school plays, and turn off the computer to cuddle up and read with his children. He is faithful to a consistent but empathy based disciplinary approach which does not allow anger to influence reactions. This approach, as it is based on empathy, is directed at the needs of the child more than toward punishment or rewards, both of which can leave a child empty and unloved.

As a father of four, who wishes to grow in compassionate love, I can envision myself joining the circle of my father and grandfathers in order to reflect upon the great "what if" question: What if I practiced mercy more often? Where would I end up? How many persons would I avoid hurting? How many words of blessing would I share with my children and grandchildren? Did I frequently decide to enter into the world of my children and base my responses upon this empathic encounter first, before reacting? It takes a micro-moment to envision a different, more compassionate response. Faithful, compassionate love can be located at the center of fatherhood and can change the world.

NOTES

1   Sigmund Freud, *Civilization and Its Discontents* (New York: W. W. Norton, 2005), p. 47.
2   Cardinal Tomas Spidlik, *The Spirituality of the Christian East*, Vol. 2 (Kalamazoo: Cistercian Publications, 2005), p. 250.
3   Vladimir Solovyov, *The Meaning of Love* (London: Lindisfarne Press, 1985).
4   Gabriel Marcel, *Creative Fidelity* (New York: Noonday Press, 1964).
5   St. Thomas Aquinas, *Summa Theologica*, Vol. 2 (New York: Benziger Brothers, 1947).
6   Aristotle, *Rhetoric*, in *Selected Works*, trans. Hippocrates Apostle and Lloyd Gerson (Grinnell: Grinnell Press, 1986).
7   Fr. Marie-Dominique Philippe, *Mary Mystery of Mercy* (Stockbridge: Marian Press, 2002).
8   Aquinas *Summa Theologica*.
9   Jean Vanier, *Community and Growth* (London: Darton, Longman and Todd, 1979).
10 Andrew Woznicki, *Karol Wojtyla's Existential Personalism* (New Britain: Mariel Publications, 1980).

PART IV

DILEMMAS FOR DAD

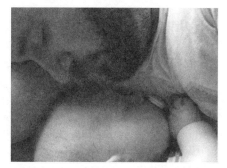

CHAPTER 13

SHOULD I LET HIM WATCH?

A Father's Philosophical Perspective on Popular Media

It's the middle of the night, and I've just gotten my newborn son Maxwell back to sleep. About an hour ago my wife poked me in the ribs and told me to check on why the baby was crying so that she could get some sleep. So, I stumbled over the dog, who bit my ankle in retaliation, fumbled my way down the pitch black hall to Mac's room, strained my back to pick him up out of his beautiful blue but painfully deep crib, cuddled his cute sack-of-potatoes body in my arms, slowly eased into the rocking chair, and gently placed his head against my chest so he could hear my heartbeat. Then, by the glow of the new television I hardly get to watch, I gently rocked him back and forth as I watched escaped psychotic murderer Michael Myers terrorize Haddonfield in John Carpenter's *Halloween*. Halfway into the symphony of screams, blood, and murder, Mac slowly drifted back to sleep.

Am I a bad dad? No doubt the movie is inappropriate for a newborn, but is it possible sweet little Mac will become an escaped psychotic murderer because of what we just watched together? I mean, we're unconditionally supportive parents and we'll still let him stay in his old room if he does escape from prison, but that won't address the problem that he's become a murderer.

Y, E10+, G,Y7, eC, E, PG?

Above is a small collection of symbols from television, film, and video game rating systems. These systems are in place to help guide parents in selecting the appropriate media for their child. Of course, I've left out a lot of symbols and entirely neglected the even more muddy "content designators." For instance, if a TV-14 symbol with a V designator appears in the little black box on your television screen, that means there is intense violence somewhere in the show. However, for a TV-MA program, the V designates graphic violence. Y7 shows are generally violence free, but an FV designator warns the viewer that there are scenes of fantasy violence. Does punching your boss while riding a unicorn count as fantasy violence? Clearly, some greater clarity could be brought to the television rating systems.

The video game rating system is slightly less ambiguous, but the cautious parent will need to pay attention to even more vague descriptors. Video game descriptors may reveal that a game contains, presumably in ascending order: cartoon violence, violent references, fantasy violence, intense violence, or violence. Unfortunately, all video game descriptors can further be qualified with a preceding designation as "mild." As such, mild intense violence must mean that the violence is not quite as intense as intense violence, but it is still more violent than fantasy violence and therefore also twice as violent as mild fantasy violence, and Tarantino-esque compared to mild cartoon violence. Seemingly old-fashioned movie ratings suddenly become so clear and easy to use.

On the other hand, popular media have rapidly expanded to include not just television, film, and video games, but also the Internet behemoth as well. The current rating systems for television, film, and video games have not yet extended to help parents make judicious decisions when it comes to the fluidity of online content. I'm at the mercy of some ingenious kid not much older than my son to invent a software program for the purpose of screening the Internet for inappropriate content.

Despite the vagueness and complexity of these rating systems, have I been a fool – a bad parent – to so brazenly disregard the omnipotent rating systems that are only trying to save poor Maxwell from corruption? As a new father and one who researches the philosophy of violent popular media, I am now forced to ask myself how to make decisions about what my son can and cannot watch as he grows older. Or should

JOSHUA BARON

I simply hand the reins over to the rating systems and simply match up numbers, letters, and age? It would take a lot less effort than, say, making an informed, reasoned parental decision.

Prominent and influential medical groups such as the American Psychological Association and the American Academy of Pediatrics consider the debate closed; that is, violent popular media negatively affect viewers, especially children. However, I contend the issue is more complex and at the very least worth closer examination. Indeed, it is easier and somewhat intuitive to believe the simplified "violent media bad" argument, but a conscientious father shouldn't fall into this trap. To guide fellow fathers beyond the hyperbole, it is useful, I hope, to explore three hypotheses regarding the influence and effect of popular media, and in particular the very scary violent popular media.[1] Despite their somewhat pretentious names, looking at each of these suppositions – the causal hypothesis, the edification hypothesis, and the catharsis hypothesis – may help me come to a conclusion about what I should let my son watch that doesn't involve simply turning my parenting decisions over to my television's V-Chip.

The Causal Hypothesis: Baby See, Baby Do

Proponents of the causal hypothesis theorize that there is a causal link between viewing violent popular media and actual violent behavior: if someone watches fictional violence they become more aggressive in real life. For example, Mac watches Patrick slap SpongeBob SquarePants. Mac mimics this violent action, sometimes slapping things, animals, and people. There are, in the causal hypothesis, two reasons why my son copies the violence he watches: in the first, children unthinkingly imitate behavior they see in popular media; in the second, children learn behavior from watching popular media. Let's address each argument.

My wife is playing with Maxwell and right in the middle of peek-a-boo he slaps when he should have booed. My wife is shocked and my son is laughing, and of course he's laughing because that is how the denizens of Bikini Bottom behave when they smack or get smacked. Mac can't understand why mommy has stopped playing peek-a-boo to ice her cheek. My son loves his mom, but treated his mother in contrast to these emotions because he doesn't understand, nor should we expect him to at this age, what is implied by his behavior or the consequences of his actions. Mac was merely imitating the action he saw on television without any thought behind the behavior. The causal hypothesis explains this scenario as the result of people, especially children, unthinkingly imitating behavior they see in popular media. Additionally, beyond act-for-act behavior mimicking, the causal hypothesis claims violent media are responsible for a myriad of forms of physical or verbal aggression.

Presumably, then, if I continue to let my son watch a young Michael Myers stab his sister repeatedly with a knife, Mac might, once able to break into the baby-proofed kitchen drawers, imitate this violent action. He might use a spatula, a teddy bear, or his finger instead of a real knife, and he might make stabbing motions at me, his mom, or Elmo, but the causal hypothesis still holds. Plus, as he ages and exposure to violent media increases, so does the refinement of the behavior.

For example, Mac is currently working on waving, and every time someone waves to him he gets better and better at waving back through imitation. In addition, he not only waves to real people, but people on television as well. Right now, any flailing of his arm is considered a wave, at least to his doting grandparents, who see it as an early sign of genius, but in a few months he will get some wrist action going, and all too soon Mac will be waving goodbye on his way to college. The point is that over time he will continue to enjoy and develop this action. Likewise, if he watches and tries to repeatedly imitate stabbing he will get better at it and more interested in performing the action. Mac may move from stabbing with his finger, to stabbing with a stick, to stabbing with a play sword, and finally to stabbing with a real knife. Before we know it, our little Mac will be waving to and stabbing people all over the place. This does seem plausible: If he imitates other actions he sees, why wouldn't he imitate violence if he watched it enough? The causal hypothesis doesn't seem too far off-base.

Second, however, the causal hypothesis also warns that children not only imitate the behavior they see in popular media, but also learn how to relate to other people by watching popular media. This form of the causal hypothesis is concerned with society, especially the youth of society, and the development of our innermost character. In philosophy, one of the strongest exhortations about the moral and social harm of popular art comes from Plato, who was mostly talking about poetry rather than the Internet. In the *Republic*, Plato, speaking through Socrates, reveals the danger of exposing society's youth too early to themes they cannot properly understand. Socrates says:

> For the young are not able to distinguish what is and what is not allegory, but whatever opinions are taken into the mind at that age are wont to prove indelible and unalterable. For which reason, maybe, we should do our utmost that the first stories that they hear should be composed as to bring the fairest lessons of virtue to their ears.[2]

Plato makes a lot of sense. Lessons and habits instilled at an early age are difficult to break, and children get these lessons from a variety of sources. Children learn about relationships by watching how other people interact. If my wife and I constantly yell to resolve disagreements about whose turn it is to do the dishes, our son learns that marriage involves solving problems with yelling.

Similarly, assume Mac is a bit older and is watching Hulk Hogan struggle against the despicable Andre the Giant, who in a fit of jealousy turns into a "heel" and challenges "baby face" Hulk Hogan to a title match on *Wrestlemania*. Hulk finally gets an opportunity, climbs to the top rope of the ring, and throws himself down on the massive Giant. Seeing this (most likely on YouTube since VHS is lame) my son climbs to the top of our couch and tosses himself onto his friend: Mac's friend failed to share his toys (classic heel move) and Mac must resolve the conflict. However, this is no longer merely "imitation": Mac has in his own way thought through this action. Mac "learned" from watching Hulk Hogan that when someone treats you badly or unfairly that the appropriate way to resolve the situation is with violence and aggression.

As such, this version of the causal hypothesis theorizes that if a child views Jackie Chan, Clint Eastwood, and Bruce Willis solving their problems with violence, he will learn the lesson that the quickest, easiest, and overall best way to solve disagreements is with a swift kick, punch, or bullet. In contrast, and as prescribed by Plato, if Mac learns about friendship and sharing (let's say from models like Big Bird or Barney) and that asking for something is a much nicer, quicker, and better way to solve disagreements, then that is what he will do in order to get a turn at the toys or a handful of cheerios from Mom and Dad. Of course, none of this applies to grandparents, who will spoil him rotten regardless of future consequences, but that's a whole other issue.

Both versions of the causal hypothesis have many proponents, a long history, and many studies that ostensibly offer proof of their claim.[3] Therefore, assuming I don't want my son to become a psychotic murderer – and I don't, really – Mac should not watch *Halloween*. Plus, if the hypothesis is correct, I should ban a lot of other stuff from being viewed. If I don't want my son to try and run my wife over with a big wheel bike, I shouldn't let him watch *The Omen*. If I don't want him to take over a small town with all his friends, I shouldn't let him watch *Children of the Corn*. And, if I don't want him to generally become more aggressive, I shouldn't let him watch violent popular media. By extension, if I don't want him doing drugs, having unprotected sex, stealing, and so forth, I won't let him watch *Kids*, *Over the Edge*, and countless other shows, films, and video games.

However, the causal hypothesis' best support comes from questionable scientific evidence. Nevertheless, in July of 2000 the influential and respected American Academy of Pediatrics, American Psychological Association, American Medical Association, American Academy of Child and Adolescent Psychiatry, American Academy of Family Physicians, and American Psychiatric Association released a joint statement touting the "over 1,000 studies" that point to a causal connection between violent media and aggressive behavior. No doubt some of these studies ostensibly lead to this conclusion, but an analysis of the claims, and the studies themselves, is far from conclusive.[4] In fact, a study by psychologists Seymour Feshbach and Robert D. Singer actually shows the reverse effect. That is, when school aged boys watched violent television they became less aggressive.[5] Studies may demonstrate an identifiable relationship between violent media and aggression, but that can be attributed to a number of other factors; for example, children predisposed toward aggressive behavior watch more violent media.

Based on the scientific evidence, I'm not totally convinced that the causal hypothesis holds: in a not trivial example, Mac hasn't seen *The Exorcist* and has still projectile vomited on me a number of times. However, as a philosopher, scientific evidence is not my only standard for proof. Plato makes a strong commonsense argument about the impressionability of young children and the negative models popular media present. My fatherly intuition, all five months of it, could never justify plopping Mac in front of *Hostel* instead of *Sesame Street*. Therefore, shouldn't I err on the side of caution and not let Mac watch anything that portrays behavior I wouldn't want him imitating or learning inappropriate lessons from? However, implicit in Plato's condemnation of poetry is the understanding that context, and not just content, matters. What if instead of teaching Mac the wrong way to behave, popular media could actually teach him the right way to behave? Then, not only should I not restrict his viewing, but I should actually encourage watching popular media.

JOSHUA BARON

The Edification Hypothesis: I Learned Something Good from Watching Something Bad

According to the edification hypothesis, viewers of popular media are just as likely to learn something positive from watching otherwise despicable behavior. Viewers may grow emotionally by identifying with fictional characters. There are two ways that positive learning comes about, both involving a level of identification and empathy.[6] First, if a slightly older Mac is watching *Schindler's List* and following the events of Oskar Schindler's life during World War II, he is likely to identify and empathize with Oskar, a response Steven Spielberg probably intended. In plain language, this means Mac relates on a certain level with the character and feels emotions similar to the character's emotions as the film progresses. At the beginning of the film, Oskar is far more concerned with making money off Jewish labor than saving Jewish lives. However, over the course of the film, Oskar's views change, and by the end he has grown emotionally. Mac, through identification and empathy, matures emotionally as well. Oskar has learned something about the value of life, respect for humanity, and the value of self-sacrifice, and thus Mac learns these lessons as well – to a lesser degree than the real Oskar Schindler, but Mac is emotionally and morally educated nonetheless.

In the above example, Mac has grown by relating and concurring with the emotions of the character. However, viewers of popular media can also learn or grow emotionally by recognizing that a character's feelings are incorrect or inappropriate. Archie Bunker from *All in the Family* or Eric Cartman from *South Park* are both bigoted, prejudiced characters. Still, both have redeemable qualities that allow audience members to identify, empathize, and – for lack of a better term – "like" them. Yet, this doesn't mean that when Archie or Eric think, say, or behave inappropriately, viewers cannot recognize that something is not quite right. In doing so, the viewer grows emotionally, recognizing and rejecting the misguided attitude or emotion displayed onscreen. Mac may never be exposed to someone as openly racist and sexist as Eric Cartman, but he can confront and rebuff that way of thinking by watching *South Park* and then carrying that lesson into the real world.

Additionally, though, these examples underscore the importance of the context, presentation, and messaging of popular media. While the content of Archie and Eric's vitriolic attacks is similar, the message and presentation is not. Likewise, the violent content of Ralph Fiennes' character sniping concentration camp prisoners in *Schindler's List* is similar to any number of first-person shooter video games, but the contexts are worlds apart.

Finally, there is something even broader to be learned from popular media that displays bad behavior: it is the lesson that the world contains some bad people and terrible events. Interestingly, Aristotle, in *The Poetics*, says that the learning we derive from such unpleasant stories is also part of the appeal to what is otherwise horrible imagery:

> Though the objects themselves may be painful to see, we delight to view the most realistic representations of them in art, the forms for example of the lowest animals and of dead bodies. The explanation is to be found in a further fact: to be learning something is the greatest pleasure not only to the philosopher but also to the rest of mankind, however small their capacity for it; the reason of the delight in seeing the picture is that one is at the same time learning – gathering the meaning of things.[7]

If we modernize this idea a little – and we need to for the purposes of this discussion – we could say that there certainly are a lot of bad things that happen in the world, and to raise our children in a world where they have no concept of bad, evil, suffering, or injustice is to fail to educate them about that world. Maybe *Halloween* isn't the best way to teach my son that evil exists in the world, but something like *Schindler's List* is used, in part, to show the violence and apathy toward human life that existed and still exists in many parts of the world. Not only do we learn that there are racist, sexist, and violent people in the world, we also learn from watching popular media how we would like to behave when confronted with bigotry, prejudice, aggression, and violence. Thus, in contrast to the causal hypothesis which too often lumps all violent content into one big category, violent popular media, given the appropriate context and presentation, provide an educational opportunity to mature one's overall character.

Unfortunately, while the edification hypothesis is an interesting and optimistic contrast to the causal hypothesis, it seems to assume a lot of high-level intellectual engagement with popular media on the part of young children, a difficult task even for adults. Popular media are almost by definition designed and used to "tune-out," not "tune-in." Message-laden media such as *Schindler's List* are the exception, not the norm. Again, then, maybe it is better to err on the side of caution and present only media that overtly present positive messages and lessons instead of assuming Mac has the capacity to empathize and identify with the right character, in the right proportion, and with the right level of critical reflection. Are we then left only with the default safe bet of the causal hypothesis? It seems we are, unless, of course, there is another reason to let Mac watch and engage with bad behavior in popular media.

The Catharsis Hypothesis: I'm So Mad I Should Pretend To Kill You

Earlier, I mentioned a study that demonstrated the reverse of the causal hypothesis. The conclusion drawn by Feshbach and Singer was that the decrease in aggression after watching violent television was the result of a catharsis effect. The catharsis hypothesis says that watching bad behavior results in a catharsis or purging of undesirable emotions or desires. Although the Feshbach and Singer theory is decades old, the catharsis hypothesis dates back at least to Aristotle. Again, in contrast to Plato, Aristotle espouses the benefits of viewing tragic plays. Aristotle uses the term "catharsis" only briefly in his *Poetics*, but it is an appropriate starting point for any discussion of catharsis. Tragic catharsis has been interpreted in a number of different ways from the brief occurrence of the concept in the *Poetics* where Aristotle offers his definition of tragedy:

> A tragedy, then, is the imitation of an action that is serious and also, as having magnitude, complete in itself ... with incidents arousing pity and fear, wherewith to accomplish its catharsis of such emotions.[8]

Aristotle's definition of tragedy specifically refers to the excitation of the emotions of pity and fear, and within Aristotle's philosophy tragedy affects the emotions of pity and fear for the consequence of pleasure and learning. However, the idea of catharsis expanded beyond pity and fear and applied to popular media has the beneficial effect of purging what would otherwise become realized and potentially harmful desires or emotions. We might call this idea "therapeutic catharsis," since it treats or cures an illness, in this case the desire to be violent or aggressive. The spectator has an illness, an inclination toward anger, violence, fear, or aggression, which needs to be cured.

However, there are two prominent therapeutic catharsis theories – homeopathic and allopathic – that offer different explanations as to how the purgation, purification, or curing of the illness is supposed to occur. First is the homeopathic theory, in which emotions or desires are purged by viewing and engaging with *similar* emotions. Second is the allopathic theory, in which emotions like anger or aggression are purged by viewing or engaging with emotions *unlike* themselves.[9]

Years into the future, and despite my best efforts, Mac has become a mischievous little man. Mac is no Damien, but he's no Wally Cleaver either. Mac is sort of like Dennis the Menace with malicious intent. Mac is often angry and frustrated, he steals and vandalizes, and no amount of therapy, medication, or time-outs is helping. Following the homeopathic theory of catharsis, if I want Mac's penchant for stealing cars to subside, I could let him play the video game *Grand Theft Auto* in order to help purge or release his misguided emotions and desires. Further, if I identify later that Mac has a general inclination towards sadistic murder akin to Showtime's charming serial killer *Dexter*, playing a few levels of *Manhunt* will help purge and satisfy his homicidal desires since gruesome, graphic murder is a major theme of this video game – Mac can even mimic the stabbing motions if I buy him a Wii.

In contrast, if I espouse the allopathic theory, I need to find a form of popular media that arouses the opposite emotions or desires. If Mac desires to harm people and is particularly uncaring, I could flood his mind with popular media that arouse compassion and caring – slim pickings, but it's out there somewhere. In doing so, I balance out the other less desirable emotions and desires. Using terminology from Aristotle's *Nicomachean Ethics*, we are forcing Mac to reach the "mean" between the excesses of his emotions. If I believe Mac is excessively stingy with money, he could watch *Citizen Kane*'s account of excessive wealth and spending to purge some of his miserly emotions and make him more generous. If Mac is excessively rash or aggressive, I could scare the heck out of him by letting him watch *A Nightmare on Elm Street*.

Can catharsis really mitigate aggression and violence? The answer is unclear. There is even less reliable and consistent scientific evidence to prove this hypothesis than the causal hypothesis. But even assuming philosophers' refinement of Aristotle's theory of tragic catharsis throughout the years, would playing *Grand Theft Auto* or watching *A Nightmare on Elm Street* really be the best way for Mac to learn to cope with his emotions? Further, any potentially beneficial cathartic effect Mac might get from violent popular media might be negated by an even more severe consequence of viewing and engaging with these images.

Gregory Currie says that fictional media such as television, movies, or video games allow us to safely engage in a sort of simulation: our desires and emotions are running "offline" as we watch popular media; we imagine ourselves in the place of others and then see how we respond emotional-ly.[10] But, what if, over time, we desire more and more vivid simulations? When I was younger, *Asteroids* or *Commando* were sufficiently violent to keep me engaged, but today they seem tame and boring. What if constant exposure necessitates more and more realistic simulations and our "offline" desires turn "online?"

Conclusion: The Decision, Like Fatherhood, is Full of Ambiguities

I can hear pre-teen Maxwell now: "Gimme a break dad, it's just a movie; it's fun." There's something to his underdeveloped entertainment hypoth-esis. Horror and action movies are fun because they take us on a thrill ride. We can have the fun of being scared with the security of knowing that we won't get hurt. For the same reason we ride roller coasters, we love to watch big explosions, car chases, and other bad behavior. We would never really rob a bank or throw our boss out the window, no matter how much we'd like to, but it is fun and exciting to make-believe and that's all it is. All this talk of identification and imitation is nonsense. Really, how many kids jumped off a building after they watched *Superman*?

However, even assuming the causal, edification, and catharsis hypoth-eses are wrong, and that popular media are just good old harmless fun, could there be a problem viewing it that way? Here's the clincher, the popular pundit buzzword: *desensitization*. But even this good old standby is ambiguous. On one hand, desensitization to violence might mean we are less likely to care about or help people subject to real violence; on the other hand, desensitization to violence might mean we will be less aroused by violence and thus less likely to be violent.

The most important conclusion to draw is that our fatherly intuitions are probably correct. Although far less substantiated and serious than the rhetoric would have us believe, there are potential harms to letting our kids watch violent popular media. Additionally, though, the representa-tion and message of the violence in *Saving Private Ryan* can be educa-tional, and the thrill of decapitating hundreds of zombies in *Dead Rising* can be cathartic and nothing more. As such, violent popular media have potential benefits as well as harms. At best it is lazy, at worst it is ignorant, to rely on content descriptors that by definition neglect to consider the context of what we watch.

Should I let him watch? Currently, the philosophical and scientific proof is insufficient to wholly support any hypothesis. However, there is a value to understanding each theory, especially their subtler implications. That is, they proffer young viewers as superficial thinkers who are impulsively reactionary. This view, conveniently, serves to relieve us as fathers from a lot of responsibility and consequently places far too much blame on the corrupting influence of popular media. Itt seems likely, though, that a number of variables, including popular media, will influence our kids' behavior and thought.

Nevertheless, we know one highly influential variable is us. Yesterday, I convinced Mac that he should laugh instead of cry when he ran his head into the wall. Our children will get out of popular media what we teach them to get out of them as we watch and engage popular media *with* them. Whether to let your child watch popular media is based more on how you watch, engage, and think about this imagery, because that, most likely, is how your children will too. We, as fathers, are the best and most influential examples, however daunting and scary that role may be. To underestimate that power and that responsibility would be a mistake.

I've got to go now. My son has just awakened, again, and we're going to watch *Halloween,* again. What can I say? It helps us all get some sleep … for now.

NOTES

1 For brevity, I will focus primarily on the issue of violence in popular media, but these theories and my analysis can easily be applied to any subject matter parents are concerned about (e.g., sex, drug use, etc.).

2 Edith Hamilton and Huntington Cairns (eds.) *The Collected Dialogues of Plato* (Princeton: Princeton University Press, 1989), p. 625.

3 See Nancy Signorelli's *Violence in the Media: A Reference Handbook* and *Violence and Terror in the Mass Media: Annotated Bibliography* (New York: Greenwood Press, 1988).

4 See Jonathan L. Freedman's *Media Violence and Its Effect on Aggression: Assessing the Scientific Evidence* (Toronto: University of Toronto Press, 2002).

5 Seymour Feshbach and Robert D. Singer, *Television and Aggression: An Experimental Field Study* (San Francisco: Jossey-Bass, 1971).

6 See Berys Gaut's "Identification and Emotion in Narrative Film," in Carl Platinga and Greg M. Smith (eds.) *Passionate Views: Film, Cognition, and Emotion* (Baltimore: Johns Hopkins University Press, 1999).

7   Richard McKeon (ed.) *The Basic Works of Aristotle* (New York: Random House, 1941), p. 1457.
8   Ibid., p. 1460.
9   Elizabeth S. Belfiore, *Tragic Pleasures:Aristotle on Plot and Emotion* (Princeton: Princeton University Press, 1992), p. 261.
10 Gregory Currie, *Image and Mind: Film, Philosophy and Cognitive Science* (Cambridge: Cambridge University Press, 1995).

DAVID S. OWEN

CHAPTER 14

FATHERING FOR SOCIAL JUSTICE

Raising Children with Open Eyes and Open Minds

"Daddy, why is her face brown?" This is a question many white parents fear yet many are asked – some version of it is a common topic of discussion among parents of four and five year olds. It is a question that can come in a variety of forms: "Daddy, why are those two men holding hands?" "Daddy, why is that woman in a wheelchair?" How parents respond to this question at the time and also how they respond in their parenting practices have a significant impact upon the degree to which their children go on in their lives to participate in or resist the cycle of racial oppression. Whether we admit it or not, parenting is a political act. Action or inaction, discussion of race or not, are all actions that have consequences for social justice. In this chapter, I want to examine in light of current understandings of oppression just how parents can raise children who will know how to resist reproducing injustice.

This is especially relevant to fathers, who occupy a historically privileged social position such that central aspects of our social identities – our maleness, our heterosexuality, our racial identity – are all often what are understood as the norms for our society generally. In my case, for example, as a white, heterosexual father, who is middle class, my particular social identity in these dimensions coincides with our culture's depictions of the "typical" or "normal" father. Having this status of normalcy means that the social system grants me privileges on the basis of these social identities, which I normally do not recognize because of the normalized status of my identity. So, as a father, I am an especially important role model for my daughter when it comes to resisting and challenging systems of oppression. If she sees me challenging a system that grants me privileges, this will have a significant impact on her own sense of responsibility for challenging these systems because a common way that early childhood learning occurs is through imitation.

Learning Difference

I want to return now to the opening question, "Daddy, why is her face brown?" My intention is to use this particular question and what parents have said about it to unpack assumptions and to clarify how the cycle of oppression can be interrupted. One particular discussion of this recently ignited a small Internet wildfire of discussion.[2] A mother wrote that when her two children visited her at work, the three-year-old asked loudly, "Mommy, why is her face brown?" The mother's initial reaction was to feel mortified, because this seemed to suggest that she had done something wrong as a parent, in particular, not having raised her children to be color-blind. But then, she says, she came to see that this question was simply a factual question about the world, like noticing differently colored eyes. Since she considered it simply a factual question, she decided to throw the question to her co-worker, who the question was about, to see how she would answer it. The co-worker simply explained that people come in a variety of colors, and the child, seemingly satisfied (or simply distracted), went on to watch a video. The mother writes that she learned something about race that day. She says she learned that recognizing differences between people is not harmful, racist, or prejudiced, but that it is natural. She further concludes that it is the judgments and discriminatory treatments that are based on these differences that do the harm. Since her child had not meant to make a racist or prejudicial judgment, then the question and her child were innocent.

I will return below to a discussion of why this is a mortifying experience for many parents, but want to turn first to the analysis that this mother gives of the question. She understands her child's question as simply noticing something factual about the world. But in what sense can it be said that this child simply "notices" something about the world? What prompts the noticing? Why notice *this* fact about the world? Idealist philosophers have long argued that what we take to be real is not independent of our minds or the human mind as such. In some sense the human mind functions in such a way that it in part or wholly constitutes or constructs what counts as reality. This seems to be especially the case when we are talking about *social* reality, for our social reality – which includes such things as social roles, identities, meanings, practices, norms of behavior, expectations, and so on – is itself socially constructed in the sense that we don't *find* this reality; we have created it. So, in this case, the fact picked out is constituted as a fact, and further, it is one worthy of noticing because our social world has historically constructed it as a *significant* fact.

What was missed in this mother's analysis is the nature of what we notice as constituted by our (socially constructed) minds. One result of a long history of racial oppression in a society is that racialized[3] differences come to have a significance and meaning, meanings that unavoidably carry value judgments about who is superior and who is inferior. While there is little doubt that the child meant no harm, it does not follow that the child had not already begun to pick up on the meaningful racialized distinctions her society has long used. Research has shown that infants as young as six months already notice differences in skin color.[4] As children are socialized and enculturated, they begin to internalize the meanings our culture attaches to racial differences. It does not take long for children in many societies to learn that being white marks one as the norm, while having a darker skin color marks one as "different."

Further, the mother concluded that while it is not the noticing of difference that is problematic, it is the judgments and discriminatory treatments that are. Of course, noticing differences that pick out what philosophers call "natural kinds," that is, categories of things that are part of the world and would continue to exist even if humanity didn't, is unproblematic. In fact, successfully picking out these natural differences is necessary for survival and flourishing. However, the sort of difference that the little boy pointed out cannot be said to be a natural kind in this way. In the modern world, skin color is not simply a natural category. In fact, it is difficult to formulate an understanding of skin color that is simply biological, for there is a continuum of skin colors that human beings have, ranging from dark brown to very light pink. Yet, we "see" human skin tones as grouped into only a handful of categories: white, black, brown, yellow, and red.

Aside from this biologically false grouping of a spectrum of skin colors into only a few categories, there is the problem of the meaning of skin color in the modern world. For complex historical reasons, skin color has come to have a meaning attached to it, with some shades being seen as superior or having more value than others. When one thinks about it, the term "race" does not simply refer to skin color – though we sometimes naïvely think it does. Instead, the ways "race" has historically been used in social practices, institutions, and law, shows that we understand visible features such as skin color as telling us something about a person's non-visible characteristics such as intelligence, athleticism, "rhythm," and so on. What this means is that noticing racialized differences is really about seeing a social system of value and not about noticing aspects of nature.[5]

Against Ignoring Difference

White parents often find themselves mortified when their children ask questions like "Why is her skin brown?" in public, and there are several reasons for this embarrassment. First, children who ask this have broken the unspoken norm that whites (or at least those "good liberal" whites who care about racial justice) do not notice or mention race in public. Second, it also suggests that the parents of the child have failed to carefully educate their children about the meanings of racial differences. Third, parents are sometimes mortified because this suggests that their child has not been exposed to people who are different from themselves – to people of color, or gays and lesbians, or people with disabilities.

Not mentioning race in public has become the norm in the post-civil rights era in the United States. Everyone is expected to be color-blind since race is not supposed to matter in our judgments and actions. Not being relevant, race is suppressed. And when it is not suppressed, and it is brought up, one is accused of either being racist – which is then invariably denied – or of playing the race card for one's own advantage.

This pressure to be color-blind has become so much the norm that it shows up in ten-year-old children. Recent research shows that eight and nine-year-old children are better at "seeing" and using racial categories than are ten and eleven-year-olds.[6] The researchers in this study conclude that this represents an anomaly in the normal development of children's ability to categorize. The older children have begun to internalize the social norm that we should not notice race, whereas the younger children understand that race is a significant feature of the social world but have not yet learned that pointing out this feature is widely considered to be problematic.

Yet this norm that people should not notice race actually functions to maintain racialized disparities. There is ample evidence that race continues to have a profound effect on modern American lives.[7] As is assumed by the color-blind attitude, these effects are unjust since what they amount to is the systematic disadvantaging of some and the systematic advantaging of others. The problem is that if the way race works in our culture continues to have unjust effects whether we intend them to or not, then ignoring race and the way it presently functions in our culture will simply allow it to continue to produce these unjust effects.

What this means for fathers, and parents in general, is that we need to discourage our children from ignoring race. Research shows that children invariably learn about racial difference at a very young age. Infants as young as six months can distinguish between skin colors in facial recognition studies, which means they are already beginning to try to make sense of this difference they find in the world.[8] And by the time they are three and four, children begin to put racial categories into practice as a central organizing feature of their shared social world.[9]

I Am Because We Are and We Are Because I Am

There are a variety of ways fathers might respond to "Why is her face brown?" One common response would be to "stick to the facts." The question is about skin color, so why not simply educate the child about the fact that people come in all different sizes, shapes, and colors? Or one might respond by explaining that skin color is determined by the amount of melanin in one's skin, and this has to do with how much sun one's ancestors were exposed to. The idea here is to simply give a straightforward biological answer to the question about skin color.

The problem with this response is that it ignores the culturally embedded meanings associated with skin color that we have inherited. Questions about skin color are not simply about biology, for as I noted above, the research shows that by the age of three and four, children are already learning that there are racialized differences and these differences carry social meanings. Even granting that the question is really only a biological one, why should parents refrain from a teachable moment by retreating from the real issue at hand: race?

If parents want to raise anti-racist children, children who will oppose any form of racial oppression, and for that matter any form of oppression, then they will need to engage in a kind of counter-education. They will need to begin educating children about the fact that we have inherited various forms of oppression and about how these oppressions are maintained. Children are already learning about oppression. They are already internalizing the social norms and practices that support and reproduce these systems of oppression.[10] Parents who want their children to be part of the solution and not the problem should begin making these norms and practices explicit and teach children how oppression is sustained in mundane, everyday practices.

Social philosophers have long understood the mutually constructive relation between the practices, values, and beliefs of a culture and individual social identities. On the one hand, the practices (which are nothing but patterns of behavior), values, and beliefs of a culture have their existence in, and are sustained by, the actions and behavior of individuals. On the other hand, individual social identities are created and maintained by the ways individuals are socialized and enculturated, processes which do not end upon the entrance into adulthood, but which are ongoing throughout our lives. Put concisely, individual behaviors create, maintain, and change culture, while the particular features of a culture become internalized in the identities of individuals.

This model of the culture-individual relation provides us with a much more sophisticated understanding of how systems of racial oppression are sustained over time. Such systems can be sustained by the intentional actions of individuals, say through intentionally racist behavior. However, they can just as easily be sustained "behind the backs of individuals" by means of a kind of cultural momentum.

Once a culture is infected by racial injustice such that some individuals are advantaged and others are disadvantaged in all major domains of social life – in the economy, the workforce, education, politics, cultural imagery of what counts as valuable, norms of interaction, and so on – then that culture becomes embedded in individuals as practices, values, and beliefs that are consistent with racial injustice. When I am socialized and enculturated into a culture that is infected by racial injustice, my own "self" becomes infected. Of course, not everyone is infected to the same degree, but no one escapes the forces of socialization and enculturation. And I go on to reproduce that racialized culture through my everyday behaviors, which against the background of the larger culture are considered "normal" and unproblematic.

It is precisely this "cycle of socialization" that needs to be disrupted in progressive, anti-oppressive parenting.[11] The key here is to accept the fact that children will inevitably internalize the social and cultural world we inhabit along with any injustice it possesses. Once this is acknowledged, then the challenge for parents is to find ways to disrupt the cycle of socialization. When your daughter or son asks, "Daddy, why is her skin brown?" this should not come as a surprise. Now, skin color is not the same thing as racialized identity, but what many neuroscientists have argued is that infants begin at this early age to attempt to make sense of this difference.[12] Thus, children are "learning" race and how it works in our culture at a very early age. Being color-blind, or refraining from pointing out racial difference, only allows this socialization and enculturation into a racialized culture to proceed uninterrupted.

If color-blindness, or more generally, an exclusive focus on the message that "we are all the same," simply permits an unjust system to be reproduced, then what can fathers do? Fathers must find ways to interrupt this cycle, and this means changing both individual identities and culturally based social practices, values, and beliefs – of both fathers and children. Parenting for social justice requires more than changing beliefs; it requires changing behavior as well as one's own sense of self. And this applies both to parents and to children.

Practicing Just Parenting

What would raising children who are anti-oppressive mean in practice? There are three aspects of anti-oppressive parenting that can be distinguished. The first has to do with what it is necessary to know or understand, the second has to do with how we teach our children to act or behave, and the third has to do with the virtues of character that should be cultivated in our children.

Given what I have said before about how individual selves and social and cultural realities mutually construct one another, it follows that we

DAVID S. OWEN

are all socialized and enculturated in such a way that we internalize significant features of our shared social world. What is internalized shows up in how we understand ourselves in our uniqueness (who I am) and in how we act (what I do). Parenting for social justice would thus mean disrupting how our children are socialized and enculturated. However, because socialization and enculturation is a process that occurs in every encounter of the individual (whether child or adult) with the social or cultural worlds, it cannot be prevented. The most parents can hope to do is to alter the patterns of socialization and enculturation sufficiently so that their children begin to learn how they can avoid reproducing the oppressive social relations and cultural meanings that they encounter.

This also means that for those parents who desire to raise anti-oppressive children, these knowledge, practice, and character shifts need to occur in the parents themselves. I cannot raise my daughter to be someone who effectively strives for more justice in the world if I do not make the very same changes in my own knowledge, practices, and character. This is quite crucial to understand. For it is too often the case that those who desire more justice in the world adopt a kind of missionary attitude: I am doing good in the world *for others*. And while it may be thought that doing good deeds changes the doer for the better, what is missing is the requirement that the doer self-consciously change herself or himself in the very same process of working for a more just world. The focus outward on the injustice in the world allows us to ignore how we embody and enact that injustice every day. This is why it is crucial not to focus one's anti-oppressive gaze solely outward, but to condition this outward activism with an inward honest self-critique and behavioral change.

Here are some concrete steps to take *with your child* to cultivate a justice-focused, anti-oppressive way of living.

Knowledge

1 Learn about the history of oppression in all of the forms it takes across the globe. This means learning the history that is not usually part of the curriculum, and includes learning about histories, cultures, and people that are not part of the mainstream, dominant white culture. Increasingly, there are more children's books that focus on suppressed histories and marginalized experiences of peoples of the African diaspora, Latin America, and Asia, as well as American Indians, Aborigines, and other original inhabitants. However, one needs to also teach children about racism, sexism, classism, homophobia, and

other forms of oppression, so they can begin to critique them. Beware of the many treatments of these topics that reduce the injustice to individual actions – oppression is not just the result of a few "bad apples," but instead is the result of collective, often unconscious participation in ways of acting that appear "normal."

2 Begin noticing how our identities – our preferences, desires, and values – are constructed in conjunction with patterns of social relations and cultural imagery and challenge your children in ways that will encourage them to begin seeing this as well. Here it is necessary to break with the standard social contract view that fully formed individuals who already have sets of preferences, desires, and values come together to form what we call "society," often merely to satisfy our own interests. We need to begin to see how individuals and societies come into existence together, each being necessary to the origins and continuation of the other. This non-individualist view of the social world is captured in the Zulu maxim *umuntu ngumuntu ngabantu*, which translates as "a person is a person through other persons." No doubt, all of this requires an age-appropriate approach. But what this means is not teaching them a false model of self-society, but instead teaching them an accurate model in somewhat simplified, metaphorical, and creative ways.

3 Pay attention to the many subtle and not so subtle ways that power infuses the social and cultural worlds. Ask yourself: How is power represented in this text, movie, video game, or image? And how is it being maintained? And, perhaps more importantly, don't focus simply on the ways power is used to oppress and dominate, but how it is used to define and maintain what counts as "normal." For what counts as normal expressly excludes from itself the abnormal, the deficient, the stigmatized. The very existence of a norm or standard of behavior means that there are some behaviors excluded – and the key question is why and how this is maintained. So ask yourself: Who is unjustly privileged in this situation, book, movie, etc. and in what ways are they (and we) prevented from seeing this privilege?

Practice

1 Reflect on how your thinking and actions contribute to the continuation of an oppressive social structure, and encourage your children to do the same. We will unavoidably reproduce oppression because we are socialized to do so. The challenge is to constantly self-monitor in

order to recognize this and to begin forming alternative assumptions, perspectives, and actions. Always ask yourself: How is this choice, action, or behavior sustaining my own privilege and at the same time limiting the choices, options, and opportunities of others?

2   Challenge others in their assumptions and behavior when it maintains privilege and oppressive structures. What we need to change is not simply individual behaviors (of a few bad apples), but the patterns of social practices that we unconsciously participate in. So it is crucial to see this change in practice as a collective effort in which we challenge each other to alter our normal ways of acting that reproduce oppression.

3   Form multiracial relationships that are authentic and be sure your children have the opportunities to do so as well. This will ensure that the blinders of privilege do not wholly prevent you from seeing either how you contribute to oppression or how your anti-oppressive actions might themselves be oppressive. Further, it is crucial, especially for young children, to witness you engaging in friendships across difference and to see you working with others in projects of social justice.

Character

1   Be courageous and encourage your children to be so. Engage in anti-oppressive practices knowing that you will make mistakes. This is inevitable. But this must not keep you from doing what is right. Letting it keep you from fully engaging in the struggle for social justice is an example of falling back on privilege to withdraw from the difficult work; an option the oppressed don't have.

2   Practice humility. Do not be overly confident or self-righteous. You do not and will not understand all there is to know about oppression, nor will you be a perfect anti-oppressive agent. Develop ways of challenging others while at the same time not demanding perfection. We all can do better, but none of us is perfect.

3   Self-reflect, self-reflect, self-reflect. As Socrates reportedly stated, "The unexamined life is not worth living." We must constantly reflect on our own assumptions and behaviors, asking, "How am I contributing to oppression?" This may be the most important aspect of parenting: teaching our children the skill of stepping outside of their own egocentric perspective so as to view their own thinking and actions from another perspective. It is only in this way that we can see the ways we are contributing to oppression. And this is a critical reason why multiracial relationships across multiple dimensions of difference are so important.

Teaching Alienation?

Assuming that as a father I can figure out how to cultivate anti-oppressive knowledge, practices, and virtues both in myself and in my child, there remains a further challenge. What it means to live a life fully committed to bringing about social justice in the world is that I and my child will become alienated from the society and culture of which we are a part. If I am successful at adopting an anti-oppressive orientation, then I will necessarily see my society and culture as unjust in the ways that they embody oppression. I will be committed not to accepting them as they are, but to changing them so that they contain more social justice.

How can I in good conscience actively encourage social alienation in my child? I will be encouraging them to be dissatisfied in their own culture, and they will feel that they lack a place or a home where they are fully comfortable. This is a serious ethical question that addresses the relation between moral action and feeling at home in one's community. Philosophers have long contemplated the relation between the two. Does being moral bring with it this sense of satisfaction or even happiness? In what way, if any, does seeking a feeling of being at home with others have a moral component to it?

Those that live a satisfied existence in an unjust society – and there are far too many that do – are living in what Jean-Paul Sartre called "bad faith." They are deluding themselves into believing they don't have any responsibility for the oppression that exists, and so they need not trouble themselves about it. But, as he would suggest, this is an inauthentic existence. We in fact are responsible for the perpetuation of oppression, whether we accept this or not. Every day, in each of my social actions, I contribute to the continuous re-creation of the social order. And I can choose either to reproduce it as it is – with its unjust structures intact – or I can choose to find ways to construct a more just social order. Accepting this responsibility that I have and living in light of it means living an authentic existence.

So the ethical dilemma of how can we justify raising alienated children can be answered in this way. While my anti-oppressive parenting may cultivate a social and cultural alienation in my daughter, she will also develop a more authentic way of living. She will come to recognize that her happiness is not achieved simply in the satisfaction of her desires, but instead her happiness is dependent upon the degree of justice in the society to which she is inextricably tied. If society is unjust and oppressive, and that society is part of who she is, then how can she be satisfied and happy in the face of that? Furthermore, seeking justice in an authentic way will require working in concert with others who share my concerns. Thus, my daughter (and I for that matter) will achieve a feeling of being at home, or happiness, within this sub-community of people concerned with social justice. It is in working with others for social justice that I create a community within which I can feel at home, and this will mitigate my feelings of alienation from the larger society.

In the end, this is what I think fathers, and parents in general, can achieve with anti-oppressive parenting. We seek to raise our children to live authentic lives that are committed to creating a more just world. This is not just a lofty hope or an abstract ideal; it is a concrete way of living in which we cultivate in ourselves and our children the knowledge, practices, and virtues for living an authentic existence in a profoundly oppressive and unjust social order.

NOTES

1 I would like to thank Avery Kolers and the editors for helpful comments that have much improved this essay.
2 See www.momlogic.com/2008/06/in_progress_1.php.
3 I intentionally use the term "racialized" rather than "racial" to signal the fact that racial categories are constructed and not naturally occurring divisions that are simply found in nature. The consensus of scholarly research in all disciplines supports this.
4 Phyllis A. Katz, "Racists or Tolerant Multiculturalists," *American Psychologist* 58, 11 (2003): 897–909.
5 I would like to thank Avery Kolers for this helpful formulation.
6 Evan P. Apfelbaum, Kristin Pauker, Nalini Ambady, Samuel R. Sommers, and Michael I. Norton, "Learning (Not) to Talk About Race: When Older Children Outperform in Social Categorization," *Developmental Psychology* 44, 5 (2008): 1513–18.
7 See, for example, Douglas Massey and Nancy Denton, *American Apartheid: Segregation and the Making of the Underclass* (Cambridge, MA: Harvard University Press, 1998); Melvin Oliver and Thomas Shapiro, *Black Wealth/ White Wealth: A New Perspective on Racial Inequality*, 2nd edn. (New York: Routledge, 2006); Michael K. Brown, Martin Carnoy, Elliot Currie, Troy Duster, David B. Oppenheimer, Marjorie M. Schultz, and David Wellman, *Whitewashing Race: The Myth of a Color-Blind Society* (Berkeley: University of California Press, 2005).

8   Katz, "Racists or Tolerant Multiculturalists."

9   Debra Van Ausdale and Joe R. Feagin, *The First R: How Children Learn Race and Racism* (Lanham: Rowman and Littlefield, 2001).

10 Ibid.

11 Bobbie Haro, "The Cycle of Socialization," in Maurianne Adams, Warren J. Blumenfeld, Carmalita Castañeda, Heather W. Hackman, Madeline L. Peters, and Ximena Zuniga (eds.) *Readings for Diversity and Social Justice* (New York: Routledge, 2000).

12 Allison Gopnik, Andrew N. Meltzoff, and Patricia K. Kuhl, *The Scientist in the Crib: What Early Learning Tells Us About the Mind* (New York: Harper, 2000).

CHAPTER 15

LIKE FATHER LIKE SON?

Challenges in the Father-Son Relationship

For a parent is fond of his children because he regards them as something of himself; and children are fond of a parent because they regard themselves as coming from him.

Aristotle, *Nicomachean Ethics*
VIII:12, 1161b18–20

Every type of parental relationship – those between mother and daughter, mother and son, father and daughter, and father and son – is different. Each has its own distinctive features and idiosyncrasies. I do not have any children, so I can't exactly say that I know what it is like to be a father. But I have been a son to two loving parents for my entire life. Since fatherhood is the theme of this book, I'd like to explore some of the peculiarities of the father-son relationship. From my perspective as a son, I seek to identify and explain what I have discovered to be a crucial ethical challenge for a father, and one that I think is more vivid and pressing in the father-son relationship than in the other parental relationships. While I may end up raising more questions than I answer, I hope that this chapter succeeds in showing that the ethical challenge I have in mind is, indeed, an important and difficult one, and perhaps one that easily goes unnoticed without due reflection.

Some of a person's features, some important ones – like one's religion and political beliefs – and some *really* important ones, like one's major league baseball allegiances – are merely accidents of one's personal history. By "accidents of one's personal history" I simply mean this: Catholics tend to raise Catholics; Democrats tend to raise Democrats; Mets fans tend to raise Mets fans. At some point in life, you may discover this. You may discover that you probably would not have the religious and political beliefs that you have, nor would you root for the team that you root for, if not for the mere fact that your parents did the same, and that their parents did the same, and that their grandparents did the same, and so on and so forth down the family tree. You ask yourself: Did I really choose these things? If I didn't, does it matter? What is at issue here, and what gives rise to the ethical challenge I spoke of in the preceding paragraph, is the idea of *autonomy*. We all strive to be autonomous to varying degrees. "Autonomy" is a word passed down to us from the Ancient Greeks. *Autos* is the Greek word for "self" and *nomos* means "law." So, in the literal sense, to be autonomous is to be a law unto oneself. But what exactly does it mean to be a law unto oneself? Philosophers are notoriously divided when it comes to autonomy – to such a great extent, in fact, that some philosophers deny that "autonomy" even has a single, coherent meaning. But we need not concern ourselves with these technicalities. And besides, I do believe that autonomy is for the most part a unified notion with a coherent meaning.

Consider Jerry, father of 21-year-old Jose. Jose is finishing up his undergraduate degree at one of the nation's top schools, where he will no doubt graduate *summa cum laude*. Jose's father, Jerry, has been a criminal defense attorney for about twenty years and has made quite a name for himself. He is a senior partner at his firm and is widely considered to be the best lawyer in his field. It would please Jerry very much if Jose would make the decision to go into law, and for a number of reasons. For one thing, Jose would be carrying on Jerry's legacy. But most of all, because Jerry is so well known and connected in his field, he would be able to open many doors for Jose and make his transition into professional life go very smoothly. Additionally, he knows that Jose would be able to earn a healthy salary in law and would be able to live a comfortable life.

Jose, however, is just not that interested in the law. He does not abhor it, but it's just not the sort of thing that makes him tick, so to speak. In fact, what he really takes a sincere interest in – what really makes him tick – is English literature of the eighteenth century. The time has now come to choose: Will it be graduate school in literature or law school for Jose? Jerry has already done the math. Three years of law school plus a six-figure salary and an abundance of connections and support versus at least six years of graduate school for a PhD, plus the travails of the academic job market, a modest level of income, and no helpful connections. Perhaps Jose would just go for a Masters degree and teach English in a high school, Jerry ponders, but that still leaves him dissatisfied. Of course, deep down, Jerry just wants Jose to be happy. But he really would prefer him to be a happy lawyer than a happy expert of eighteenth-century English literature.

Jose is very well aware of his father's preferences. As far back as Jose can remember, his father always tried to instill in him, as best as he could, a deep respect for the practice of law. But it's just not Jose's thing. Eighteenth-century English literature is his thing, and the decision to pursue it is a decision he can truly embrace. It is a decision he can make autonomously. The decision to pursue law, on the other hand, would not be a genuinely autonomous decision for Jose because it's not what *he* truly values and wants. Sure, he would be happy to please his father. But deep down, in his heart of hearts, he would not be able to genuinely embrace such a decision.

When we think of the autonomous person, we think of someone like Jose choosing to pursue literature: someone whose life is marked by the fact that it is a product of *him* – *his* reason, *his* values, *his* decisions. In other words, we think of someone who directs his life by his own judgment and lives in accordance with what he truly values. His way of life is embraced "from the inside," we might say. And quite naturally, when we think of the non-autonomous person, the sort of person who comes to mind is someone whose life is directed, in some way, by some entity other than him. On the extreme end, we might think of a slave or someone living under an oppressive regime, or in general someone who lives at the call and mercy of others. On the less extreme and more common end, we might think of someone who chooses a certain profession simply because it is expected of him by others. We might think of Jose choosing to pursue law. Simply put, our common intuitions of autonomy are best exemplified by the statement "I'm in charge here." Or, perhaps Frank Sinatra said it best when he said, "And through it all, I did it *my* way."

We also closely associate autonomy with independence. It makes sense to say that someone who, for whatever reasons, needs to rely heavily on the help of others is thereby less autonomous, and perhaps this is often true. But I do not think that the absence of dependence thoroughly captures the idea of autonomy. Someone can make himself rich and thus less dependent, and yet he may still lack autonomy. He may still be poor at making his own decisions, at figuring out what it is that *he* truly wants in life and why, and at executing a plan to achieve those things. And this is how I want us to think of the autonomous person: a person who knows what *he* wants and why, and makes his choices in life accordingly.

How important is autonomy? How important is it that we direct our lives solely by our own judgment and live in accordance solely with what we truly value? Perhaps you are of the mindset that this is a silly question, and so obviously the answer is something like *extremely important*. After all, you might ask, what could be better for a person than his own development of a plan of life that he judges to be good for himself? Not many people, I would imagine, want to live in a way contrary to their own independent judgment of what is best. On the other hand, you may agree that autonomy is indeed important. Yet you may believe it's just not *that* important. There are other values that, when push comes to shove, can be more important than the value of autonomy. Philosophers who argue about the value of autonomy tend to fall into one of these mindsets. According to one view, autonomy is a sort of *foundational value*, meaning that the value of any life pursuit depends, *in some way*, on whether it is embraced "from the inside" and thus autonomously chosen. According to the second view, autonomy is just one value among many, and sometimes we have to make tradeoffs.

Of which view of autonomy does the example of Jerry and Jose speak in favor? The first view says that autonomy is a foundational value, and so the value of some life pursuit depends *in some way* on whether it is autonomously chosen. Notice my emphasis of "in some way." In what way, exactly? Let us suppose, for now, that on this view, if some life pursuit is not chosen autonomously, then it can have *no value* to an individual. According to this view, if Jose chooses to pursue law, he is in some trouble. Since his choice would not be autonomous, and since the value of the pursuit depends on whether it is autonomously chosen, the pursuit could not have value for him at all. The second view says that autonomy is just one value among many and there are times when other values can trump the value of autonomy. According to this view, if Jose chooses to pursue law, the pursuit *might* still have a lot of value for him even though it is not autonomously chosen. Perhaps another value in Jose's case is more important and is thus being favored. Money and security are, no doubt, important values. Perhaps, in Jose's case, they outweigh the value of autonomy.

I think that most of us would say that the right decision for Jose to make is to pursue literature. Not all of us, but the majority of us (even if it turns

ANTHONY CARRERAS

out to be only a slight majority) would feel this way, I believe. The idea that "if it's not what you really want, then you won't get anything out of it" does have a considerable amount of stock in many societies. So we may seem to be moved in favor of the foundational view of autonomy. And I think that some version of the foundational view is right. But as we are currently understanding it, it is simply too strong. Non-autonomous choices can have *no value at all* to an individual? None at all? Well, that's just false. A smoker, for example, who is somehow forced from the outside to quit his habit may not be an autonomous quitter, but he is surely healthier for it. He surely gets some value out of quitting. Sometimes we can do our loved ones favors by preventing them from making bad choices, even though those choices would have been autonomous choices.

And even Jose might still get something good out of pursuing a career in law, even though it's not what he truly wants. He'll have money and security, after all, and ample means to support his family should he choose to have one. It would be wrong to simply dismiss these values. Yet, it would be just as wrong to think that autonomy is merely one value among many. A more reasonable version of the foundational view would say something like the following: while non-autonomous lives may still have value, the *best* kind of life is an autonomous life. In order to get the best of what life has to offer, one has to be autonomous. Autonomy is connected to other values in that in order to get the *most* out of those other values, one has to choose them autonomously. On this view, we can grant that Jose would get some value out of pursuing law. But, he could never get as much out of it as he would if he chose it autonomously.

I had hoped for the example of Jerry and Jose to make clear what this all has to do with fatherhood and the father-son relationship. Let me now attempt to clarify this in detail. The autonomy of one's child is surely of concern to any parent, and it plays a role in all of the parental relationships. However, I think that in the father-son relationship the autonomy of the child is especially precarious, at least potentially. Sons tend to look up to fathers in a peculiar kind of way – sort of in the way that a student looks up to his most valued teacher. A father, to a son, often serves as a kind of moral ideal, an exemplar. To a great extent sons do seek the approval and endorsement of their fathers, and perhaps even more so sons fear falling short in their fathers' eyes and disappointing them.

The quote by Aristotle that I showcased at the start of this essay is particularly relevant here. As he says, sons are fond of their fathers because they naturally see themselves as coming from their fathers. There is something perfectly natural about a son wanting to be just like his dad.

This is one source of the ethical challenge. The other source lies in the natural tendencies a father has towards his son. As Aristotle tells us, a father is fond of his son because, naturally, he sees his son as something of himself. Fathers have a natural and instinctive desire to mold their sons in their own image. Jerry certainly has this desire, but to a detrimental degree, I think. While it is perfectly natural for a father to take pride in his son's feats and accomplishments because he sees his son as an extension of himself, there is a fine line between wanting your son to do well and wanting to create a miniature version of yourself in your son.

And this is where the ethical challenge comes into play. On the one hand, fathers want to instill values in their sons and show them the way. As moral ideals, they have every opportunity to do this. A son naturally wants to be like his dad, and at the same time a father has a natural desire to mold his son in his own image. On the other hand, fathers want to foster autonomy in their sons. We all want our life path to be of our own making – a product of our own reflective judgment and endorsement, and a father naturally wants this for his son. But how, then, is a father to balance the use of his inevitable influence with the need to foster autonomy? This is the fundamental question. Both are important, yet it seems that the favoring of one is done at the expense of the other. The more you use influence, the greater the risk to autonomy. The more you foster autonomy, the less influence you can use. It is difficult for me to answer this question. After all, I'm not a dad. But as a son who has seen his own father tread carefully around the line between using influence and fostering autonomy, and as someone who believes that autonomy is deeply important, naturally I think that the question is deeply important.

The question is made even more difficult by the fact that, more often than not, interferences with autonomy can be quite subtle, especially with respect to the father-son relationship. Take Jerry and Jose, once again. It would be one thing for Jerry to interfere with Jose's autonomy by openly and explicitly urging him to pursue law instead of eighteenth-century English literature. That would be clear-cut enough and probably more objectionable.

Is the answer to the question simple, then? Is the answer for Jerry to simply lay off, if he cares about Jose's autonomy? Not quite. In fact, I do not think it is a stretch to say that Jerry has already, at least potentially, interfered with Jose's autonomy simply by virtue of being who he is – of having his legacy, career, and stature; of impressing upon Jose since he was a boy that the law is a wonderful profession. Suppose for a moment that Jose genuinely wanted to become a lawyer, and so became one.

In that case, wouldn't it be perfectly legitimate to ask: Would he really have chosen that path if not for his father? Now, even if the answer to this question is "no," that does not mean that Jose did not choose law autonomously. But should it make us suspicious?

The tension between using influence and fostering autonomy manifests itself in the father-son relationship in a number of ways no doubt. One way in which it manifests itself – the way that I have emphasized throughout this essay – is when it comes to choosing one's profession. In family-run businesses it is common for the offspring to be groomed from an early age to eventually take over the reins.

My father is a veterinarian who has owned his own practice for the last twenty-some odd years. Neither I nor my younger brother found our paths in veterinary medicine. I guess it just wasn't our thing. When we were younger, we spent some amount of time working there, but we were certainly never "groomed" in any sort of way (that was saved for the animals). And now, as our father looks towards retirement, there is the question of what to do with the place, since it obviously cannot be passed down to either my brother or me. Since it's natural for a father to want to have himself live on, in a sense, through his son, I've always wondered why he never tried to push it on us a little bit more. He had told us stories about how when he was as young as 12-years-old he was helping his father, who was a large-animal veterinarian, with surgery on horses and the like. Why, I've wondered, did he not have us doing similar things all the time? Now, I've never really asked him, so I can't be sure what the answer is. But, knowing my father, I think the answer has something to do with autonomy. It was important to my father that if either of us had chosen veterinary medicine, that it was a choice made "from the inside." To whatever extent he may have had a desire to be like Jerry – a desire to mold his son into another him – he overcame it.

Back to our main question: Given that sons have a natural desire to be like their fathers, and given that fathers have a natural desire to mold their sons in their own image, how is a father to balance the use of his inevitable influence with the need to foster autonomy? Philosophers tend to be trouble-makers, sometimes providing more questions than answers to questions. I have mainly tried to show that this question is very important, easily overlooked, and has different answers depending on how important one believes autonomy to be. The more important you believe autonomy is and the closer you come to holding some version of the foundational view, then the more hesitant you might be to try to instill certain values. The less important you believe autonomy to be and the closer you come to holding the view that autonomy is just one value among many, then the opposite will probably be the case. Still, I should like to attempt to sketch out an answer to this vexing query, or at least suggest ways to navigate the challenge.

Navigating the challenge requires a father to honestly reflect on the importance of autonomy. I have tried to give some reasons for why I think some version of the foundational view is the correct one. Again, that view says that while non-autonomous lives may still have some value, the *best* kind of life is an autonomous life. In order to get the best of what life has to offer, one has to be autonomous. Autonomy is connected to other values in that in order to get the *most* out of those other values, one has to choose them autonomously. This is because when you choose something autonomously, you get to fully experience all of the value of that choice. This is because you sincerely believe that the choice has value for you, and if you are in fact correct about this, you will reap the benefits.

Let me try to illustrate what I mean by this with an analogy. Suppose that you were forced to spend an entire day blindfolded. The blindfold would, of course, make it difficult for you to get around. But the fact that you wouldn't be able to see the objects around you would not mean that there were in fact no objects. You'd occasionally bump into them and in general would be able to sense them with your other senses. But due to your blindfold, you would not be able to experience them as fully as someone who had the use of his eyes. What I am suggesting is that someone who does not make autonomous choices is wearing a kind of value-blindfold. Those choices may still end up having some value to him if the choices are, in fact, good for him (even though he does not endorse them as good, since he makes the choices non-autonomously). Analogously, the blindfolded person bumps into things and has some experience of objects even though he cannot see them. But in both cases, due to the blindfold, something very important is missing that would otherwise make the experience far richer than it is. When some course of action, the value of which you do not recognize or endorse, is forced on you – and "force" can come in many different varieties and flavors, as the Jerry-Jose example shows – you cannot fully experience all of the value of that course of action, even if it is in fact good for you in some way.

Now, if you agree with this view, then as a father, navigating the challenge will also involve controlling your natural desire to mold your son in your own image. You may, of course, reject the foundational view. But if you do, make sure that your rejection of it is the result of honest reflection on the matter rather than the result of the aforementioned natural desire. The fact that a view conflicts with some strong desire you have is not a reason for thinking that the view is false.

But assuming you are on board with the foundational view and assuming you are able to control your natural desire to mold your son in your own image, then all that's left is to figure out where the line should be drawn between instilling values and fostering autonomy. This is no easy question. It is of course important for a father (or for any parent for that matter) to instill values. It's important to be responsible, caring, and honest, for example. These are the sorts of things any parent should try to instill in his or her children. Indeed, these are the sorts of things parents try to instill in their children before their children are even old enough to have the capacity for autonomy. But when it comes to more specific sorts of values – like one's profession, one's significant other perhaps, or one's personal philosophy – in most cases it is wise to adopt as a general rule to err on the side of autonomy. There's a simple question you might ask yourself in such cases, a question Jerry would have been wise to ask himself regarding Jose and pursuing a law career: Is this what *he* truly wants? Or is this just what I want?

Yes, there may be exceptions. A father may have strong reasons for thinking that his son is making such a big mistake that he sincerely believes he has no choice but to intervene, and I'm not denying that in such cases intervention would be appropriate. Such cases are probably rare, but certainly not inconceivable. Still, such cases do not disprove the general rule I suggest ought to be adopted. Without autonomy, one risks waking up one day to the thought, "This life I've been living isn't really mine." To be able to reflect on the values in one's life and on the choices one has made to achieve those values, and to be able to say that these are values that I truly endorse, choices that I made of my own accord, is immensely satisfying. It is, in itself, a great value. We are deprived of that when we are deprived of our autonomy.

CHAPTER 16

FATHER'S IDEALS
AND CHILDREN'S LIVES

Visiting a beautiful Hindu temple in Goa last year, my family was given a short tour by one of the priests, who explained the origin and the design of the temple. Afterwards, the priest made a prediction: my son (age twelve) would become a great scientist, but my daughter, who is five, would follow in my footsteps and become a philosopher. My son ignored the prediction, but surprisingly my daughter took it seriously: a few months later she said to her kindergarten teacher, "Do you know that I am a philosopher?" I don't put too much credence in the priest's prediction. As my son told me later, *most* fathers want to hear such things, and it was clear that a request for a donation was in the offing.

Still, like many fathers I have aspirations for my kids – I mean, beyond mere happiness and moral decency. My son will be a scientist or a doctor.

He will continue his interests in violin and acting. My daughter shall indeed follow in Dad's footsteps and become a philosopher – better than me of course, although she will always acknowledge her debt to Dad. She will practice gymnastics, ballet, and piano. Both my kids will also give me grandchildren. But these are, I hope, mere wishes that shall never be forced upon them.

When a father (or mother) impels his kids to accept his conception of the good life, he is acting paternalistically. Usually, this term is understood as pejorative, but it really means acting like a father. While the corresponding feminine term, "maternal," can be used pejoratively, it is typically considered a good quality, indicating care, compassion, and concern for others. To be maternal is to be nurturing, certainly not a bad quality, even for men. But the very idea of "father" appears to have an implicit negative connotation. Is this significant? Maybe. At least there is a need to explain the virtues of fatherhood, if indeed there are any. Surely we cannot be content with any conception of fatherhood that implies the fundamental illegitimacy of being a father. We need, therefore, to distinguish the duty to *respect* the autonomy of adults from the duty to *develop* the autonomy of children.

Now, it makes sense that my peers would object were I to tell them which activities they ought to be pursuing, but it is puzzling why paternalism regarding my own kids would be wrong. Isn't it okay to give guidance to my kids? Don't they need to be guided, given that they are too young to be trusted to make complex decisions regarding their lives? When is it wrong to have ideals for our kids?

This is a very subtle issue and there really are no easy answers. Nevertheless, as in many practical and pressing issues where there are numerous considerations demanding sensitive ethical judgment, philosophy can be of great assistance. Philosophy offers clarity and once we are clear about an issue it is usually easier to see the right path. I argue that it is wrong to force ideals on one's children. However, if I am right about this, it does not follow that the good father must never guide his children. Good fathers guide their children by applying wisdom regarding human nature and knowledge of their own kids' character. Further, and perhaps most importantly, fathers can and should guide their children by "sharing life" with them. I begin by considering what it means to force an activity on one's kids.

I don't mean "force" to necessarily imply any brutality, but merely that the child's own wishes or intentions are either ignored or disregarded. If I force my kids to do or value some pursuit, even for their own good, I risk causing them great unhappiness: they might never experience the fulfillment of life in accordance with their own personal constitution, developed through their own decisions and efforts. Suppose my son is really not inclined to play violin. He dutifully practices and indeed acquires some talent, but he never truly loves the instrument. Perhaps he was, all along, more inclined to be a drummer; or maybe he would have been better served by developing some other talent – freestyle skiing or gardening – and the time devoted to practicing violin inhibits the development of these talents. Part of the problem is that the parent has to choose from a vast array of activities (and no one knows enough about all possible activities to help his kids choose them) and pursuit of one necessarily has implications for the pursuit of others. True, I can be a doctor, philosopher, violinist, skier, and philatelist, as well as a husband and father, but real talent takes time and effort. No one can do everything well. However, the problem is deeper than simply not being able to choose to pursue all worthwhile activities. People also need to be authors of their own destiny – or at least to feel that they are.

Why should we care whether we are authors of our own destiny? It is possible that this is merely a prideful demand for independence or sovereignty, but something more significant is at stake. Actually, there are two plausible considerations. One relatively superficial reason is that the individual herself is in the best position to determine what activities will allow her to flourish. The idea is that I know myself best, so I ought to be the one who chooses my activities. I say this is a relatively superficial consideration because it is clear that I may not – even as an adult – know myself better than others know me. Most children do not know themselves well enough or know about enough activities to make wise decisions about their activities. That said, I often know quite well whether I'll enjoy an activity: even as a ten-year-old, I knew very well that I would enjoy scuba diving, and I was quite certain that skydiving would be downright unpleasant for me! So, we want to make our own choices regarding our activities because we are more likely to get these decisions right. While young kids cannot be left to make their own decisions, there is every reason to allow children increasing opportunity to make choices regarding their lives. By the time a child reaches late adolescence, in the standard case, she should be making most of her own decisions regarding her life. However, there is a deeper reason why people need to make their own decisions regarding their life paths.

The deeper reason stems from the importance of meaningful activities in a person's life. A happy or flourishing life implies engagement in meaningful activities.[1] A life lived without activities that are meaningful to the person will be empty and directionless; indeed, without meaningful

JEFFREY MORGAN

activities I am alienated from my own life. To see why, we have to think about what makes something meaningful to a person. For an activity to be meaningful for me, I have to accept its goals and strategies as my own.[2] I must engage in it "from the inside," as a reflection of my deepest identity. If you paternalistically choose my activities for me, I might experience them as alien, as a reflection of you, not me. This is because I do not identify with the activity. My sense of myself – my self-esteem – is not tied up with the activity. If I do well, great; but I'm not going to go into depression just because I'm not successful at an activity that wasn't really my choice in the first place. However, I noted that you might experience the activity as alien, but this isn't quite right. The issue isn't entirely one of choice of activity, but whether one comes to embrace the activity.

Choice, then, is a bit of a red herring, a distraction. Consider this: you are a student in a university program that requires you to take a history course. Although you have no interest in history, you dutifully albeit resentfully take the course. At first, the long readings are hard and boring, but as you get further along you begin to see the beauty of well-written history. You learn how history demands a deep understanding of the human condition. Perhaps you occasionally begin to read history on your own, or even develop an interest in exploring a particular historical issue, such as the history of baseball or the Japanese occupation of China. There is an obvious analogy to parenting here. Many times we acquire an interest in meaningful activities as a direct result of our parents' influence. Dads who introduce their kids to activities often bestow a great gift on their children: a lifelong love of rugby, stamp collecting, or botany. The problem is that children are often limited by their fathers' interference.

So forcing one's children to participate in activities that Dad has chosen is probably not the best option. Although there will be occasions in which children do develop a passion for these activities, often this will lead to alienation and rebellion. It will be too hard to get these choices right. The problem is that if we eschew the force option, we may be tempted to simply wait until the kid reveals who they are and what they would like to pursue in life. There are two ways we could take this: either I insist on a clear statement of their goals ("Daddy, I want to be a magician"), or I am content with interpreting their goals from their actions, including direct statements such as the above. The first option at least has the virtue of respecting their independence, but presupposes that the child has a clear conception of her interests. This isn't really plausible, especially for younger children. For older children, it is more plausible, but for many activities or lifestyles there is a prolonged training period that is best begun in early childhood. This is true of many athletic activities, artistic disciplines, and intellectual activities. I know a woman who began figure skating training as a adult – while I applaud her courage, it is clear that the best skating is done by people in their teens and twenties, and takes years to achieve. (I'll come back to this point.) So waiting for the child to literally state her goals, while it respects the child in one sense, is not typically going to be in the best interests of the child. What about the option of interpreting their goals from their overall behavior?

This option is more plausible. Of course, it assumes that I am very good at interpreting the behavior of my children. I need to study the overall behavior of my son and infer that he has an interest in medicine or Greek language or ice hockey. I may get it all wrong. There is no way around this problem, but there are ways in which I can improve my chances of accuracy. The contemporary American philosopher Robert Noggle[3] suggests one way.

Drawing on some ideas from John Rawls,[4] Noggle suggests that we can develop a hierarchy of goods for any person. His idea is that the problem of choosing for our kids need not be one of lay psychological analysis. Rawls himself uses the concept of a primary good, something that is good for anyone, regardless of their desires. Some examples are "rights and liberties, opportunities and powers, income and wealth."[5] Noggle further distinguishes basic goods (those essential to life itself, such as food, shelter, and clothing) and pre-primary goods, which are essential to appreciating any primary good. One such pre-primary good is what he calls "moral agency." This includes a rich understanding of oneself as having a past, present, and future (including understanding that what seems important today may seem less significant later), a sense of moral decency, and a conception of the good (a worldview) – without which, he says, one would be a "lost soul." Further, after primary goods, we need to pursue secondary goods, which do not hurt anyone, but are valuable to most people. Possible examples are religious commitment and a capacity to enjoy music or have deep friendships. Finally, once these goods are satisfied, it is acceptable to pursue specialized goods, which are valued only by particular people and depend on particular characteristics of individual people. For example, a specialized good might be training in figure skating or in higher mathematics. This hierarchy of goods can guide parents in making decisions regarding the interests of one's children.

The basic idea is that while children lack the maturity to make important decisions for themselves, parents should make these decisions, balancing the child's short- and long-term interests. The parent is merely a surrogate for the future authority of the child. As a father, therefore, I can

JEFFREY MORGAN

guide my kids' lives, but only on the basis of ensuring their own interests are satisfied. Fortunately, children are not so different in their general interests – basic, pre-primary, primary, and secondary goods – although there might be distinctions at the level of specialized goods or in how we satisfy secondary goods (for instance, whether my kids should be raised to be Christians or Buddhists). So, as a father, I can be confident that I must guide my children's lives and that I will not go too far wrong if I focus initially on goods that are common to all children. I don't need to be a super-sensitive psychologist for this. Still, I wonder how I will decide whether to initiate them into competitive hockey, ballet, or tae-kwon-do, or cause them to join the air cadets, attend an elite school, or learn to snowboard. In the remainder of this chapter we will consider religious initiation. Is this form of influence acceptable?

Can I legitimately raise my child as an evangelical Christian or orthodox Muslim or member of the Fundamentalist Church of Jesus Christ of Latter Day Saints (the polygamous sect of which Warren Jeffs and Winston Blackmore have been leaders)? For many fathers, this is a "no-brainer": to refrain from such religious initiation puts the child's very soul in jeopardy. Also, it would have the consequence of destroying family harmony – how can parents worship wholeheartedly without including their kids in the traditions and rituals? However, if you consider religious initiation in light of the child-centered model presented above, it is clear that there is an issue.

What is religious initiation? Obviously, this varies significantly from faith to faith and according to the strength of commitment of the parents, but it will often include attendance at religious services, religious training, baptism and confirmation, choosing family activities, and limiting access to literature and the child's social circle. One goal of religious initiation is to give one's child a faith that will serve him well throughout his life. A second but closely related desire will be to share life with one's children, participating with shared joy in festivals, celebrations, and milestones. Some parents will say that such initiation is their god-given right, but if we think of kids as distinct persons with their own rights and dignity, then this is implausible. Surely we must base any justification of religious initiation on the interests of the child. Let's apply the strategies suggested by Noggle's analysis.

We should begin by making a few assumptions. First, there are multiple justifiable religious traditions, so we must recognize that children may reasonably choose religious lives distinct from those of their parents.[6] Were we able to establish that there is a single correct religion, the issue would be much simpler. Second, religion is in many respects optional:

one can live a satisfactory life without any religious commitment whatsoever. Third, for those with sincere religious commitment, faith is often a central element in their identity; rejecting faith is possible only at the cost of a deep identity crisis. Fourth, once established in the child, religious faith is often difficult to overcome or change. So the power parents have to influence their kids' faith is truly significant. Finally, let's recognize that compelling religious parents to refrain from raising their own kids within their particular faith would likely result in serious harm to the family unit. Because religious faith is often a central element in a person's sense of who they are, driving a wedge between parents and children by preventing parents from sharing their deepest selves with their kids would often do more harm than good. So, given these assumptions, would it be acceptable to compel children to subscribe to one's faith?

Noggle himself says that it is acceptable. His argument, in a nutshell, is that every child has to take on some worldview or the other, so parents might as well impose theirs. We should take a moment to consider what this means. He is claiming that each person has a fundamental conception of the good – a set of fundamental values that guide his decisions – and that the secondary values of family continuity justify allowing parents to instill theirs on the child. Obviously, the moral legitimacy of the worldview is presupposed here (no Nazis!). In addition, Noggle points out that we need to remind ourselves that we are acting on behalf of the child, implying that we must be sensitive to the child's emerging character or identity. I can raise my child to share my faith, but only if that appears to be consistent with his emerging identity. If the adolescent child resists, then we are wrong to continue to force our faith on the child.

We can however question two moves in Noggle's argument. First, we should be concerned with his assumption that everyone has a worldview. If, on the one hand, what is meant is that everyone has a set of fundamental convictions that constitute a more or less well-defined "ism" (for example, aestheticism, atheism, or liberalism) or a religion (such as Christianity, Islam, or Sikhism) then he is wrong. We simply do not need a publicly namable set of precepts to guide us in our lives. The absence of such a set of fundamental convictions does not in itself make us directionless, provided we have goals or ideals that we have ourselves chosen. Marriage, parenthood, career, leisure activity, and moral purposes (working for world peace or fighting human rights abuses) can all give direction to one's life without constituting a single religion or "ism." On the other hand, if Noggle simply means that we each have fundamental values, then this won't support his claim for the right to impart a worldview to the child.

The child of course needs to acquire moral values (truth-telling, promise-keeping, care for others, justice, refraining from harming others, etc.), but there is no reason that the child cannot be taught to acquire her own personal values. A child can learn the importance of integrity and identity, for example, without being made to adhere to a single set of values. So, either way, Noggle exaggerates the degree to which each of us has a worldview, and therefore he exaggerates the right of parents to instill theirs in the child. This leads me to support a somewhat weaker right for parents, namely the right to guide family life, as supported by David Archard.[7]

Archard supports the right of parents to determine the activities and structures of the family. This is part of the compensation for taking on the duty of raising children, but also stems from the fact that there is really no alternative – the state would make an extremely poor substitute! Thus, they may choose to attend soccer games, spend summers camping in the mountains, or attending church services. They may choose to have close relations to extended family members, to keep to themselves, or even to live communally with family or friends. Usually, some of these values will be passed on to the child, but this does not imply a right to impart them. I can take my son skiing, cycling, and hiking, but this does not imply that I can compel him to acquire an appreciation for these activities. The right to guide family life is much weaker than the right to impart a worldview on one's children, but still permits parents a privileged place in their children's lives.

So is it legitimate for me to raise my child within a particular religious tradition? Well, it depends on what exactly we mean. If the question is whether I have a moral right to impose my own particular religious convictions and practices on the child, then the answer is clearly, "No, there is no such right." But can I set the parameters of family life (along with my wife, of course!)? Then the reply is "Yes, provided that one recognizes the growing capacity of the child to choose alternate forms of life for herself."

Paternalism is tricky because, while nobody appreciates a busy-body who sticks his nose into other people's business and tries to determine the way in which they live their lives, it seems that as fathers we can and should guide our children's lives. This is part of the traditional model of fatherhood, but I argue that this model is limited. If we are talking about guidance with regard to universal values, basic, pre-primary, and primary goods, then I am clearly in support of paternalism. However, when the values are not universal, then I support a far weaker form of guidance: gentle initiation as part of family activity, along with teaching the importance of choice, autonomy, and integrity in a flourishing life.

To conclude now, I want to consider a special case that may present a challenge for this account of paternalism.

Many possibly meaningful activities require significant guidance by parents at ages too early for us to reliably predict whether children will meaningfully pursue them. Consider musical training. Some instruments, such as the violin, require years of effort to attain proficiency – as one who began his violin training after turning forty, I can attest to this! Furthermore, they are best begun at an age when the child is not in a position to know whether the activity is likely to be of serious interest as an adult. Now, while some children seem to enjoy practice, most kids need to be compelled to do so. They are not capable of balancing their short- and long-term interests, so there will be many occasions when practice seems far less attractive than other activities in which they might engage. Is it okay for Dad to compel the child to practice?

Learning to play a musical instrument is a secondary good – good for most people who achieve it, but one that hurts no one – so this good must be weighted less than primary goods. However, for most children of moderate affluence, there will be opportunity to pursue some such goods. Consequently, fathers can legitimately compel practice, but only in light of the child's emerging identity. As her identity becomes clear, we must moderate or even eliminate this demand. However, learning to play a musical instrument *well* is a specialized good, requiring long hours of practice over many years, usually foregoing other childhood activities. Some kids practice four or more hours per day. This has ramifications for the child's overall wellbeing; as noted above, intense focus on a single activity necessarily limits the time one could spend on other activities. Such cases are troublesome because while the child who possesses special promise in music or ice hockey (think of Wolfgang Amadeus Mozart and Wayne Gretzky) often leaves the world a better place, they themselves may suffer to some degree. Moreover, we are seldom in a position to be confident that a child is indeed displaying a high degree of raw talent. I may think that my kid is the next Gretzky, but how can I know? And would it be legitimate to limit his exposure and participation in other activities in the *hope* that he is so talented?

I am afraid not. Mere hope for an increased talent is not sufficient to justify limiting the child in this way. We need more than hope. Fortunately, in the vast majority of cases, superior promise, interest, and future happiness coincide. So Noggle's model works well. That is, the child who has such a latent talent will have an interest in the activity and will be made happy by participating in it. The parent's role will be to facilitate the ongoing development of the talent. While there might be children who later regret participating in the given activity, the best predictors will be talent and interest. Happily, children who show superior latent talent will likely flourish through their activities and will contribute to the happiness of others too.

Where does this leave us with respect to the issue of whether I can choose activities for my children? Do I have a right to be paternalistic? Well, it all depends on what you mean. No father knows for certain what activities or commitments will allow his child to flourish, although it is clear that there are interests that all children share. Furthermore, we each have our own interests and capacities and these will necessarily color the manner in which we raise our children. We know that other equally competent dads will not share our visions of life. So if paternalism means forcing one's kids to accept one's ideals, I think the answer is clearly "no." However, if it means guiding one's children by working with them towards goals that reflect their individual character and disposition, then I think that fathers can be assured that they not only have a right to be paternal, but even have an obligation to be so.

NOTES

1 In this argument, as well as in the chapter generally, I assume that the family has at least sufficient wealth to pursue leisure activities. Of course, many families do not, one of the great disgraces of our world.

2 See Harry Brighouse's *On Education* (New York: Routledge, 2006) for a defense of this point.

3 Robert Noggle, "Special Agents: Children's Autonomy and Parental Authority," in D. Archard and C. McLeod (eds.) *The Moral and Political Status of Children* (Oxford: Oxford University Press, 2002).

4 John Rawls, *Political Liberalism* (New York: Columbia University Press, 1993).

5 Noggle, "Special Agents," p. 192.

6 In noting that there are multiple reasonable religious convictions I might be seen as undermining the possibility of reasonable religious conviction more generally. However, it is possible to have a strong belief in Christian doctrine while noting that there are other equally reasonable people who have different views. We must however distinguish between religious belief and belief about religious belief in order to do this. While this might undermine some forms of religious conviction, I believe that as responsible citizens and parents we cannot insist on the legitimacy of any one religious faith.

7 David Archard, *Children: Rights and Childhood* (London: Routledge, 1993).

CHAPTER 17

DADS AND DAUGHTERS

Wisdom for a Winding Road

I'm the only male in my home. I'm not complaining about this, but merely stating a fact. My wife, three daughters, and two dogs are all female (we aren't sure about the fish or the hermit crabs). While fatherhood is a challenge for all who take the relationship and role seriously, it seems to me that dads with daughters have an extra challenge because they've never been a daughter and so don't know what it's like to be a daughter. More generally, dads don't know what it's like to be a woman in the society in which we live. Given this, dads with daughters have some additional issues to face and things to learn compared to fathers who have only sons (not that raising boys is an easy job). Being the dad of a daughter is like traveling a winding road that you've never been on before. You don't know what's around the next bend, how sharp this blind curve is, or where the next rest area lies (if there is one!). The trip can be scary, anxiety-producing, and demanding, and there is no GPS for raising daughters. But there are some things that can help. Talking with your wife, mom, and other women about their experiences can help you understand the road they've traveled. As she grows up and is able to do so, talking to your daughter can help as well. Philosophy, perhaps surprisingly, can also help.

In this chapter we'll look to philosophy to provide a bit of wisdom as we consider some of the particular challenges faced by dads with daughters in contemporary society. Philosophy at its best should not only guide us into truth, but it should help us apply that truth to life in the right way. And this is just what wisdom is, applying truth to life in the right way. Many of the points I raise also apply to dads with sons, though the applications and implications that I discuss often will be unique to those who have daughters. With all of this in mind, the goal of this chapter is to provide some practical wisdom for dads with daughters to help them in their task of helping those daughters to flourish.

Interests and Obligations

One question of great interest to moral philosophers is this: Where do our moral obligations come from? There are of course many answers given to this question, but one plausible answer is that our obligations towards others are in part based on their fundamental interests.[1] A *fundamental interest* is something that is vitally important to human life. Human beings have many such interests, such as physical and psychological wellbeing, close personal relationships, and the freedom to pursue a satisfying and meaningful life. While we are unable to help satisfy the fundamental interests of all of the people that we come into contact with, dads are especially well positioned to help their daughters flourish by contributing to their physical and psychological health, having close relationships with them, and assisting them in discovering and pursuing a life that is both satisfying and meaningful. Given that our daughters have these fundamental interests, and given that we have great potential for helping them satisfy these interests, it is quite reasonable to think that dads have a duty to do just that. Now you might be thinking that the demands of diaper-changing, toddler-corralling, or teenager-guiding are more than enough to fill your days. And you'd be right. However, we dads can help our daughters flourish in the midst of all of our other duties.

There are many issues related to these ideas that could be discussed, too many to cover in one chapter. However, I think that the fundamental interests alluded to above are closely connected to the wisdom made available to us by both ancient and contemporary philosophers related to three things: self-knowledge, moral development, and contributing to the common good. If dads with daughters can make some progress in these areas, I believe that their relationships with their daughters will be enhanced and their daughters will have a much better chance of living happy and fulfilling lives. For example, several years ago, when my oldest daughter was eight, our church was spending the day doing much of the deferred maintenance on school buildings in our town. She and I were painting a wall in a classroom, and she turned to me and said, "This is really *fun*." I've done my share of painting over the years, and "fun" isn't the first word to jump to mind. However, we were contributing to the common good in a small but significant way, and in so doing she felt happier and more fulfilled. And I'm glad I was there, standing next to her, to share that moment.

Self-Knowledge

Know thyself. This command to acquire self-knowledge is reported to have been inscribed over the temple at Delphi in ancient Greece. Many philosophers have discussed whether and to what extent we can truly know ourselves. I believe a significant degree of self-knowledge is not only possible, but also essential for parents, including those of us who are fathers of daughters. It's also true that our knowledge of ourselves can grow wider and deeper if we are reflective in the midst of being a dad. There is much to say about the relationship between self-knowledge and fatherhood, but here I want to focus on the importance of two aspects of self-knowledge that can help us be better dads.

First, we need a certain sort of emotional self-knowledge if we are to excel as fathers, and this is something that many men still lack in our culture. To acquire this kind of knowledge, we need to ask ourselves certain kinds of questions that we may tend to avoid. What sorts of things tend to get to me emotionally? (Almost everything my teenage daughter says to me, you might be thinking.) Why do I react so strongly to certain words and situations? (Because I haven't had a full night's sleep since our daughter was born two years ago, you say.) Knowing ahead of time what sort of situations and speech has the tendency to rouse some of our more negative emotions can help us avoid losing our cool and speaking cruelly to our daughters or making a big deal out of something that just isn't a big deal. This is important to think about, given that how a father relates to his daughter can have a deep impact on much of her emotional inner life and her perception of her own value.

I think one thing that has the potential to spark our more negative emotions as dads is that we have a strong desire for control. For whatever reason, many of us believe that we can control our lives, and are frustrated when reality resists this belief and its correlating desire. For example, when my daughters were preschool age, we had a junk drawer in our kitchen that they were drawn to in order to rifle around in search of some important treasure. While this is a bit embarrassing to admit, for some strange reason I was annoyed when they would mess up this already messed up drawer. In retrospect, I came to realize that my annoyance was rooted in a desire to have some control. This was during a stage in my life when I had little control over some big aspects of my life. I was in graduate school, and it seemed like so much related to my career was outside of my control. Given this, I was grasping for control wherever I could try to find it. It all seems so silly now, but once I realized this, it was easier to lighten up about the junk drawer (as well as many other things). This sort of self-knowledge is something we can help our daughters gain as well. If we are attentive and in a sense study our daughters, we'll be able to help them acquire self-knowledge, which is not only important in our relationships with them, but in helping them live a fulfilled life. When we identify some similarities between us and our daughters, we can talk about these with them and share how to capitalize on the positive aspects and minimize the more negative ones. For example, if a child is especially sensitive towards the thoughts of others, this can be a negative thing if they are overly concerned with what others think of her. However, this sensitivity can be put to good use as she is attentive to the needs and interests of her family and friends. This type of self-knowledge can be quite conducive to a fulfilled, happy, and purposeful life.

Second, a more general and also very important aspect of self-knowledge has to do with what contemporary philosopher Charles Taylor calls our *strong evaluations*.[2] These include our judgments about right and wrong, our beliefs about what is better or worse and higher or lower. Taylor isn't referring to our beliefs about such things as whether it is better or worse to have a designated hitter in Major League baseball, or the proper way to make a mint julep. (Not that these are small matters, mind you.) Rather, our strong evaluations are our judgments about what is good, what is moral, and what does or does not have value, especially as it relates to what makes life meaningful and worthwhile. These sorts of evaluations are also crucial parts of our identity, of our selves, and so it is important that we know what we believe about such things and why we believe what we do. It is also important to talk about these sorts of issues with our daughters because communicating about them can foster closeness in the father-daughter relationship.

This involves not only sharing our thoughts with our daughters, but also listening to them as they mature and develop their own set of strong evaluations.

Moral Development Through Humility, Courage, and Wisdom

Many dads devote large amounts of time and significant amounts of money to the intellectual development of our daughters. Many of us do the same to help our girls grow as athletes, artists, or musicians. And this is all well and good. Part of helping our daughters be truly happy is helping them to discover and develop their talents and pursue things about which they are passionate. However, I have a suspicion that many of us give less focused time and energy to something that is just as important – if not more important – to the true happiness of our daughters: their moral development. I don't mean to suggest that we entirely neglect this area, as most parents teach their daughters basic values like fairness, respect for others, and honesty. Yet if our daughters are to truly flourish and be fulfilled, they'll need more than these basic values. They'll need to develop other important moral virtues as well, including humility, courage, and wisdom.

The process of moral development is complex, but philosophers do offer some wisdom that is useful. For example, Aristotle suggests that growth in virtue is a lot like growth in other skills, insofar as it takes practice. If you want to excel at soccer, it takes practice. Similarly, if you want to become a just person, Aristotle advises you to go perform just actions. In light of this, dads should give their daughters opportunities to grow in the virtues by engaging in activities where they can practice them. For example, if your daughter excels at a piano recital, she can learn humility by sharing the credit for her accomplishment with her teacher. She could also learn to practice courage on the soccer field, for example, by taking risks and being willing to fail in front of others as well as practice the limited physical courage that such a sport involves. Finally, we can help our daughters grow in wisdom as we uncover some of the myths that our culture reinforces in the minds of young women and girls. But in order to do these sorts of things, we'll need a clearer understanding of humility, courage, and wisdom.

Humility is a virtue that is connected to self-knowledge, and it would be a great topic for conversation with a daughter when she's intellectually capable of doing so. Humility can be difficult to understand, but a good starting point is to take it to be "a mean between the unjustified low regard of self-denigration and the loftiness of arrogance or excessive pride."[3]

Many wrongly confuse humility with self-denigration and low self-esteem. The humble person should take credit when it is deserved, and as fathers we should encourage this. As a college professor, I've come across many excellent students, and the majority of the ones that are truly excellent have been females. The problem is that many of them are still plagued with self-doubt. There are likely some psychological and sociological explanations for this, given the sexism still present in society and the sorts of challenges that females face because of this. What is important at present is that this form of self-doubt is not humility. It is a deficient form of this trait. When someone is truly excellent related to academics, sports, or the arts, humility does not require that she deny this fact. Each of my own daughters excels at certain things and it would be wrong to teach them that they don't. If humility required us to have false beliefs about our gifts and talents in this way, it would not be a virtue because a true virtue should not demand that we have false beliefs.

At the other end of the spectrum is arrogance or excessive pride. Humility counters this tendency because the humble person realizes that she deserves some of the credit for her accomplishments, but credit should also go to others in her life, such as coaches, teachers, family, and friends. We rely on others in a variety of ways, and humility enables us to realize and accept this dependence.

Nancy Snow points out that there are other forms of humility as well.[4] One of these that could be helpful to dads is what she calls existential humility. This is humility related to our general finitude as human beings, the mental and emotional experience one might have looking at the Grand Canyon, Niagara Falls, or the ocean. This feeling of smallness before the greatness of nature, the awe one can feel in such situations, is a form of humility that can help us see our own limitations more clearly. These limitations aren't necessarily bad; they are just a part of the human condition.

Practically speaking, if we want to foster this form of the virtue of humility in our children it might be beneficial to expose them to some of the natural wonders of the world, both large and small. The sense of awe and finitude one gets before a view of the Rocky Mountains or even the night sky away from the light pollution many towns and cities emit can put things in perspective, including our own cares and concerns. Another way to foster humility in our daughters is to be humble as dads. One way to demonstrate this is to apologize and ask our daughters to forgive us when we fail them in small or large ways. This not only provides them with an example of humility, but it also fosters forgiveness and intimacy in our relationships with them.

Courage is another crucial virtue that fathers would be well advised to try to instill in their daughters.[5] Historically and for many in contemporary times, courage is seen as a predominantly masculine virtue, exemplified by soldiers on the battlefield and others who face adversity and the risk of personal injury or death for some greater good. There are other forms of courage, however, that we should acknowledge in order to fully understand it and which our daughters can benefit from possessing. It takes courage to refuse to give into despair in trying circumstances, such as when someone or a loved one faces a terminal illness. Our daughters will need courage in other contexts as well. There are many obstacles that girls and women must face in society because they are female, such as unequal pay for equal work, the ubiquitous sexual objectification of women, and other forms of sexism still present in the world. Facing illness, harassment, and prejudice but refusing to be defeated by these is courageous. This is one place where our lack of knowledge about what it's like to be a woman in our society can be a hindrance, and some conversations with the women in our lives can help us understand what our daughters face and enable us to better encourage them to be courageous in the midst of such challenges.

Fathers can demonstrate another kind of courage, the courage of putting one's own projects and goals on hold for the good of someone else. According to contemporary philosopher Richard White, this is a neglected dimension of the virtue of courage.[6] Historically, it is women who have done this (and still often do this today) in the context of the family. Fortunately, there are men who put their careers on hold in order to stay at home with their young children, and hopefully in the future creative forms of childcare as well as job sharing will be more widely available. However, there is something courageous about refusing to assert oneself for the good of someone else. While this can be taken to an unhealthy extreme, in its proper form such a refusal of self-assertion requires courage. Some girls and women can be too willing to sacrifice themselves and their interests for others, and it takes courage to refuse to do so. But there are times when courage enables us to sacrifice our own interests for the good of others, and this is an important component of a good moral character. Dads should both exemplify and encourage this in their daughters.

Wisdom is a virtue that involves the intellect, but it is a moral virtue as well. While there is no consensus among philosophers about the true nature of wisdom (which is ironic given that philosophy means "the love of wisdom"), we can get enough of a handle on this concept to help dads with daughters. The wise person knows the means to achieving good ends, and also knows the value that certain ends possess.[7] This means that wisdom enables us to discover the best way to achieve our goals, and it also enables us to see which goals are worth trying to achieve. Wisdom is not some esoteric trait, but rather it is intensely practical. It is a necessity for living a good human life. Given this, dads need to help their daughters grow in wisdom.

How can fathers help their daughters become wise? There are three traits that consistently emerge when the lives of wise individuals are examined: curiosity, versatility, and critical thinking.[8] In what follows, I'll explore these traits briefly and give some practical suggestions for cultivating them in our lives and the lives of our daughters.

A curious person wants to learn. She wants to understand new things, motivated by a sense of wonder at life and the world around her. Children are, as any parent knows, naturally curious. At some point during the preschool years, they almost incessantly ask "Why?" This is often a sign of curiosity and it is incumbent upon parents to foster rather than squelch this curiosity. Questions about words, animals, society, religion, and a variety of other topics are often broached by our kids, and we should encourage this. When we don't know something, we can admit it and look for answers together, whether this has to do with a question about dinosaurs that a five-year-old daughter asks, or a question about connections between science and religion that a fifteen-year-old daughter poses. A crucial part of wisdom is a persistent sense of curiosity about humanity, the world, and the universe. This is the kind of curiosity dads need to encourage, rather than the kind of curiosity present in the popular culture's fascination with celebrity.

A second aspect of wisdom is versatility. We live in an age of ever-increasing specialization regarding knowledge and competence, but a wise person has a broad range of interests. She is not obsessed with only one or two things (whether philosophy or the *Twilight* book series). Of course, our daughters will likely go through phases where their interests are captured by books like *Twilight* (and probably not philosophy!), and this isn't necessarily something to worry about. However, over time it is best for them to have a range of interests, as this is part of being a wise person. Learning about new things and trying them out are good for our daughters and could uncover a hidden talent or passion that may contribute to their happiness and the happiness of others. Giving our girls opportunities to try music, art, or sports can cultivate versatility not only by participating in these activities, but in learning about them as well. A trial and error approach in these areas also takes some courage, and this is one illustration of the way in which growth in one virtue also results in growth in other virtues.

Of special importance here for dads is the need to *show* versatility as a way of loving our daughters. We need to take an active interest in what our daughters are involved in, even if their interests don't mirror our own. My father-in-law did this with his girls by coaching soccer and learning about photography, among other things. This is a wise thing to do as a dad. It also communicates love and care for our daughters by making them feel appreciated, valued, and loved, especially when their interests are different from our own.

A final trait of the wise person is being a good critical thinker. Critical thinking involves the ability to use sound judgment, to discern what is true from what is false. A critical thinker pursues knowledge and employs a variety of skills in the quest. Critical thinking involves making distinctions – sometimes very subtle distinctions – that are present among different ideas and values. It also involves understanding ideas and their connections with one another, as well as the evidence that can be marshaled for or against an idea. A good critical thinker also looks for and identifies assumptions people make, and thinks through the possible problems and objections that could be given to a claim. And a good critical thinker is also open-minded, being willing to change her mind when the evidence leads her to do so.

Developing these and other skills of critical thinking is crucial for our daughters because there are so many false and harmful ideas propagated by our culture. As dads, we want our daughters to know that their value is not dependent upon the false standards of beauty embraced by popular culture. We want them to know that their character is what matters most. We live in a time in which elementary school-aged girls think their thighs are fat. When this occurs, there has been a lapse in critical thinking. And while our daughters will need to be at a certain level of cognitive development to do so, we need to help them critically evaluate the judgments and values that they encounter in their lives. One practical thing to do is to *identify assumptions* made in commercial advertising with your daughter. Whether related to cars or hair color products, there are assumptions about the value of human beings, what will bring us happiness, and the status of women that need to be challenged. By identifying these assumptions and talking them over with our daughters, we are helping them grow in wisdom. Ask them what assumptions are present, and what they think. You may be surprised at what they uncover. Even though we dads don't have identical experiences, we can still be there for our daughters to talk through such issues. And we may have learned some lessons from our own journeys that could be helpful for our girls.

A final piece of practical advice related to the cultivation of wisdom is this: limit your daughter's screen time. This includes television, movies, video games, computers, and mobile devices. These things aren't bad, and my kids spend time using them all. But one downside of the information age is that it exposes us to a lot of facts without deepening our understanding of life and how to live it. Too much time spent in front of screens prevents kids from developing their creative and reflective sides, both of which are important aspects of a good human life.

In the next section, we'll look at one final aspect of a good life, contributing to the common good.

Character and the Common Good

Part of the reason given above for helping our daughters develop morally is that having good character is conducive to their own happiness and fulfillment. There is another important reason for doing this, and that is that virtuous people will also contribute in a variety of ways to the common good.

Some are suspicious of the notion of a common good, as they fear that the needs and interests of the many will necessarily trump the needs and interests of the individual. The way that I'm thinking of the common good is connected with the idea of fundamental interests discussed at the beginning of this chapter. A commitment to the common good is a commitment to the welfare and flourishing of everyone. Of course, it is beyond our ability to ensure that this occurs, but a person of good character will do her share to meet the physical needs of others, and she will do what she can to help them flourish and be happy. This will require virtues like compassion and patience. In the end, if one of our basic commitments in life is to the welfare of others in the community and in the world, we end up being happier and more fulfilled as a result. When we live for something larger than the self, we have a better shot at being truly happy. Given this, we should try to demonstrate and foster in our daughters a commitment to the common good. Whether in her career, community service, or role as a wife or mother, dads can encourage their daughters to make meaningful and valuable contributions to the good of other people.

Encouraging our daughters in any and all of these pursuits is significant. Something of particular importance is helping our daughters match their gifts, talents, and passions with the common good. For example, there are particular fields in which women are underrepresented. If one of my daughters ends up having both the ability and passion to pursue a career in such a field, like philosophy, then it is important that I help her overcome the barriers that will stand in her way. This contributes to the common good because she could be a role model for others and help empower them to pursue a career in the field as well. This can help bring about more justice and equality in society, which are key components of the common good. Of course, we must be careful not to impose such things on our daughters, as our primary responsibility is to help them discover and pursue a life that will bring them true happiness and contribute to the common good.

In sum, and as readers of this chapter likely know, being a dad is both demanding and rewarding. The ideas presented above are meant to be goals and not burdens, and there will be bumps along the way as we try to figure out how to be a good dad. There is much more to say, but one key point to draw from this chapter is that part of being a good dad is to put your daughter's interests before your own as you seek to love and care for her and help enable her to live a happy and fulfilling life.

Further Down the Road

All dads make mistakes. Just ask their daughters. But if there is a foundation of love, of unconditional commitment to the good of your daughter as you help her acquire self-knowledge, encourage her moral development, and try to instill in her a commitment to the common good, then you and she will be able to navigate your relationship in ways that are fulfilling to you both. And while the road changes as your daughter is eight, 18, 38, and beyond, I believe that there is always a place for Dad on that journey with her, especially if he continues to provide her with the kind of love and support that she needs and that he is uniquely qualified to give.

NOTES

1   The following is partially drawn from my book *Conceptions of Parenthood: Ethics and the Family* (Burlington: Ashgate, 2007), pp. 76–7.

2   Charles Taylor, *Sources of the Self* (Cambridge, MA: Harvard University Press, 1989), p. 4.

3   Joseph Kupfer, "The Moral Perspective of Humility," *Pacific Philosophical Quarterly* 84 (2003): 266.

4   Nancy E. Snow, "Humility," *Journal of Value Inquiry* 29 (1995): 203–16.

5   The following discussion of courage draws heavily from Richard White, *Radical Virtues* (Lanham: Rowman and Littlefield, 2008), pp. 13–41.

7   Ibid., p. 33.

8   Philippa Foot, *Virtues and Vices and Other Essays in Moral Philosophy* (Oxford: Clarendon Press, 2002), p. 5.

9   James S. Spiegel, *How to be Good in a World Gone Bad* (Grand Rapids: Kregel Publications, 2004), pp. 181–5.

APPENDIX A

Cookie Recipes for Dads

Here are two delicious cookie recipes for dads. The first is my father's double chocolate chip cookie recipe (made for the Christmas season). The second is my "healthy" reinterpretation of that recipe.

Dr. Joseph Cavanaugh's Double Chocolate Chip Cookies

Ingredients

- 1.75 cups all-purpose flour
- .25 tsp baking soda
- 1 cup margarine
- 1 tsp vanilla extract
- 1 cup white sugar
- .5 cup dark brown sugar
- .33 cup unsweetened cocoa
- 2 tbs milk
- 6 oz chocolate chips

Directions

- Preheat oven to 350 degrees
- In the bowl of an electric mixer, crème the margarine, vanilla, and sugars
- Turn the speed down; add the cocoa, flour, baking soda, and milk
- Add the chocolate chips

- Grease cookie sheets and drop cookies by spoonful onto sheet
- Bake for 12 minutes
- Cool on a wire rack

Dr. Dan Collins-Cavanaugh's Reduced Calorie and Reduced Fat Black and White Chocolate Chip Cookies

Ingredients

- 1 cup wheat flour
- .75 cups all-purpose flour
- .5 tsp baking soda
- .5 cup light butter
- 1 cup non-fat yogurt
- 2 tsp vanilla
- .5 cup brown sugar
- 2 cups Splenda
- .33 cup unsweetened cocoa
- 2 tbs skim milk
- .25 cup semi-sweet chocolate chips (preferably minis)
- .25 cup white chocolate chips (minis again, if you can find them)

Directions

- Preheat oven to 350 degrees
- In the bowl of an electric mixer, crème butter, vanilla, brown sugar, and Splenda
- Turn down slightly and add yogurt
- Turn down more and add flours, baking soda, cocoa, and milk
- Add chips
- Drop by spoonfuls onto baking sheets sprayed with cooking spray
- Bake for 8–10 minutes (it is very important not to over-bake low-fat baked products)
- Cool on a wire rack

Note: Low-fat baked goods need to be stored in a refrigerator, preferably in single layers with wax paper between each layer, in an air-tight container.

Approximate nutritional information for reduced-sugar/reduced-fat version (36-cookie batch): 63 calories, 2.5 g fat, 1.5 g protein, 8.5 g carbs.

APPENDIX B

Wisdom of Youth

Some of our contributor's children share their deep thoughts about fatherhood and philosophy. Enjoy!

What Does Your Dad Do?

Mary (age 7): "He is a scientist. He uses chemicals and takes care of them."

Paul (age 3): "Daddy goes to work and picks me up. Sissy doesn't go to work."

Jasmine (age 6): "He is a teacher who makes big people listen, put up their hand to ask a question, and think very hard."

Conner (age 5): "Daddy teaches the people!"

Bernadette (age 2): "He pumps gas."

While brushing his teeth Aidan (age 5) asks his father for instruction on using dental floss. It turns out that he thought his dad was some sort of specialist on oral hygiene: a "flossopher."

One day, Aidan's (age 6) dad wants to look at a small cut on his back to make sure it was healing properly. But when he lifts Aidan's shirt to look at the cut, Aidan indignantly pulled his shirt down and said, "Stop! You're not that kind of doctor. You're a doctor of philosophy, and I don't have philosophy!"

What Is A Father?

Silas (age 5): "Someone who takes care of people."

Elizabeth (age 10): "Someone who chooses to take care of and love children."

Kieran (age 4): "They catch babies."

What Have You Learned From Your Dad?

Mary (age 7): "Not to talk to someone when they are talking to someone else, especially if it is Mommy."

Silas (age 5): "How to fight, wrestle, shave a beard, and how to wind up a clock."

Liz (age 10): "How to choose a boyfriend someday."

Catherine (age 7): "How to ride a bike."

Jasmine (age 6): "He taught me about numbers, adding, and subtracting."

Paul (age 3): "I learn from my Mommy."

What Is Philosophy?

Elizabeth (age 10): "It's about history."

Elena (age 5): "You know, it's like that book I have. Is this full and this empty? Or is this empty and this full?"

Catherine (age 7): "It has to do with drinking alcohol."

Leona (age 12): "The study of boring stuff."

Jasmine (age 6): "It's a sort of mathematics involving supersonic numbers."

Other Bits of Wisdom

An adult friend of the family has Ben (age 3) on her lap and tells him that he smells good. "Are you wearing cologne?" she asks. "No," says Ben, "I wear pull-ups."

Ben's (age 5) aunt asks him when he might visit her again, to which his mother responds, "Maybe after February." His aunt says, "That would be fabulous!" But Ben corrects her: "No, that would be March."

Balogun: "My kids are fond of calling me 'Dad Agbari.' In Yoruban, 'Agbari' refers to the 'skull' which represents intelligence. They call me this because I always find ways around their clever pranks, by logically analyzing situations."

When you grow up, what do you want to be? Do you want to be a mommy? "No," Grace (age 3) said, "I want to be a daddy so I can be the one to answer the phone."

After learning the Old Testament story of Daniel being saved from the lion, Drew (age 4) made a lion mask with tears running down the lion's face. Why? Drew said, "I drew him crying because he wanted to eat Daniel but he couldn't."

What will you do after kindergarten? Conner (age 5) responds, "After kindergarten, I will go to college, and daddy will be my teacher!"

Emma (age 4): "I know why we lock the door when we leave. It's so people don't move in when we're gone."

Final Thoughts on Daddies

What is your favorite thing about your daddy? Katelin (age 6): "He loves me." How do you know that your daddy loves you? "Because he gives me kisses and hugs and because he plays with me."

What is the difference between a mommy and a daddy? Kieran (age 4): "Daddies have little boobies and mommies have big boobies."

Katelin (age 6): "Daddies are funny. Daddies are nice. Daddies are good readers. I don't know how to say this … daddies are talented!" What are some of a daddy's talents? "Loving their babies, hugging, and kissing."

NOTES ON CONTRIBUTORS

AMMON ALLRED, PhD, is Visiting Assistant Professor of Philosophy at the University of Toledo. He has also held visiting positions at York College of Pennsylvania, Shippensburg University, the University of Pennsylvania, and Villanova University, where he received his PhD. He researches and writes primarily in the areas of contemporary continental philosophy, aesthetics, and philosophy and literature. He is pretty sure that he used to have hobbies. Now he has two kids, Elena and Jasper, instead.

MICHAEL W. AUSTIN is an associate professor of philosophy at Eastern Kentucky University. His philosophical interests focus on issues related to morality and the good life. He has written two books on ethics and the family, *Conceptions of Parenthood* (2007) and *Wise Stewards* (2009). He has edited *Football and Philosophy* (2008) and *Running and Philosophy* (Wiley-Blackwell, 2007). Mike has decided that it is easier to write about parenting than to actually engage in the practice, though he does both.

ABIODUN OLADELE BALOGUN, PhD, is an Assistant Professor of Philosophy at Olabisi Onabanjo University, Ogun State, Nigeria, where he currently serves as the Sub-Dean, Faculty of Arts Postgraduate Programs. His papers have appeared in international journals such as *Nordic Journal of African Studies*, *Journal of Pan African Studies*, and *Philosophia*. His research interests are in African philosophy, philosophy of education, and philosophy of mind. When not engaged in deep thought and writing, he enjoys hanging out with his marvelous children and with his lovely wife, Temitope.

MICHAEL BARNWELL, PhD, has been an Assistant Professor of Philosophy at Niagara University since earning a dual doctorate degree in both philosophy and religious studies from Yale University in 2005. His primary interests are in medieval philosophy and philosophy of religion. He has a forthcoming book investigating the utility of medieval theories of the will for solving contemporary problems related to negligent omissions. While there are many things – such as cutting the grass and pulling weeds – he would (and sometimes does) negligently omit, fatherhood is not one of them.

JOSHUA BARON, MA, is a graduate student in the Department of Philosophy at Temple University and teaches in the Department of Philosophy and Religious Studies at McDaniel College. His research interests are in aesthetics and ethics, particularly as they relate to violent imagery. As a new dad, Josh is learning to do all his work in between diaper changes, feedings, and temper tantrums – his son's, that is.

ADRIENNE BURGESS (Research Manager at the Fatherhood Institute) writes widely on fatherhood. Her groundbreaking book *Fatherhood Reclaimed: The Making of the Modern Father* (1997) helped set a new agenda on fatherhood in the UK, and has been published in translation throughout the world – as has *Will You Still Love Me Tomorrow?* (2002), in which she presented, in an accessible form, the huge body of research on couple relationships. Her main Fatherhood Institute research summary – *The Costs and Benefits of Active Fatherhood* – as well as smaller summaries on separated families; fathers, mothers, work, and family; maternal and infant health in the perinatal period; young fathers; antisocial behavior and fatherhood; and so on – are widely used by policy makers and practitioners alike. Adrienne is also co-author, with other Institute trainers, of its highly regarded *Toolkit for Father-Inclusive Practice* and *Invisible Fathers: Working with Young Dads* – a resources pack for practitioners. Adrienne speaks and trains on fatherhood in the UK, the US, and Australia.

ANTHONY CARRERAS received his BA from Drew University with honors in philosophy and his MA in philosophy from Georgia State University. He is now a PhD candidate at Rice University, specializing in ancient Greek philosophy and writing a dissertation on motivation and the self in Aristotle's account of friendship. In addition, he loves teaching and has taught courses at Georgia State, Houston Community College, and Rice. In his spare time, which he tries to make as ample as possible, he enjoys being in his hometown of New York City, playing tennis, making music, spending time with his fiancée, Adrienne, and trying to make the gray hairs come early by being a diehard New York Mets fan.

DAN COLLINS-CAVANAUGH, PhD, is an associate professor in the Department of Art, Music and Philosophy at the Prince George's Community College. His recent publications include "Does the Salary Cap Make the NFL a Fairer League?" in *Football and Philosophy* (2008). His philosophical interests include philosophy of sport and ethics. His advice to new fathers is simply this: love trumps competence.

SCOTT A. DAVISON earned BA and MA degrees from Ohio State University and MA and PhD degrees from the University of Notre Dame, before landing in Morehead, Kentucky. There he became Professor of Philosophy and Coordinator of the program of Philosophy and Religious Studies at Morehead State University, where he works in metaphysics, the philosophy of religion, and ethics. Most importantly, though, in Morehead he became the proud father of two boys and a girl, which makes everything else seem like straw.

KIMBERLEY FINK-JENSEN has an MA from the Department of Anthropology at the University of British Columbia and a degree in physical therapy from the University of Manitoba. Her interest in fatherhood began with late-night musings with her partner following the births of their two children. For her graduate research, she interviewed first-time fathers about pregnancy, birth, and early parenthood. She currently spends most of her time explaining to friends and family what narrative analysis is and why anyone should care.

DAN FLORELL, PhD, is an assistant professor in the Psychology Department at Eastern Kentucky University with a specialty in school psychology. He is a licensed psychologist and nationally certified school psychologist (NCSP). His research interests focus on the use of technology by adolescents, specifically in regard to bullying and cyber bullying. In addition, he is a father of two little girls who continually teach him that parenting books don't have all the answers.

ANDREW KOMASINSKI, MA, is working through ideas of human personhood, drawing from elements of contemporary ethics, Chinese philosophy, and Kierkegaard. He received his MA from Loyola Marymount and is presently pursuing his PhD in philosophy at Fordham University. Andrew and his wife will adopt in the future, by which point he plans to develop superhuman abilities: the patience of a Saint Bernard, the compassion of a Border collie, and the seeing eye of a German shepherd.

STEPHEN JOSEPH MATTERN, MA, is Instructor of Health Care Ethics at St. Francis Medical Center College of Nursing in Peoria, Illinois. He is a Licensed Clinical Professional Counselor (LCPC, NCC) and a Certified Occupational Therapy Assistant and has spoken to academic and ecclesial audiences extensively on such topics as marriage, relationships, and the nature of professional relationships. He enjoys planting and growing varieties of tomatoes and potatoes and is intensely engaged in the relentless search for the perfect cup of espresso. He is also known to play a fierce game of dodge ball with his children.

JEFFREY MORGAN, PhD, is at the University of the Fraser Valley, Canada. He teaches courses on ethics, Indian philosophy, and philosophy of education. Currently, he is writing on the ethics of private schooling. His two children keep him younger than he ought to be, but are his greatest source of philosophical wisdom.

LON S. NEASE is a PhD student in the philosophy department at the University of Cincinnati. He holds an MA in philosophy from the University of Kentucky where he studied phenomenology and existentialism. He has published on post-Kantian ethical theory and has previously done editing work for Hackett. Lon loves to travel, loves being with his daughter, and has managed to combine those passions by dragging her all over the world during their family vacations.

DAVID S. OWEN is Associate Professor of Philosophy and Director of Diversity Programs for the College of Arts and Sciences at the University of Louisville. His research interests are mainly in social philosophy, including critical race theory, philosophy of social science, and the Frankfurt School. He has previously published *Between Reason and History: Habermas and the Idea of Progress* (2002) and is currently working on developing a critical theory of whiteness that will explain the structural and unconscious mechanisms by which racial oppression is reproduced. He is regularly awakened from his parental slumbers by his daughter's continuous development – for as soon as he thinks he has parenting mastered, his daughter changes the rules of the game.

J. K. SWINDLER, PhD, is Professor and Chair of the Department of Philosophy at Illinois State University. He took all his degrees at the University of Kansas. His dissertation won the Review of Metaphysics Dissertation Essay Contest and led to publication of his book, *Weaving: An Analysis of the Constitution of Objects*. In recent years he has been at work on a book on collective responsibility and has published essays on many aspects of the problem in numerous journals. He has served as president of the Southwestern Philosophical Society and the Central States Philosophical Association and for 15 years as editor of *Southwest Philosophy Review*. He has two grown sons who by now cannot help but associate fatherhood with philosophy.

ANDREW TERJESEN is currently a visiting Assistant Professor at Rhodes College in Memphis. He has previously taught at Washington and Lee University, Austin College, and Duke University. His interests are in ethics and moral psychology, especially the role of empathy and sentiments in morality. He has explored those interests in his scholarly work as well as essays in *Serial Killers – Philosophy for Everyone* and in the Wiley-Blackwell Pop Culture and Philosophy series, including *The Office and Philosophy* (2008), *X-Men and Philosophy* (2009), and *Heroes and Philosophy* (2009). He dedicates this essay to his father in the hopes that it will make up for a lifetime of polo shirts, golf balls, pajamas, and other not very imaginative Fathers' Day gifts.

STEFFEN WILSON, PhD, is an Associate Professor in the Psychology Department at Eastern Kentucky University. She enjoys teaching courses on child and adolescent development, as well as a career development course for undergraduate students. Her current research interests include investigating the impact of a sense of belonging at the university on the success of college students. While she is not a father, she is the mother of a young son and daughter. She sees the positive impact that fathering has had on her children, and she hopes this book will inspire fathers to enjoy the ride of parenthood.